ACTRESSES OF THE RESTORATION PERIOD

If any thing be overlooked, or not accurately inserted, let no one find fault, but take into consideration that this history is compiled from all quarters.

From the title page of *Some Account of the English Stage...* 1832.

ACTRESSES OF THE RESTORATION PERIOD

MRS ELIZABETH BARRY AND MRS ANNE BRACEGIRDLE

SUSAN MARGARET COOPER

PEN & SWORD
HISTORY

AN IMPRINT OF PEN & SWORD BOOKS LTD.
YORKSHIRE - PHILADELPHIA

First published in Great Britain in 2023 by
PEN AND SWORD HISTORY
An imprint of
Pen & Sword Books Ltd
Yorkshire – Philadelphia

ISBN 978 1 39906 480 4

A CIP catalogue record for this book is available from the British Library.

Typeset in Times New Roman 11/13.5 by
SJmagic DESIGN SERVICES, India.
Printed and bound in the UK by CPI Group (UK) Ltd.

Pen & Sword Books Limited incorporates the imprints of Atlas, Archaeology,
Aviation, Discovery, Family History, Fiction, History, Maritime, Military, Military
Classics, Politics, Select, Transport, True Crime, Air World, Frontline Publishing,
Leo Cooper, Remember When, Seaforth Publishing, The Praetorian Press,
Wharncliffe Local History, Wharncliffe Transport, Wharncliffe True Crime and
White Owl.

For a complete list of Pen & Sword titles please contact
PEN & SWORD BOOKS LIMITED
47 Church Street, Barnsley, South Yorkshire, S70 2AS, England
E-mail: enquiries@pen-and-sword.co.uk
Website: www.pen-and-sword.co.uk

Or
PEN AND SWORD BOOKS
1950 Lawrence Rd, Havertown, PA 19083, USA
E-mail: Uspen-and-sword@casematepublishers.com
Website: www.penandswordbooks.com

Contents

Acknowledgements   vii

Prologue   viii

**Part One: Mrs Elizabeth Barry
(1658–1713)**

Chapter One	Restoration Theatre and Its Environs	2
Chapter Two	Mrs Barry's Roots	29
Chapter Three	Would She Make An Actress?	34
Chapter Four	The Famous Mrs Barry	37
Chapter Five	Not a Very United Company	46
Chapter Six	Nice and Settled at Lincoln's Inn Fields	53
Chapter Seven	Fame Brings Its Price	60
Chapter Eight	Mrs Barry's Latter Stage Years	70
Chapter Nine	A Welcome Retirement But a Tragic Death	86

**Part Two: Mrs Anne Bracegirdle
(1671–1748)**

Chapter Ten	Unlocking Anne's Ancestry	94
Chapter Eleven	The Play House, Anne's New Home	102
Chapter Twelve	Fresh-faced Anne Bracegirdle, the Darling of the Stage	109
Chapter Thirteen	A Happy Company at Lincoln's Inn Fields	113

Chapter Fourteen   A Discomforting Rival   145

Chapter Fifteen   A Long and Happy Retirement with the
Inevitable Consequence   156

Epilogue   164

Repertoire of Plays performed by Mrs Barry and/
or Mrs Bracegirdle   168

Bibliography   172

Appendix I   *A pindarique ode, humbly offer'd to the*
Queen, on the victorious progress of Her
Majesty's arms, under the conduct of the
Duke of Marlborough   176

Appendix II   Will of William Congreve of Saint Clement
Danes, Middlesex. Probate:
03 February 1729. PROB 11/621/422.
The National Archives, Kew.   181

Endnotes   185
Index   196

Acknowledgements

In creating this work, four invaluable theatre history sources must be acknowledged: *A Biographical Dictionary of Actors, Actresses, Musicians, Dancers, Managers & Other Stage Personnel in London*, 1660-1800 by Philip H. Highfill, Jr., Kalman A. Burnim, and Edward A. Langhans. [1973]-1993; The incomparable Mr Colley Cibber's *An Apology for the Life of Mr. Colley Cibber*, 1740; *Eighteenth Century Drama, Censorship, Society and The Stage - The London Stage,* whose data is provided by various participating libraries; *The Restoration Theatre* by Montague Summers, 1934.

Further acknowledgment must be made of the following, which enabled important relevant research on the work: Archive.org; British History Online; EEBO (Early English Books Online); London Metropolitan Archives; Northamptonshire Record Office; Ohio State University Press; Oxfordshire History Centre; Project Gutenberg; The British Library; The National Archives; University of Nottingham; University of Pennsylvania.

Finally, my personal thanks to my wonderful husband for his unconditional support of my passion for research and writing.

S.M.C.

Prologue

The cessation of England's Commonwealth in 1660 brought about not only the restoration of an exiled, impoverished king, but at last an end to the drawn-out and bitter puritanical regime. Protector Oliver Cromwell (1599-1658) had cast his oppressive will over England's green and once pleasant land for far too long and, following his demise in 1658 and the subsequent failure of his son Richard Cromwell (1626-1712) to govern as second Lord Protector, *his* reign lasting a mere two hundred and sixty-four days, the monarchy was once again restored. The coronation of King Charles II (1630-1685) was held on 23 April 1661. Among much jubilation, the king finally took his rightful place upon the throne as ruler of England, Scotland and Ireland.

Most of the populace embraced the change and the inhabitants of the Capital were no exception. The Londoners' pursuit of amusement, drinking, gambling, and leisure was inherent. Their insatiable appetite for the barbaric spectacles of bull and bear-baiting or staged cock fights and their love of fairs, street entertainments, pleasure gardens, brothels and taverns had not been fully slaked during Cromwell's miserable prohibitions. Even enjoying traditional Christmas celebrations and Twelfth Night festivities was seen as a sin.

The reality of Commonwealth tyranny must have really hit home when this intolerable order was read: *Die Veneris, Septemb. The 2. 1642. Ordered by the Lords and Commons Assembled in Parliament, that this Ordinance concerning Stage-Playes be forthwith Printed and Published. John Browne Cler. Parliament*:

> Whereas the distressed Estate of Ireland, steeped in her own Blood, and the distracted Estate of England, threatened with a Cloud of Blood by a Civil War, call for all possible Means to appease and avert the Wrath of God, appearing in these Judgements; among which, Fasting and Prayer, having been often tried to be very effectual, having been lately and are still enjoined; and whereas Public Sports do not well agree

with Public Calamities, nor Public Stage-plays with the Seasons of Humiliation, this being an Exercise of sad and pious Solemnity, and the other being Spectacles of Pleasure, too commonly expressing lascivious Mirth and Levity: It is therefore thought fit, and Ordained, by the Lords and Commons in this Parliament assembled, That, while these sad causes and set Times of Humiliation do continue, Public Stage Plays shall cease, and be forborn, instead of which are recommended to the People of this Land the profitable and seasonable considerations of Repentance, Reconciliation, and Peace with God, which probably may produce outward Peace and Prosperity, and bring again Times of Joy and Gladness to these Nations.[1]

The closure of the playhouses, so dear to the citizens' hearts, had been the meanest attack on their cruelly withheld liberties, as can be seen in this passage from dramatist, poet and musician, Richard Flecknoe (c.1600-1678):

RICHARD FLECKNOE, 1653.

From thence passing on to Black-fryers, and seeing never a *Play-bil* on the Gate, no Coaches on the place, nor *Doorkeeper* at the *Play-house* door, with his *Boxe* like a *Church-warden*, desiring you to remember the poor *Players*, I cannot but say for *Epilogue* to all the Playes were ever acted there:

Poor House, that in dayes of our Grand-sires
Belongst unto the mendiant *Fryers:*
And where so oft in our Fathers dayes
We have seen so many of Shakespears *Playes.*

A whimzey written from beyond seas, about the end of the year, 52, to a Friend lately returned into England.

Miscellania, or Poems of all sorts with divers other Pieces. Written by Richard Fleckno. . . . London, Printed by T. R. for the Author, M.D.C.LIII. [8vo]. pp. 141, 2.[2]

Charles II was well-known for his love of science, the arts, flamboyant dress, his fondness for the playhouse and his most pleasurable wont, the company and moreover the bedding of beautiful females. These apparently free and easy times now brought expectation of a more liberated culture for those who approved of his morals.

On 15 January 1662, Letters Patent were granted by King Charles II to Sir William D'Avenant (1606-1668) and Thomas Killigrew Esq (1612-1683).

William Davenant, who was knighted in 1643 by Charles I (1600-1649), had a colourful life. He was born in Oxford in 1606 the son of John Davenant who ran the Salutation Tavern, later known as the Crown Tavern, at 3 Cornmarket Street in the town. William was one of eight children born in Oxford to the Davenants. Their first six children, born in London, had all died in infancy and were laid to rest in St James Garlickhythe. It was believed by some however that the famous playwright, poet, and actor William Shakespeare (1564-1616) was William Davenant's godfather, and even rumoured that 'the Bard' could have been his father.

William Davenant left Oxford after a short period there as a student which came to nothing. He became a page to Frances Stewart (nee Howard), Duchess of Lennox and Richmond, Countess of Hertford (1578-1639). While in London, at the age of twenty-four, he became infected with syphilis. A common outcome of this disease was an erosion of the tissues of the nose, which in William's case can be clearly seen in an engraving of him, but this apparently unsightly disfigurement didn't exclude him from becoming Poet Laureate in 1638.

He was a great supporter of the Royalist cause during the English Civil Wars, joining the king's army at the beginning of the conflict but, on the Monarch's defeat, he fled to Paris where he was appointed Emissary to France and later made Lieutenant Governor of Maryland. However, he was captured at sea and sentenced to death in 1650, but apparently was reprieved with the intervention of John Milton (1608-1674) who at that time was serving as a civil servant under the Commonwealth. William Davenant spent a year incarcerated in the Tower of London, but was released the following year. Because of Parliament's strict laws of censorship, he cleverly turned one of his rooms at his house in London into a private theatre where it is believed that the first performance of an English opera, *The Siege of Rhodes*, written by him, took place in 1656.

William was once again imprisoned in 1659, after taking part in the Cheshire uprising following the death of Oliver Cromwell and, on his release shortly after, he again fled to France. After the Restoration of Charles II, William returned to England where, along with Thomas

Killigrew, he became a patentee on the reopening of two London theatres; the Duke's under Davenant and the King's under Killigrew.

Surprisingly, Thomas Killigrew's life had taken a similar path to that of Davenant. He was born into a large family of twelve. His father, Sir Robert Killigrew (1580-1633), was a courtier and politician and had been knighted by King James I (1566-1625) in 1603. Thomas, at a young age, like William, became a page to King Charles I. Thomas followed Prince Charles, the future Charles II, into exile in 1647 and from 1649 to 1651 he travelled to Paris, Geneva and Rome, and later was appointed the exiled king's representative in Venice.

At the Restoration, he returned to England and was made Charles II's Groom of the Bedchamber and Chamberlain to Queen Catherine (1638-1705). At Court, Killigrew held the reputation of a wit, gaining the title of the king's fool and jester. Nonetheless, Thomas did have the honour of being boxed on the ears at Court in an act of lese-majesty by the infamous John Wilmot, 2nd Earl of Rochester (1647-1680). Rochester was banned from the Court but, as a favourite, was soon returned by the king.

The historic Letters Patent were a watershed for females to be given the right to act upon the stage in a professional capacity for, until this change, female roles were the privilege of male actors only. A favourite among these was Edward Kynaston (c.1640-1706), who apparently portrayed a very convincing woman. The famous diarist Samuel Pepys (1633-1703) called him *the loveliest lady that ever I saw in my life* after watching him act in *The Loyal Subject*, a tragicomedy by playwright John Fletcher (1579-1625). Today's remnants of the custom must surely be the Molly in traditional Morris sides and the Dame in pantomime. These innovative Letters Patent would allow theatre audiences an entirely different view of stage performances than the plays' previous all-male counterparts, thus adding a certain amount of credible genteel elegance, sweetness of voice and natural beauty. Although not thought of as a respectable career for women, there were no shortages of females willing to enter the profession.

Although a lengthy document, the Letters Patent give such clear and precise conditions that must be adhered to in the building and running of Restoration theatre. Therefore, I feel that selected excerpts will set the scene suitably. Nevertheless, it is not until the penultimate paragraph that the permission for women to act on the stage is set out:

> CHARLES the second, by the Grace of God, king of England, Scotland, France, and Ireland, defender of the faith, &c. to all to whom all these presents shall come, greeting,

Whereas our royal father of glorious memory, by his letters patents under his great seal of England bearing date at Westminster the 26th day of March, in the 14th year of his reign, did give and grant unto Sir William D'avenant (by the name of William D'avenant, gent.) his heirs, executors, administrators, and assigns, full power, licence, and authority, That he, they, and every of them, by him and themselves, and by all and every such person and persons as he or they should depute or appoint, and his and their laborers, servants, and workmen, should and might, lawfully, quietly, and peaceably, frame, erect, new build, and set up, upon a parcel of ground, lying near unto or behind the Three Kings ordinary in Fleet-Street, in the parishes of St. Dunstan's in the west, London: or in St. Bride's, London; or in either of them, or in any other ground in or about that place, or in the whole street aforesaid, then allotted to him for that use; or in any other place that was, or then after should be assigned or allotted out to said Sir William D'avenant by Thomas Earl of Arundel and Surry, then Earl Marshal of England, or any other Commissioner for building, for the time being in that behalf, a theatre or play-house, with necessary tiring and retiring rooms, and other places convenient, containing in the whole forty yards square at the most, wherein plays, musical entertainments, scenes, or other the like presentments might be presented... .

And whereas we did, by our letters patents under the great seal of England, bearing date the 16th day of May, in the 13th year of our reign, exemplifie the said recited letters patents granted by our royal father, as in and by the same, relation being thereunto had, at large may appear.

And whereas the said Sir William D'avenant hath surrendered our letters patents of exemplification, and also the said recited letters patents granted by our royal father, into our Court of Chancery, to be cancelled; which surrender we have accepted, and do accept by these presents... .

And we do hereby, for us, our heirs and successors, grant unto the said Sir William D'avenant, his heirs and assigns, full power, licence, and authority, from time to time, to gather together, entertain, govern, priviledge and keep, such and so many players and persons to exercise and act tragedies, comedies, plays, operas, and other performances of the stage, within the house to be built as aforesaid, or within the house in Lincoln's Inn Fields, wherein the said Sir William D'avenant doth now exercise the premises; or within any other house, where he or they can best be fitted for that purpose, within our cities of London and Westminster, or the suburbs thereof; which said company shall be the servants of our dearly beloved brother, James Duke of York, and shall consist of such number as the said Sir William D'avenant, his heirs or assigns, shall from time to time think meet... .

And that it shall and may be lawful to and for the said Sir William D'avenant, his heirs and assigns, to take and receive of such our subjects as shall resort to see or hear any such plays, scenes and entertainments whatsoever, such sum or sums of money, as either have accustomably been given and taken in the like kind, or as shall be thought reasonable by him or them, in regard of the great expences of scenes, musick, and such new decorations, as have not been formally used.

And further, for us, our heirs, and successors, we do hereby give and grant unto the said Sir William D'avenant his heirs and assigns, full power to make such allowances out of that which he shall so receive, by the acting of plays and entertainments of the stage, as aforesaid to the actors and other persons imployed in acting, representing, or in any quality whatsoever about the said theatre, as he or they shall think fit; and that the said company shall be under the sole government and authority of the said Sir William D'avenant, his heirs and assigns. And all scandalous and mutinus persons shall from time to time be by him and them ejected and disabled from playing in the said theatre.

And for that we are informed that divers companies of players have taken upon them to act plays publicly in our said cities of London and Westminster, or the suburbs thereof, without any authority for that purpose; we do hereby declare our dislike of the same, and will and grant that only the said company erected and set up, or to be erected and set up by the said Sir William D'avenant, his heirs and assigns by virtue of these presents, and one other company erected and set up, or to be erected and set up by Thomas Killigrew, Esq. his heirs or assigns, and none other shall from henceforth act or represent comedies, tragedies, plays, or entertainments of the stage, within our said cities of London and Westminster, or the suburbs thereof; which said company to be erected by the said Thomas Killigrew, his heirs or assigns, shall be subject to his and their government and authority, and shall be styled the Company of Us and our Royal Consort.

...That no actor or other person employed about either of said theatres, erected by the said Sir William D'avenant and Thomas Killigrew, or either of them, or deserting his company, shall be received by the governor or any of the said other company, or any other person or persons, to be employed in acting, or in any matter relating to the stage, without the consent and approbation of the governor of the company, whereof the said person so ejected or deserting was a member, signified under his hand and seal. And we do by these presents declare all other company and companies, saving the two companies before mentioned, to be silenced and suppressed.

And forasmuch as many plays, formerly acted, do contain several profane, obscene, and scurrilous passages; and the womens parts therein have been acted by men in the habits of women, at which some have taken offence: for the preventing of these abuses for the future, we do hereby straitly charge and command and enjoyn, that from henceforth no new play shall be acted by either of the said companies, containing any passages offensive to piety and good manners, nor any old or revived play, containing any such offensive passages as aforesaid, until the same shall be corrected and purged, by the said masters or governors of the said respective companies, from all such offensive and scandalous passages, as aforesaid. And we do likewise permit and give leave that all the womens parts to be acted in either of the said two companies for the time to come, may be performed by women, so long as these recreations which, by reason of the abuses aforesaid, were scandalous and offensive may by such reformation be esteemed, not only harmless delights, but useful and instructive representations of humane life, to such of our good subjects as shall resort to see the same.

...In witness whereof, we have caused these our letters to be made patents. Witness our self at Westminster, the fifteenth day of January, in the fourteenth year of our reign.

By the King. HOWARD.[3]

The permission for females to act in their natural roles, and indeed at times even to don men's attire, must have caused resentment in some of their male counterparts. And no doubt, at the outset, women actresses were looked upon with great suspicion, not only by the actors themselves, whose careers were somewhat in jeopardy, but by much of the audience who viewed these newcomers as no more than women of easy virtue. But in time they rivalled their opposite numbers, not only in roles of tragedy and comedy but they also enjoyed the added advantages of a natural beauty, a sweet singing voice and their captivating dancing of jigs. Such cavorting was a favourite among audiences and in particular with rakes, bucks, debauchers and wits who craved sight of the dancers' legs, and who off-stage lusted after them. In turn, such lechers proffered rich gifts of jewels and money to any who may be willing to accept them. And for a lucky few who caught the eye of the king, dukes, earls and wealthy men of quality, a luxury lodging or even the offer of a good marriage was the reward for such sexual favours. Two examples are pretty, witty, Nellie Gwyn (1650-1687), who relinquished the stage for the royal bed and moved into a fashionable house in Pall Mall which boasted a silver bed for her troubles and the actress Margaret (Peg) Hughes (c.1645-1719), who became the mistress of Prince Rupert of the Rhine, Count Palatine, Duke of Cumberland (1619-1682), cousin to Charles II. Peg and their only child, Ruperta (Hughes) Howe (1671-1726), reaped vast wealth heaped upon them by the dashing cavalier.

***

This work is the story of two celebrated Restoration actresses and close friends; Mrs Elizabeth Barry (1658-1713) and Mrs Anne Bracegirdle (1671-1748), whose early family circumstances and stage careers were very similar. In later life however, their reputations took very different paths and so that is where their similarity ends.

PART ONE

Mrs Elizabeth Barry (1658–1713)

Chapter One

Restoration Theatre and Its Environs

Now, for the difference betwixt our Theaters and those of former times, they were but plain and simple, with no other Scenes, nor Decorations of the Stage, but onely old Tapestry, and the Stage strew'd with Rushes, (with their Habits accordingly) whereas ours now for cost and ornament are arriv'd to the heighth of Magnificence.

Richard Flecknoe: A short Discourse
of the English Stage, 1664.

Seventeenth-century London was a dangerous place, its streets and alleyways fraught with danger from many quarters for the unwary, especially after dark. After the playhouses closed for the evening, the 'better sort' of the audience made their way swiftly by coach to the safety of their homes. But for those that were on foot, the lack of street lighting made the city's walkways very menacing indeed. This was the often undesirable atmosphere of Restoration London in which the actresses Mrs Elizabeth Barry and Mrs Anne Bracegirdle, with many of their contemporaries, lived and worked.

The theatre districts, particularly those of Drury Lane and Covent Garden, were famous for their prostitutes, jilts, nightwalkers, whores, doxies, call them what you will, who took advantage of potential clients emerging from the theatres; *here were found the wits in the afternoon, and rakes at night*. These areas were well-known too for common thieves, pickpockets and for drunken unruly behaviour on the streets and in the drinking establishments, where all manner of unsavoury characters loitered.

Irish writer, playwright, and politician, Sir Richard Steele (1672-1729), co-founder of *The Spectator* along with his friend, essayist, poet, playwright and also politician, Joseph Addison (1672-1719), had this to say of Drury Lane in Volume 1 of The Tatler, 1709.

White's Chocolate-house, July 25.

There is near Covent Garden a street known by the name of Drury, which, before the days of Christianity, was purchased

2

by the Queen of Paphos, and is the only part of Great Britain where the tenure of vassalage is still in being. All that long course of building is under particular districts or ladyships, after the manner of lordships in other parts, over which matrons of known abilities preside, and have, for the support of their age and infirmities, certain taxes paid out of the rewards for the amorous labours of the young. This seraglio of Great Britain is disposed into convenient alleys and apartments, and every house, from the cellar to the garret, inhabited by nymphs of different orders, that persons of every rank may be accommodated with an immediate consort, to allay their flames, and partake of their cares. Here it is, that when Aurengezebe thinks fit to give a loose to dalliance, the purveyors prepare the entertainments; and what makes it more august is, that every person concerned in the interlude has his set part, and the prince sends beforehand word what he designs to say, and directs also the very answer which shall be made to him.

Aureng-zebe is a Restoration drama by playwright and first Poet Laureate, John Dryden (1631-1700), written in 1675 and the last he wrote in rhymed verse, and believed his best heroic work.

One tavern in particular, the Rose, on the east side of Brydges Street, (now Catherine Street), was *frequented by courtiers and men of letters, of loose character, and other gentry of no character at all*. This tavern certainly held a reputation for unruly behaviour.

In the play *The Morning Ramble; or, The Town Humour*, 1672, a comedy by Henry Nevil Payne (d.c.1710), there are some scenes reflecting the kind of events that took place in the Rose Tavern such as *drunken broils, midnight orgies and murderous assaults*. These agitators were often men of fashion referred to as hectors, who might find sadistic pleasure in *running through of some fuddled toper, whom wine had made valiant*. Such were the dangers then, that a man walking a short way from the Rose Tavern to the Piazza *must venture his life twice*.

An excerpt from an amusing lengthy poem, *The Rake Reform'd: A Poem in a Letter to the Rakes of the Town*, 1718, by A. G. Gent, (Abraham Glanvill), depicts a typical rake's night on the town, beginning at Bradbury's, a noted gaming table. Needless to say. the Rose Tavern has a mention too:

> ...To *Bradbury's* at five I did repair,
> Whose chief Frequenters Cheats and Bubbles are;

Where butter'd Squires, mercenary grown,
Too late repent the luckless Mains they've thrown;
Where scatter'd Dice, and broken Boxes show,
The losing Chance, and my unsuccessful Throw
And we by new-coin'd Oaths the Bankrupt Gamester know.
If there Success did on my Wishes wait,
And well-thrown Casts declar'd my prosp'rous Fate;
With Transport to th' half-acted Play I run,
And there by changing Boxes sav'd my Crown:
Inflam'd with Lust, and burning with Desire,
I sought a Punk to cool my amorous Fire,
With eager Eyes the crouded Pit survey'd,
Where Masks, and Velvet-Scarves the Jilts betray'd,
And to the singled She, my well-known Marks convey'd.
Not far from thence appears pendant Sign,
Whose Bush declares the Product of the Vine,
Where to the Travellers Sight the full-blown *Rose*,
Its dazzling Beauties doth in Gold disclose,
And painted Faces flock in Tally'd Cloaths:
Thither conducted I embraced the Whore,
And when enjoy'd I kick'd her out of Door;
Madam discharg'd, I still renew'd the Bowl,
To chear my Senses and obscure my Soul,
Whilst to my Brains Vapours confus'd did rise,
And double Tapors sparkled in my Eyes;
Fancy in airy Dreams aloft was tost,
And vanquish'd Reason in the Height was lost:
In vain I strove to use my faultring Tongue,
Imperfect Accents on the Palate hung;
The swelling Bumpers did my Senses charm,
And Draughts repeated did my Soul disarm;
Glasses diffus'd in broken Fragments lay,
And Cloaths disdain'd with Wine did my Excess betray.
At dead of Night when the unequal Moon,
By silent Steps was mounted to her Noon,
And vocal Watchmen took their solemn Rounds,
Whilst *Twelve a Clock* echo'd in distant Sounds,
With giddy Brains and more uncertain Feet,
I left the *Rose* and sally'd in the Street;...[1]

Restoration London certainly was fraught with danger, where one could easily die at the point of a sword over a trivial argument, often flamed by alcohol.

On the night of Monday 18 May 1696, a young actor, Hildebrand Horden, reportedly one of the most handsome of his day, was killed *in a frivolous, rash accidental Quarrel* at the bar of the Rose Tavern by a Captain Elizeus Burges, who was taken into custody. *The London News Letter* later announced, in November 1697, that Captain Burgess *who killed Mr. Horden the player, has obtained his majesties pardon*, the king then being William III (1650-1702). Incredibly, the alleged murderer Burgess, who had also killed Henry Bourchier Fane (c.1671-1696), an elder brother of Charles Fane, 1st Viscount Fane (1676-1744), in a duel on 12 April 1696 at Leicester Fields, was later appointed Captain General and Governor in Chief of Massachusetts Bay in New England.

Certain London taverns were definitely not places to venture into by the more respectable citizens about town. To give a flavour of what one could expect to experience once inside those grubby tavern walls, here is a piece that sets the scene perfectly. It is taken from *A Walk round London and Westminster, exposing the Vices and Follies of the Town*, by translator and satirist Thomas Brown (1662-1704). This is taken from *The Third Volume of the Works of Mr. Tho. Brown*, 1719. Volume four of the 1911 *Encyclopædia Britannica* sums up Brown and his works pretty accurately: *He was the author of a great variety of poems, letters, dialogues and lampoons, full of humour and erudition, but coarse and scurrilous. His writings have a certain value for the knowledge they display of low life in London*:

> ...a *Tavern* is a little *Sodom*, where as many Vices are daily practis'd as ever were known in the great one. Thither *Libertines* repair to drink away their Brains and piss away their Estates; *Aldermen* to talk Treason, and bewail the Loss of Trade; *Saints* to elevate the Spirit, hatch Calumnies, coin false News, and reproach the Church; *Gamesters* to shake their Elbows, and pick the Pockets of such Cullies who have no more Wit than to play with them; *Rakes* with their *Whores*, that by the help of Wine they may be more imputed and more wicked, and do those things in their Cups, that would be a Scandal to Sobriety; *Lovers* with their *Mistresses*, in hopes to wash away that Modesty with the Soothing Juice, which had been a Hindrance to their Happiness, so that they may fall to without

Grace, and give a pleasing Earnest to each other of their future Affections: Thither *Sober Knaves* walk with *Drunken Fools*, to make cunning Bargains, and over-reach them in their Dealings, where, cloaking their mental Reservations with a grave Countenance, they will tell more Lies about a Hogshead of Tobacco, than Tavernier in his Travels does about Mount *Ætna*. Thither *Young Quality* retire to spend their Tradesmens Money, and to delight themselves with the Impudence of lewd Harlots, free from the Reflections or Remarks of their own Servants, whilst their Ladies at Home are doing themselves Justice after the like Manner, and perhaps, for want of better Opportunity, are glad to break a Commandment with their own Footmen. Thither *Bullies* Coach it to kick Drawers, and invent new Oaths and Curses, and in Feasting, Rattling and Blustering, to lavish away that scandalous Income call'd a Petticoat-Pension, tho' doom'd the next Day to a Threepenny Ordinary. Thither run *Sots* purely to be drunk, that they may either wash away the Reflections of their own past Follies, or forget the Treachery of their Friends, the Falsehood of their Wives, the Disobedience of their Children, the Roguery of their Lawyers, the Bitchery of their Paramours, or the Ingratitude of the World, that they may drown the Remembrance of past Evils in the Enjoyment of the present: Thither *Beaux* flock to show their Vanity, drink Healths to their Mistresses, boast of Conquests they never made, praise Beauties they never saw, brag of Duels they never fought, censure Books they never read, damn Authors they never knew, talk familiarly of Noblemen they had never the Honour to speak to, commend the Virtue of Women they have made Whores, and rob those of their Reputation they could never conquer. Thither *Cowards* repair to make themselves valiant by the Strength of their Wine; Fools to make themselves witty in their own Conceits; *Maids* to be made otherwise; *Married Women* to cuckold their Husbands; and *Spendthrifts* to be made miserable by a ridiculous Consumption of their own Fortunes. In short, no People are Customers to that Warehouse of Debaucheries, where *Rakes* and *Extravagants* surfeit their vicious Appetites at the Price of their own Ruin, but what are less careful of their own Good, than they are of their Vintners, except such who have a strong Guard upon their Purses, and a stout Bridle to

their Appetites, and they may venture to sip off half a Pint at
a Sitting, without the Danger of contracting an ill Habit, that
may at last expose them to the World's Contempt, under the
scandalous Plague of an empty Pocket.[2]

Following Brown's education at Newport and Oxford, he worked as a
schoolmaster for a short time at Kingston-upon-Thames before moving to
the Grub Street district of London. The pleasures of London afforded him
a libertine lifestyle which he later regretted. Although his satirical works
gained him many enemies, Jonathan Swift (1667-1745) thought highly
of Brown's work, with Joseph Addison declaring in *The Spectator* on
Wednesday 14 July 1714: *Some of our authors indeed, when they would be
more satirical than ordinary, omit only the vowels of a great man's name,
and fall most unmercifully upon all the consonants. This way of writing
was first of all introduced by T_m Br_wn, of facetious memory, who, after
having gutted a proper name of all its intermediate vowels, used to plant it
in his works, and make as free with it as he pleased, without any danger of
the statute.* Thomas Brown died on 16 June 1704 and was buried in the east
cloister of Westminster Abbey.

Even away from taverns, dangerous arguments were had, one such
involving the famous soldier and statesman, John Churchill, later 1st Duke
of Marlborough (1650-1722) and dramatist and poet Thomas Otway
(1652-1685). The cause of this altercation was a playhouse orange-wench:

> In a letter, dated 23rd June, 1679, from John Verney in
> London to Sir Richard Verney, of Claydon House, *comitatu*
> Bucks, mention is made of an event which was causing great
> talk: "Churchill, for beating an orange wench in the Duke's
> playhouse, was challenged by Capt. Otway (the poet), and
> were both wounded, but Churchill most. The relation being
> told the King by Sir John Holmes, as Churchill thought to his
> prejudice, he challenged Holmes, who fighting disarmed him,
> Churchill."[3]

This whole affair was alluded to in some lines of the prologue to the
tragicomedy, *The Young King; or, The Mistake*, believed performed at
the Duke's Theatre in the summer of 1679, by the talented Aphra Behn
(1640-1689), playwright, poet, translator and fiction writer, and one of
the first English women to attempt to earn a living by writing. For a short
period, Aphra had been employed by Charles II as a spy in Antwerp, which

circumstance left her seriously in debt. One option to alleviate her lack of funds was to embark on writing. Although one of the most productive playwrights of her time, she continued to be hampered by poverty and debt until the day she died, on 16 April 1689. Soon after, she was buried in the East Cloister of Westminster Abbey.

The Theatre pit certainly seemed a hive of activity where *Men of Quality, particularly the younger Sort, some Ladies of Reputation and Vertue, and abundance of Damsels that hunt for Prey, sit all together in this Place*:

> *They're Sparks who are of noise and nonsence full,*
> *At Fifteen witty and at Twenty dull;*
> *That in the Pit can huff, and talk hard words,*
> *And briskly draw Bamboo instead of Swords:*
> *But never yet Rancounter cou'd compare*
> *To our late vigorous* Tartarian *War:*
> *Cudgel the Weapon was, the Pit the Field;*
> *Fierce was the Heroe, and to brave to yield.*
> *But stoutest hearts must bow; and being well can'd,*
> *He crys, Hold, hold, you have the Victory gain'd.*
> *All laughing call—*
> *Turn out the Rascal, the eternal Blockhead.*
> *—Sounds, cry* Tartarian, *I am out of Pocket:*
> *Half Crown my Play, Six pence my Orange cost;*
> *Equip me that, do you the conquest boast.*
> *For which, to be at ease, a gathering's made,*
> *And out they turn the Brother of the blade.*
> *—This is the fruits of idleness and ease.*
> *Heaven bless the King that keeps the Land in peace,*
> *Or he'll be sweetly serv'd by such as these.*[4]

There is a delightful piece to be found, a *Prologue: Against the Disturbers of the Pit*, in *The Works of the Earls of Rochester, Roscomon, and Dorset...*:

> GENTLE Reproofs have long been try'd in vain
> Men but despise us, while we but complain;
> Such Numbers are concern'd for the wrong Side,
> A weak Resistance still provokes their Pride,
> And cannot stem the Fierceness of the Tide.
> Laughers, Buffoons, with an unthinking Croud
> Of gaudy Fools impertinent and loud,

Insult in ev'ry Corner. Want of Sense,
Confirm'd with an outlandish Impudence.
Among the rude Disturbers of the Pit,
Have introduc'd ill Breeding and false Wit.
To boast their Leudness here young Scow'rers meet,
And all the vile Companions of the Street,
Keep a perpetual Bauling at the Door,
Who beat the Baud last Night? Who bilkt the Whore?
They snarl, but neither fight, nor pay a Farthing;
A Play house is become a meer Bear-Garden.
Where ev'ryone with Insolence injoys
His Liberty and Property of Noise.
Should true Sense, with revengeful Fire come,
Our *Sodom* wants ten Men to save the Town;
Each Parish is infected; to be clear,
We must lose more, than when the Plague was here.
While ev'ry little Thing perks up so soon,
That at Fourteen it hectors up and down,
With the best Cheats, and the worst Whores in Town;
Swears at a Play, who should be whipt at School,
The Foplings must in Time grow up to Rule;
The Fashion must prevail to be a Fool.
Some pow'rful Muse, inspired for our Defence,
Arise, and save a little common Sense.
In such a Cause, let thy keen Satire bite,
Where Indignation bids thy Genius write;
Mark a bold leading Coxcomb of the Town,
First single out the Beast, then hunt him down;
Hang up his mangled Carcass on the Stage,
To fright away the Vermin of the Age.[5]

Even Robert Gould (*c.1660-c.1708*), in *The Play-House. A Satyr*, 1685, spells out in no uncertain terms the dangers of the playhouse:

...The Fops in Scarlet swearing the Play:
Nor yet unduly they themselves acquit,
For Fustian on the Stage, too, goes for Wit.
A Harmless Jest, or Accidental Blow,
Spilling their Snuff, or touching but the Toe,
With many other things too small to name,

Does blow these Sparks of Honour to a Flame:
For such vile Trifles, or some Viler *Drab*,
'Tis in an Instant *Damn me*, and a *Stab*.
No mild Perswasion can these Brutes reclaim;
'Tis thus to Night, to Morrow 'Tis the same.
What a long List might Justice here Produce
Of Blood, of Fighting, Banning and Abuse?
What *Weekly Bill*, for Number, can compare
To those that have been basely Butcher'd here,
Within the Compass but of Twenty Year?
One Actress has at least, to name no more,
Been her own self the Slaughter of a Score.
Murder's so Rife, with like Concern we hear
Of Man kill'd, as Baiting of a *Bear*.
All People now, the Place is grown so ill,
Before they see a *Play* shou'd make their *Will*:
For with much more Security, a Man
Might take a three Years Voyage to *Japan*…

Robert Gould was orphaned aged thirteen, at which time he entered domestic service as a footman to a Lady. By the age of twenty, Gould was in the employ of Charles Sackville, 6th Earl of Dorset (1643-1706), where he possibly learned to read and write, later earning a living as a poet, satirist and author. According to Montague Summers, in his Notes to Appendix I, *The Play-House, A Satyr*, he *became a patron and staunch friend of James, Earl of Abington, who employed the poet upon the family estate at Rycote, Oxon.*

In an excerpt from one of Gould's famous works, a poem, *Love given over; or, A Satyr against the pride, lust and inconstancy &c. of woman*, variously attributed to him and Thomas Brown, a woman's lust is satirised in no uncertain terms. Do I detect an element of misogyny here!:

…And now, if so much to the World's reveal'd,
Reflect on the vast Stores that lie conceal'd,
How, oft into their Closets they retire,
Where flaming Dil— does inflame desire,
And gentle Lap-d—s feed the am'rous fire.
How curst is Man! when Brutes his Rivals prove,
Ev'n in the sacred Business of his Love!
Unless Religion pious thoughts instill,

Show me the Woman that wou'd not be ill,
If she conveniently could have her will.
And when the Mind's corrupt, we all well know,
The actions that proceed from't must be so.
Their guilt's as great who any ill wou'd do,
As theirs who actually that ill pursue,
That they would have it so their Crime assures;
Thus, if they durst, most Women would be Whores.
That is (and 'tis what all men will allow)
There's many wou'd be so that yet seem vertuous now,…[6]

It is pretty clear that the ungentlemanly conduct ever-present in the notorious pit, often didn't in any way adhere to *The Young Gallant's Academy; or, Directions how he should behave himself in all places and company as in an ordinary, in a play-house etc.*, by *Sam. Overcome*, 1674. Sam Overcome was a pseudonym of Samuel Vincent, and his publication was largely drawn from *Gull's horn-book*, 1609, by Thomas Dekker (c.1572-1632).

The following is an amusing excerpt from chapter five in the publication, giving detailed instructions on how a young man should conduct himself on a visit to the playhouse. However, it is obvious, from historic references regarding behaviour in the pit, that many young men, and for that matter some women too, ignored etiquette and lived by their own intemperate rules:

> *Instructions for a young Gallant how to behave himself in the*
> Play-house.

> The *Theatre* is your *Poets-Royal Exchange*, upon which their *Muses* (that are now turned to Merchants) meeting, barter away that light Commodity of words, for a lighter ware than words, *Plaudities*, and the breath of the great Beast, which (like the threatnings of two Cowards) vanish into Air.

> The *Play-house* is free for entertainment, allowing Room as well to the *Farmers Son* as to a *Templar*; yet it is not fit that he whom the most Taylors bills make room for when he comes, should be basely, like a Viol, cased up in a corner: Therefore, I say, let our Gallant (having paid his *half Crown*, and given the Door-keeper his *Ticket*) presently advance himself into the middle of the *Pit*, where having made his Honor to the rest of the Company, but especially to the Vizard-Masks, let him pull

out his Comb, and manage his flaxen Wig with all the Grace he can. Having so done, the next step is to give a hum to the China-Orange-wench, and give her her own rate for her Oranges (for 'Tis below a *Gentleman* to stand haggling like a *Citizens wife*) and then to present the fairest to the next Vizard-mask. And that I may incourage our Gallant not like the Trades-man to save a shilling, and so sit but in the Middle Gallery, let him but consider what large comings-in our pursed up sitting in the *Pit*.

1. First, a conspicuous Eminence is gotten, by which means the best and most essential parts of a Gentleman, as his fine Cloaths and Perruke, are perfectly revealed.
2. By sitting in the *Pit*, if you be a Knight, you may happily get you a Mistress; which if you would, I advise you never to be absent when *Epsom Wells* is plaid: for,

We see the Wells *have stoln the* Vizard-masks *away*...[7]

Those particularly unruly theatre-going men had gained such a reputation, documented in many publications, including Thomas Brown's *Amusements Serious and Comical, Calculated for the Meridian of London. 1700.* The last paragraph is most descriptively amusing and comical and, if anything, portrays Brown's talent for observation:

Amusement V.
The Play-House.

THE *Play-House* is an Inchanted Island, where nothing appears in Reality what it is, nor what is should be. 'Tis frequented by Persons of all Degrees and Qualities whatsoever, that have a great deal of Idle Time lying upon their Hands, and can't tell how to employ it worser. Here *Lords* come to Laugh, and to be Laugh'd at for being there, and seeing their Qualities ridicul'd by every Triobolary Poet. Knights come hither to learn the Amorous Smirk, the *A la mode* Grin, the Antick Bow, the Newest-Fashion'd Cringe, and how to adjust his Phiz, to make himself as Ridiculous by Art, as he is by Nature.

Hither come the Country Gentlemen to shew their Shapes, and trouble the Pit with their Impertinence about Hawking, Hunting, and their Handsome Wives, and their Housewifery.

There sits a *Beau* like a Fool in a Frame, that dares not stir his Head, nor move his Body, for fear of incommoding his Wig, ruffling his Cravat, or putting his Eyes, or Mouth out of the Order his *Maitre de Dance* had set it in, whilst a *Bully Beau* comes Drunk into the Pit, Screaming out, *Dam me*, Jack, *'Tis a Confounded Play, let's to a* Whore *and spend our time better.*

Here the Ladies come to shew their Cloaths, which are often the only things to be admir'd in or about 'em. Some of them having Scab'd, or Pimpled Faces, wear a Thousand Patches to hide them, and those that have none, scandalize their Faces by a Foolish imitation. Here they shew their Courage by being unconcerned at a *Husband* being *Poison'd*, a *Hero* being *kill'd*, or a Passionate Lover being *Jilted*; And discover their Modesties by standing Buff at a Baudy Song, or a Naked Obscene Figure. By the Signs that both Sexes hang out, you may know their Qualities or Occupations, and not mistake in making your Addresses.

Men of *Figure* and Consideration, are known by seldom being there, and Men of *Wisdom* and Business, by being always absent. A *Beau* is known by the Decent Management of his Sword-Knot, and Snuff-Box. A *Poet* by his Empty Pockets: A Citizen by his Horns and Gold Hatband: A Whore by a *Vizor-Mask*: And a Fool by Talking to her. A Play-House *Wit* is distinguish'd by wanting Understanding; and a *Judge* of Wit by Nodding and Sleeping, till the falling of the Curtain, and Crowding to get out awake him...[8]

You could imagine playhouse China-orange-wenches just turning up randomly at the theatres, and selling their wares. Yet, this seems not to be the case, as in February 1662/3 the authorities of the Theatre Royal, who included Thomas Killigrew, granted to Mrs Mary Meggs, a widow also known as Orange Moll, *on payment of one hundred pounds, full, free, & sole liberty, licence, power, & authority to vend, utter, & sell Oranges, Lemons, fruit, sweetmeats, & all manner of fruiterers & Confectioners wares & commodities.* She paid six shillings and eight pence a day and could trade throughout the house, but apparently not in the upper gallery. Mrs Meggs' privileged licence lasted for thirty-nine years!

Hopefully, Orange Moll's own reputation was not one that was generally bantered about. *Collin's walk through London and Westminster, a poem in burlesque*, 1690, is an amusing work by Devonshire-born writer and wit Thomas D'Urfey (Tom Durfey) (1653-1723). In the poem, Country Collin, on his visit to London, is taken to the playhouse where he observes sights unfamiliar to his bucolic living. D'Urfey was a prolific writer, composing during his lifetime some five hundred songs and thirty-two plays!:

> …The Beau that rambles from the Boxes
> To the middle Gallery where the Pox is;
> The Cully too that makes a show
> With Punk in the side box below,
> From whence his Heart e're she can ask it,
> Leaps into th' Orange-Wenches Basket;
> There Pants, and Praises the dam'd Features
> Of that most Impudent of Creatures;…

D'Urfey added a further judgement; *The Character of an Imprudent Play-House Orange Wench, being there every day acted, I think needs no further Comment*. It seems clear that this West-Country wit was not over-enamoured of the fruit sellers, or perhaps he simply had an aversion to oranges.

And here we have musings on the playhouse audience, with an excerpt from *Prologue at Oxford*. 1673:

> …A Lover thus to's Mistriss does impart,
> The treasure of his purse as well as heart;
> For that of which She has an equal part,
> What pleasure is it to give you delight,
> When most of you are fit to Judge and write.
> Here none t' appear fantastick take great pains,
> Or under huge white Perr'wigs have no brains;
> No blustring Bullyes come in here half drunk,
> For Chyna Oranges and love to Punck;
> To fly at Vizard Masks talk Nonsence loud,
> And with their noise out-vye Bear-baiting Croud
> Poets should be above such Judges rais'd,
> To be condemn'd by such is to be prais'd:
> But to his Nursery of Art and Wit,
> Our Poets humbly all their Pens submit.
> To you what 'ere they can invent is due,
> Since all that's Wit and Art is taught by you…[9]

But what of the playhouse itself? One often alludes to the romanticism of a candlelit theatre, with its players dressed in colourful attires of the best silks, satins and lace, much akin to its audience. The air filled with the smell of sweet oranges and with lovers' intrigues acting out their own scenes in the boxes. All in all, a very pleasant place to see and be seen while awaiting patient hours before that day's performance began.

There is a contemporary description of the King's Theatre recorded by Count Lorenzo Magalotti (1637-1712) who accompanied Prince Cosimo III of Tuscany (1642-1723) on his visiting England in 1669. The prince attended the playhouse on 25 April and was seated in His Majesty's box:

> ...going towards evening to the King's theatre, to hear the comedy, in his majesty's box. This theatre is nearly of a circular form, surrounded, in the inside, by boxes separated from each other, and divided into several rows of seats, for the greater accommodation of the ladies and gentlemen, who, in conformity with the freedom of country, sit together indiscriminately; a large space being left on the ground-floor for the rest of the audience. The scenery is very light, capable of a great many changes, and embellished with beautiful landscapes. Before the comedy begins, that the audience may not be tired with waiting, the most delightful symphonies are played; on which account many persons come early to enjoy this agreeable amusement. The comedies which are acted, are in prose; but their plots are confused, neither unity nor regularity being observed; the authors having in view, rather than any thing else, to describe accurately the passions of the mind, the virtues and the vices; and they succeed the better, the more the players themselves, who are excellent, assist them with action, and with the enunciation of their language, which is very well adapted for the purpose, as being a variation, but very much confined and curtailed, of the Teutonic idiom, and enriched with many phrases and words of the most beautiful and expressive description, taken both from ancient and modern languages...[10]

Be that as it may, the reality of that crowded and stifling building, measuring in length on the outside some one hundred and thirteen feet, would, to a modern audience seem unbearably cramped. The stage itself together with the tiring-rooms occupied sixty-four feet, with three feet for the orchestra leaving less than half the building's length for the audience. It is difficult to determine the sort of capacity of such a Restoration playhouse, but it is thought that some one thousand people could have been seated at any one time, with over half occupying the pit.

To begin with, the majority of the wooden seating, particularly the ten rows in the pit, would have been very basic, with no backboard and covered with green cloth. The only form of lighting would have been by wax candles, presenting the danger of fire being sparked in the crowded building. The candles' flickering presence, along with the odour of burnt wax and smoke would, I'm sure, have been quite bothersome.

The smell of oranges, lemons and other fruit being consumed would no doubt have been a welcome distraction from the smell of the audience, whose own personal body stench must have been quite overwhelming. But considering that personal hygiene in those days was less than basic, including the wealthy and poor alike, Restoration noses were probably far more accommodating in close confinement than would be today's nostrils.

This brings me to public conveniences… there *were* none! No doubt one would make sure to empty one's bowels or bladder, or both, beforehand. But if taken short during a performance, the answer would often have been to vacate in order to evacuate in the nearest dark alley. Nevertheless, if this was not possible, then the inevitable would transpire. How theatregoers today take for granted the convenience of good sanitation, hot and cold running water, comfortable seating, heating, air conditioning and electric illumination; things now so common for us. It wasn't until 1881 that the first theatre in London, the Savoy, had incandescent electric lightbulbs installed.

Of course, a hidden danger in the packed building could be that of deadly diseases, the playhouses themselves being breeding grounds for such as smallpox and tuberculosis. However, people would be readily infected with syphilis during liaisons beyond the playhouse.

It is worth noting words written in the diary of Samuel Pepys for Thursday 6 February 1668, when he and his wife attended the playhouse on a very popular occasion:

> …at noon home to dinner; and my wife being gone before, I to the Duke of York's playhouse, where a new play of Etheriges called She would if she could. And though I was there by 2 a-clock, there was 1000 people put back that could not have room in the pit; and I at last, because my wife was there, made

shift to get into the 18*d* box - and there saw; but Lord, how full
was the house...

And what of the players themselves? Acting was not the easiest of
employments, the players spending long hours and weeks rehearsing new
plays, often in full costume. Some performances required the players to
dance, sing and sometimes to stage mock fights with weapons, when a
sudden lack of concentration by a combatant could easily cause real harm.
I know these incidents to be true, as an eighteenth-century ancestor of mine,
Roger Bridgwater, who was a London stage actor, accidentality inflicted a
serious wound on a fellow player during a performance:

> To break a leg is a well-known theatrical term wishing good
> luck to a performer prior to their going on stage, but to stab a
> fellow actor on stage would be going a little too far. Yet such
> an incident did occur at Drury Lane on the 15th of September
> 1739! The play was Mariamne, a tragedy (literally), written
> by English poet, biographer and translator, Elijah Fenton
> (1683-1730). Roger was acting the part of Sohemus, first
> Minister, and fellow actor, singer and dancer James Rosco
> (d.1761) was playing the part of Sameas, the King's Cup-
> bearer. The part of Salome, the King's sister, was played
> by Mrs. Stevens, stage name of Priscilla Wilford, later the
> third Mrs. John Rich (c.1713-1783). In the fight scene, Act
> V scene IV, Roger accidentally stabbed poor Rosco, but
> luckily he survived and thankfully didn't hold a grudge
> against Roger. By October, Rosco was back on the stage.
> Nonetheless, the incident did add an element of realism to
> the play.[11]

That unfortunate 'shot in the dark' so to speak, would certainly not have
slaked the Elizabethan or Restoration audience's appetite for gore on the
stage. Originally, bladders filled with the blood of a sheep or a calf were used
to good effect, and later a sponge of blood became the choice of weapon
for realism. Surreally, these bloody events were often depicted in comedies
as well as in scenes of historic martyrdom. The players were also required
to act the part of being brutally tortured on the rack or the wheel, and were
seen suffering the pincers and fire, or even being hanged, for which it is
believed a dummy figure was used, thank goodness. This leads me onto an
amusing anecdote in Richard Steele's *The Spectator*, on Friday 16 March

1711, on the use of smoke and fire during a performance of *Rinaldo and Armida*:

> ...We had also but a very short Allowance of Thunder and Lightning; tho' I cannot in this Place omit doing Justice to the Boy who had the Direction of the Two painted Dragons, and made them spit Fire and Smoke: He flash'd out his Rosin in such just Proportions, and in such due Time, that I could not forbear conceiving Hopes of his being one Day a most excellent Player. I saw, indeed, but Two things wanting to render his whole Action compleat, I mean the keeping his Head a little lower, and hiding his Candle.

And back to the red stuff. Two years earlier, Steele remarked in *The Tatler*, on Wednesday 13 February 1709:

> ...I must own, there is something very horrid in the public executions of an English tragedy. Stabbing and poisoning, which are performed behind the scenes in other nations, must be done openly among us, to gratify the audience.
>
> When poor Sandford was upon the stage, I have seen him groaning upon a wheel, stuck with daggers, impaled alive, calling his executioners, with a dying voice, cruel dogs and villains! And all this to please his judicious spectators, who were wonderfully delighted with seeing a man in torment so well acted. The truth of it is, the politeness of our English stage, in regard to decorum, is very extraordinary. We act murders to show our intrepidity, and adulteries to show our gallantry: both of them are frequent in our most taking plays, with this difference only, that the first are done in sight of the audience, and the other wrought up to such a height upon the stage, that they are almost put in execution before the actors can get behind the scenes...

It seems then, that Restoration audiences were certainly not averse to the sight of bloody drama. Probably they were acclimatised to such barbarity from an early age, with real murders, public executions, and street and tavern fights with victims succumbing to a violent end from brutal woundings inflicted by knife or sword. So it would appear that playhouse spectators were somewhat accustomed to real violence and so were not unduly perturbed witnessing the depiction of it in the form of stage entertainment. But no doubt some in the audience, of a more sensitive nature, were only too pleased to see an earlier murdered victim alive and well reciting the Epilogue.

Apart from the players, the theatre behind the scenes was a very busy, bustling place. There was an army of workers all playing their parts, ensuring the smooth running of performances. These included managers, box-keepers, door-keepers, house tailors, dressers, carpenters, painters and wardrobe keepers, all earning their livings from theatre entertainment.

Then, as today, the audience would see the players on stage effortlessly performing their roles, seemingly without any knowledge of the hectic back-of-stage activities.

The stage props and costumes themselves were an essential part of any production, and were stored away in readiness for when they were needed. Here is an except from a delightful piece, *The Stage: A Poem*:

HIGH o'er the Stage there lies a rambling
  Frame,
Which Men a Garret vile, but Play'rs the Tire-
  room name;
Here all their Stores (a merry Medley) sleep,
Without Distinction huddled in a Heap.
  HUNG on the self same Peg, in Union rest
Young TARQUIN'S Trowsers, and LUCRETIA'S Vest,
Whilst without pulling QUOIVES ROXANA lays
Close by STATIRA'S Petticoat her Stays;
Hard by a Quart of bottled Light'ning lies,
A Bowl of double Use, and monstrous Size;
Now rolls it high, and rumbles in its Speed,
Now drowns the weaker Crack of Mustard-seed;
So the true Thunder all array'd in Smoak,
Launch'd from the Skies now rives the knotted
  Oak,
And sometimes nought the Drunkard's Pray'rs
  avail,
Ah sometimes condescends to sower Ale.
Near these sets up a Dragon-drawn Calash,
There a Ghost's Doublet delicately slash'd,
Bleeds from the mangled Breast, and gapes a
  frightful Gash,

In Crimson wrought the sanguine Floods abound,
And seem to gutter from the streaming Wound.
Here IRIS bends her various painted Arch,
There artificial Clouds in sullen Order march,
Here stands a Crown upon a Rack, and there
A WITCH'S Broomstick by great HECTOR'S Spear;
Here stands a Throne, and there the CYNICK'S
    Tub,
Here BULLOCK'S Cudgel, there ALCIDE'S Club.
Beads, Plumes, and Spangles, in Confusion rise,
Whilst Rocks of Cornish Diamonds reach the Skies.
Crests, Corslets, all the Pomp of Battle join,
In one Effulgence, one promiscuous shine.[12]

On 19 March 1666, Samuel Pepys visited the Theatre Royal at a time when it was closed to the public due to it undergoing alterations. Here he sums up how different the theatrical items looked in their unglamorous surroundings:

> …after dinner we walked to the King's play-house, all in dirt, they being altering of the Stage to make it wider– but God knows when they will begin to act again. But my business here was to see the inside of the Stage and all the tiring roomes and Machines; and endeed, it was a sight worthy seeing. But to see their clothes and the various sorts, and what a mixture of things there was, here a wooden leg, there a ruff, here a hobby-horse, there a Crowne, would make a man split himself to see with laughing–and particularly Lacys wardrobe, and Shotrell's. But then again, to think how fine they show on the stage, by candle-light, and how poor things they are to look now too near-hand, is not pleasant at all…

And who could resist transcribing such an amusing Inventory as that in *The Tatler*, on Friday 15 July 1709. No one could disagree that Steele and Addison possessed humour!:

> St. James's Coffee-house, July 15.

> It is now twelve o'clock at noon, and no mail come in; therefore I am not without hopes, that the town will allow me the liberty which my brother news-writers take, in giving them what may

be for their information in another kind, and indulge me in doing an act of friendship, by publishing the following account of goods and movables.

This is to give notice, that a magnificent palace, with great variety of gardens, statues, and waterworks, may be bought cheap in Drury Lane; where there are likewise several castles to be disposed of, very delightfully situated; as also groves, woods, forests, fountains, and country seats, with very pleasant prospects on all sides of them; being the movables of Ch——r R——ch, Esq.; who is breaking up housekeeping, and has many curious pieces of furniture to dispose of, which may be seen between the hours of six and ten in the evening.

The INVENTORY.

Spirits of right Nantes brandy, for lambent flames and apparitions.

Three bottles and a half of lightning.

One shower of snow in the whitest French paper.

Two showers of a browner sort.

A sea, consisting of a dozen large waves; the tenth bigger than ordinary, and a little damaged.

A dozen and a half of clouds, trimmed with black, and well conditioned.

A rainbow a little faded.

A set of clouds after the French mode, streaked with lightning, and furbelowed.

A new-moon, something decayed.

A pint of the finest Spanish wash, being all that is left of two hogsheads sent over last winter.

A coach very finely gilt, and little used, with a pair of dragons, to be sold cheap.

A setting sun, a pennyworth.

An imperial mantle, made for Cyrus the Great, and worn by Julius Cæsar, Bajazet, King Harry the Eighth, and Signior Valentin.

A basket-hilt sword, very convenient to carry milk in.

Roxana's night-gown.

Othello's handkerchief.

The imperial robes of Xerxes, never worn but once.

A wild-boar, killed by Mrs. Tofts and Dioclesian.

A serpent to sting Cleopatra.

A mustard-bowl to make thunder with.

Another of a bigger sort, by Mr. D——is's directions, little used.

Six elbow-chairs, very expert in country-dances, with six flower-pots for their partners.

The whiskers of a Turkish bassa.

The complexion of a murderer in a band-box; consisting of a large piece of burnt cork, and a coal-black peruke.

A suit of clothes for a ghost, viz., a bloody shirt, a doublet curiously pinked, and a coat with three great eyelet-holes upon the breast.

A bale of red Spanish wool.

Modern plots, commonly known by the name of trapdoors, ladders of ropes, vizard-masks, and tables with broad carpets over them.

Three oak cudgels, with one of crab-tree; all bought for the use of Mr. Pinkethman.

Materials for dancing; as masks, castanets, and a ladder of ten rounds.

Aurengezebe's scimitar, made by Will Brown in Piccadilly.

A plume of feathers, never used but by Oedipus and the Earl of Essex.

There are also swords, halberts, sheep-hooks, cardinals' hats, turbans, drums, gallipots, a gibbet, a cradle, a rack, a cart-wheel, an altar, a helmet, a back-piece, a breast-plate, a bell, a tub, and a jointed baby...[13]

Stage costumes for Restoration players were elaborate, colourful and with plenty of sparkle though, one way or another, took mainly the form of Restoration attire. As Summers comments, *Indeed there were very few female characters that wore any but modish costumes, which would have been strictly en regle for a jaunt to the Park or the New Exchange.... But I have no doubt that although when Pepys saw Heywood's rather clumsy chronicle Queen Mary and Queen Elizabeth were in their native habits, the many characters who surrounded them differed little if at all in their costumes from the ordinary clothes in vogue during August, 1667. I conceive that most of the actors might have walked straight from the boards into the streets without exciting attention or remark.*

However, there are always exceptions to the rules, as can be seen from one of Pepys' diary entries for Thursday 24 January 1667:

> ...and, anon, at about 7 or 8 a-clock comes Mr. Harris, of the Duke's playhouse, and brings Mrs. Pierce with him, and also one dressed like a country-maid, with a straw hatt on, which at first I could not tell who it was, though I expected Knipp—but it was she, coming off the stage just as she acted this day in *The Goblins*—a merry jade...

Several pendant chandeliers, hanging from the proscenium arch, would have aided the costumes to look their best. For safety's sake, the chandeliers were placed well in front of the curtain, their light illuminating the stage apron and the players' heads. There were footlights too, the early ones consisting of a few separate, smelly oil lamps. Later, a device known as *the floats* came into being, and consisted of a number of cotton wicks, running through large round pieces of cork. These floated on oil contained in a long narrow tin box that was placed over a trapdoor in front of the stage.

There were several trapdoors, which rose and sank, strategically placed on the floor of a Restoration theatre, and used for various purposes. The larger ones, behind the curtain, were used for set pieces of scenery of a large size, sometimes with a group of characters upon them, whereas on the apron stage, there were smaller trapdoors where just one or two people could appear from below. All this seems to point to the fact that there would have been a considerable cellar room under a Restoration theatre.

Many of these theatre innovations and devices were put into practise at the suggestion of the great leading actor Thomas Betterton (c.1635-1710) when he had returned from his stay in Paris, after examining the theatres there at the request of Charles II. One outcome of his reconnaissance was the inclusion on the English stage of shifting scenes that replaced the old tapestry scenery.

The costumes, particularly those for principal characters, were often designed for showy, luxurious richness, made from fine velvets, silks and lace, rather than for creating detailed historical accuracy, particularly as a large part of the audience would view the stage from a distance. It is believed that the minor players, albeit costumed, would be dressed in plainer clothes.

The Restoration fashion for the wearing of full-bottomed periwigs was also a major part of the costume ensemble, not only for actors but for the actresses too, when their breeches role required them to dress in man's attire.

An excerpt taken from The Prologue to the Reader, in *Thyestes a tragedy*, by John Wright, Gent. 1674:

> ...Nor Love, nor Honour here the Author show'd:
> Nay, what is worse, no Bawd'ry A-la-mode.
> No Amorous Song, nor a more Amorous Jigg,
> Where Misses Coats twirl like a Whirlegig,
> And such who next the Lamps themselves dispose,
> Think thus to recompence the stink of those,
> While she that Dances jilts the very eyes,
> Allowing only these Discoveri's
> A neat silk Leg, and pair of Holland Thighs...[14]

Thomas Davies, writing as late as 1784, remarks on the former players' liking for the wig:

> The heads of the English actors were, for a long time, covered with large full-bottomed perriwigs, a fashion introduced in the reign of Charles II. which was not entirely disused in public till about the year 1720. Addison, Congreve, and Steele, met at Button's coffee-house, in large, flowing, flaxen, wigs; Booth, Wilks, and Cibber, when full-dressed, wore the same. Till within these twenty-five years, our Tamerlanes and Catos had as much hair on their heads as our judges on the bench.—Booth was a classical scholar, and well acquainted with the polite arts; he was conversant with the remains of antiquity, with busts, coins, &c. nor could he approve such a violation of propriety; but his indolence got the better of his good taste, and he became a conformist to a custom which he despised. I have been told, that he and Wilks bestowed forty guineas each on the exorbitant thatching of their heads...[15]

The running of a playhouse was a serious business, and its main aim was to make a profit ensuring payment of salaries for all who worked there, from the lowest paid to the highest. In the 1690s, an experienced actor could be paid fifty shillings a week, today's equivalent would be some three hundred pounds, a good wage in those days. Even so, an experienced actress was paid far less and would receive no more than thirty shillings a week. It appears that the famous Mrs Barry was an exception to this rule, commanding a weekly salary equivalent to her experienced male counterparts except that

Betterton, who performed alongside Elizabeth, would earn a whopping five pounds a week! To be fair to him, his managerial skills, as well as his acting prowess, were no doubt reflected in his salary.

Some of the highest earners, by fair means or foul, usually the latter, were the theatres' door-keepers and box-keepers. Their job was to collect money from theatregoers as they entered the building for the day's performance. There are various amusing accounts of the keepers' cunning in monetary matters; In a treatise *The Actor's Remonstrance, or Complaint, for the Silencing of their Profession and Banishment from their several Playhouses*, dated 24 January 1643, printed after the closing of the theatres by Parliament, it mentions: *Nay, our verie doore keepers, men and women, most grievously complain that by this cessation they are robbed of the privilege of stealing from us with licence; they cannot now seem to scratch their heads where they itch not, and drop shillings and half crown pieces in at their collars.*

Samuel Pepys, always in the thick of things, was conned of a shilling when he, his wife and their maid Deb Willet went to the playhouse to see *The Spanish Tragedy*, on Monday 24 February 1668: *I was prettily served this day at the Playhouse door where, giving six shillings into the fellows hand for us three, the fellow by legerdemain did convey one away, and with so much grace faced me down that I did give him but five, that, though I knew the contrary, yet I was overpowered by his so grave and serious demanding the other shilling, that I could not deny him, but was forced by myself to give it him.*

Astonishingly, a shilling here, a half crown there, could add up to a tidy sum over the years, as can be seen from the following:

> In a letter to Lord Berkley, Buckingham desired him to tell a certain lady, that he had resolved to swear by no other than Joe Ash; 'and, if that,' said his grace, 'be a sin, it is as odd an one as ever she heard of.' Joe Ash was, it seems, a box-keeper at Drury-lane play-house. How this man could merit this distinction I know not, unless he lent the duke money to supply his necessities, which were often very urgent. Box-keepers, whatever they may be now, by the managers keeping an eye over their conduct, were formerly richer than their masters. A remarkable instance of it I heard many years since. Colley Cibber had, in a prologue, or some part of a play, given such offence to a certain great man in power, that the playhouse, by order of the lord-chamberlain, was shut up for some time,

Cibber was arrested, and the damages laid at ten thousand pounds. Of this misfortune Booth and Wilks were talking very seriously, at the playhouse, in the presence of a Mr. King, the box-keeper; who asked if he could be of any service, by offering to bail Cibber.— 'Why, you blockhead,' says Wilks, 'it is for ten thousand pounds.'____ 'I should be very sorry,' said the box-keeper, 'if I could not be answerable for twice that sum.' The managers stared at each other; and Booth said, with some emotion, to Wilks, 'What have you and I been doing, Bob, all this time? A box-keeper can buy us both.'[16]

Ten thousand pounds at that time seems a staggering sum for verbal offence aimed at someone, whether it be at a great man in power or otherwise. And what is the more unbelievable is that a mere box-keeper had the means to offer such a vast sum for bail. Now, I am not saying that Mr King was an unscrupulous sort of fellow but, either way, there must have been a method in his madness, he no doubt desiring the re-opening of the theatre as soon as possible in order to continue his lucrative employment.

The theatres themselves were no safe haven from unruly behaviour, it being so far removed from that of today's considerate and attentive audiences. The following is a piece regarding eighteenth-century theatre, but no doubt little had changed from the seventeenth-century establishments:

In the theatre, the better sort, with the ladies, occupied the boxes; no disreputable or drunken persons were admitted it was thought ill-mannered for a man to keep on his hat during the performance; the pit —there were no stalls—was occupied almost entirely by men, especially by young lawyers, young City men, and students who had read the play and were all ready with their criticism. As to the upper boxes nothing is said; we may imagine that they were frequented by the lower class. The footmen, for many years, had their own gallery, and very often proved noisy critics; order, if necessary, was preserved among the gods by the butchers of Clare Market, who were steady patrons of the theatre and staunch upholders of the actors.[17]

The cost of entry to the theatres remained constant for a very long time. Admission to the upper gallery was one shilling, the middle gallery eighteen pence, the pit half a crown and the boxes were four shillings.

In John Timbs' *Club Life of London,* 1866, he mentions the market's butchers' keenness for the playhouse; *Clare Market lying between the two great theatres, its butchers were the arbiters of the galleries, the leaders of theatrical rows, the musicians at actresses' marriages, the chief mourners at players' funerals.*

To expand further on the dangers for theatregoers, there is an interesting account of an incident that occurred at the Theatre Royal, Drury Lane during a performance of *The Scornful Lady*. This was a benefit play for the actress Mrs Anne Oldfield (1683-1730) who was also in the cast:

> A circumstance is related as having happened at a representation of this play, which may serve as a useful hint to those who are apt, on the most trivial occasions, to appeal to what are most absurdly called the laws of *honour*: At a representation of *The Scornful Lady*, many years ago, for the benefit of Mrs. Oldfield, several persons of distinction were behind the scenes: among others, Beau Fielding came; and, being always mighty ambitious of showing his fine make and shape, as himself used vainly to talk, he very closely pressed forward upon some gentleman, but in particular upon one Mr. Fulwood, a barrister of Gray's Inn, an acquaintance of Mrs. Oldfield. Mr. Fulwood, being a gentleman of quick resentment, told Mr. Fielding he used him rudely; upon which he laid his hand upon his sword but Mr. Fulwood instantly drew, and gave Mr. Fielding a wound of twelve inches deep in the belly. This putting the audience into the greatest consternation, Mr. Fulwood was, with much entreaty, persuaded to leave the place. At length, out of respect to Mrs. Oldfield, he did so, and went to the theatre in Lincoln's Inn Fields, where, the same evening, *The Libertine* was acted. Mr. Fulwood went into the pit, and, in a very few minutes, cast his eye upon one Captain Cusack, to whom he had an old grudge, and there demanded satisfaction of him. Captain Cusack, without the least hesitation, obeyed the summons. They went into the field, and, in less than half an hour, word was brought into the house, that Mr. Fulwood was killed on the spot, and that Captain Cusack had made his escape.[18]

Life for those frequenting these notoriously unsavoury areas was in general intimidating so, as a rule, safety in numbers on the perilous neighbouring streets of Covent Garden and Drury Lane must have been essential.

But not all danger was in the form of criminality. The hazards of disease, and moreover risky medical intervention in an attempt to cure the same would often end in death after a surgeon's interference. Horrific accidents with horse-drawn vehicles involving passengers and pedestrians alike and the simple extraction of a rotten tooth which could easily lead to septicaemia and death are two such examples. These are just the tip of the iceberg of all the possible disasters faced in everyday life in a crowded metropolis.

What a dangerous environment for a vulnerable fifteen-year-old girl to find herself living in.

Chapter Two

Mrs Barry's Roots

There are often mysteries attaching to the family roots of Restoration actresses, and Elizabeth Barry's are no exception. All in all, the lack of factual documentation prior to her becoming an actress is frustrating to say the least. Even after exhaustive research, which did reveal some tantalising possibilities, alas next to nothing conclusive could be gained. So to date, an author writing of Mrs Barry's ancestry still has to rely on sparse and, it has to be said, somewhat questionable evidence.

According to bookseller and publisher Edmund Curll (c.1675-1747) in his biography of Elizabeth Barry, her father was a *gentleman of an ancient family and good estate*, a Mr Robert Barry, Barrister at Law, later known as Colonel Barry through his raising of arms for King Charles I during the English Civil Wars. This generous act apparently depleted his estate and so made difficulties for his family. In other accounts, her father is named as Edward Barry, so there is immediate confusion as to who Elizabeth's father really was. In *The history of the English stage, from the Restauration to the present time. Including the lives, characters and amours, of the most eminent actors and actresses. With instructions for public speaking; wherein the action and utterance of the bar, stage, and pulpit are distinctly considered* by Thomas Betterton, believed to have been written in collaboration with Edmund Curll and published in 1741, there are, on page thirteen, chapter two, *Memoirs of Mrs. Barry*, beginning with:

> *Elizabeth Barry* was the Daughter of *Robert Barry*, Esq; Barrister at Law; a Gentleman of an ancient Family, and good Estate.
>
> At the Beginning of the Civil Wars, when King *Charles* invited all his Loyal Subjects to take up Arms in his Defence, Mr. *Barry* raised a Regiment for his Majesty's Service, composed of his Neighbours and Tenants, equipping and maintaining them a considerable Time at his own Expence. This, as it ever after, made him known by the Title of Colonel *Barry*, it also so far incumbered his Estate, as to oblige his

29

Children, when grown up, to make their own Fortunes in the
World.

The Lady *D'Avenant*, who had been several Years a Widow,
and a particular Friend of Sir *William D'Avenant*, having the
greatest Friendship for Col. *Barry*, took his Daughter, when
young, and gave her a good Education. Lady *D'Avenant* made
her not only her Companion, but carried her wherever she
visited. Mrs. *Barry* by frequently conversing with Ladies of
the first Rank and best Sense, became soon Mistress of that
Behaviour which sets off the well-bred Gentlewoman.

Let's hope that Lady D'Avenant *was* a particular friend of Sir William, as
she was his third wife, having several sons by him!

Sir William Davenant met Henrietta Maria du Tremblay of
St Germaine Beaupré during his stay in France, probably
about 1646. He may have been married at that point, but the
facts concerning his first wife are very dim; it is probable
that Henrietta Maria was also then married, though facts of
her life at this time are equally scarce. At any rate, the pair
may well have had an affair, as Davenant's *Gondibert* implies.
About a decade and one wife later, Sir William came back to
France, wooed and won the lady (then, apparently, a widow),
and brought her back to England in 1655. The couple moved
into Rutland house, in which Sir William planned to present
his "operas."[1]

Lady Davenant survived her husband by twenty-three years and was buried
in the old vault at St Bride's Church, Fleet Street, on 24 February 1690/1.

Considering *The history of the English stage* was published some twenty-
eight years after the death of Elizabeth Barry in 1713, one does feel a little
unsure of its reliability as to the parentage of the actress. Edmund Curll was
apparently notorious for publishing biographies of famous people which
included inaccuracies and inventions. Was this the case with Elizabeth's
biography? Twenty-eight years is a long time to remember accurate details
of someone's life, unless of course contemporary notes had been made by
the author, Curll, which is very doubtful.

There are no references regarding the identity of Mrs Barry's father
other than to those of a Robert or an Edward noted above. The *Robert Barry*
account has been accepted universally as the truth. However, with research,

there has not been found, so far, reference to anyone who would truly fit the bill of either a Robert or an Edward Barry, both supposedly Barrister at Law and Royalist Colonel. Intriguing.

As Lady Mary Davenant was of French birth, one wonders whether Mrs Barry was taught by her to speak and write the language, although there appears no evidence for this. But to have been educated by Lady Mary and seemingly her companion from a young age, she might have at least learned something of the language and a certain amount of French sophistication too.

Whatever the truth of her lineage, of good estate or otherwise, there was one who thought her bloodline stemmed from the lowest quarter and, with the lack of evidence, who are we to argue that this might or might not have been the case. The old proverb *no smoke without fire* does spring to mind. Within an extremely lengthy poem, *The Play-House. A Satyr*, 1685, by Robert Gould, the author wrote these damning lines on Elizabeth Barry who played Zara in *The Mourning Bride*, with Betterton as Osmyn:

> ...When, let our Plays be acted half an Age,
> W'ave but a third Days Gleaning of the Stage?
> The rest is yours:— and hence your Sharers rise,
> And once above us, all our Aid despise:
> Hence has your *Osmin* drawn his Wealthy Lot,
> And hence has *Zara* all her Thousands got:
> *Zara!* That Proud, Opprobrious, Shameless Jilt,
> Who like a Devil justifies her Guilt,
> And feels no least Remorse for all the Blood sh'has spilt.
> But prithee *Joe*, since so she boasts her Blood,
> And few have yet her Lineage understood,
> Tell me, in short, the Harlot's true Descent,
> 'Twill be a Favour that you shan't repent.
>
> Truly said *Joe*, as now the Matter goes,
> What I shall speak must be beneath the Rose.
> Her mother was a common Strumpet known,
> Her Father half the Rabble of the Town.
> Begot by Casual and Promiscuous Lust,
> She still retains the same Promiscuous Gust,
> For Birth into a Suburb Cellar hurl'd,
> The Strumpet came up Stairs into the World.
> At Twelve she'd freely in Coition join,

And far surpass'd the Honours of her Line.
As her Conception was a Complication,
So its Produce, alike, did serve the Nation;
Till by a Black, Successive Course of Ills,
She reach'd the Noble Post which now she fills;
Where, *Messalina* like, she treads the Stage,
And all Enjoys, but nothing can Asswage!...[2]

Earlier in the poem, both Betterton and Mrs Barry are also lampooned:

...These little Shifts, grown useless for the Stage,
I'm forc'd to follow to sustain my Age.
Our Sharers, now so insolent are they,
We Under-Actors must like Slaves obey;
and toil and drudge, while they divide the Pay.
Not *Busby* more Tyrannically Rules,
Than *Bet____n* among his Knaves and Fools:
But most to me is his ill Nature shown,
Because my Voice is with my Palate gone:
Not that I faster than the rest decline;
Both Men and Women in my Failing joyn,
and *B____y's* Breath is grown as rank as mine...[3]

By the time these words were written, Elizabeth had become an experienced actress over some ten years, following her first recorded performance at the Dorset Garden Theatre in 1675, at the age of seventeen, as Maid Draxilla in *Alcibiades* by Thomas Otway. The dramatist's infatuation with Mrs Barry caused him perpetual heartache, she never reciprocating his advances. Poor Otway died, it is said, chocking on a mouthful of beggarly bread, love-lorn and poverty-stricken.

This is just one of many undated passionate letters Otway wrote to Mrs Barry:

TO MADAM——

COULD I see you without passion, or be absent from you without pain, I need not beg your pardon for this renewing my vows, that I love you more than health, or any happiness here, or hereafter. Every thing you do is a new charm to me; and though I have languished for seven long tedious years of desire, jealously despairing; yet every minute I see you, I still discover something new and more bewitching. Consider how I love you; what would not I renounce, or enterprize for you! I must have you mine, or I am miserable, and nothing but knowing which shall be the happy hour, can make the rest of my life that are [is] to come tolerable. Give me a word or two of comfort, or resolve never to look with common goodness on me more, for I cannot bear a kind look, and after it a cruel denial. This minute my heart aches for you; and, if I cannot have a right in your's, I wish it would ache till I could complain to you no longer.

Remember poor OTWAY.[4]

Chapter Three

Would She Make An Actress?

Initially, all had not gone to plan for this aspiring actress, to the point of her being dismissed from the company.

> …There was, it seems, so little Hope of Mrs. *Barry* at her first setting out, that she was, at the end of the first Year, discharg'd the Company, among others, that were thought to be a useless Expence to it…[1]

This sacking could have been curtains for Elizabeth's career, but there was someone in the wings who had noticed some potential in her. Even though she was not a beauty, according to actor and dramatist Anthony Aston (*c.1682-c.1753*): *And yet this fine Creature was not handsome, her Mouth opening most on the Right Side, which she strove to draw t'other Way, and at Times composing her Face as if sitting to have her Picture drawn. She was middle-siz'd, and had darkish Hair, light Eyes, dark Eyebrows, and was indifferently plump.* And Aston was also known to remark that Mrs Barry; *was woman to Lady Shelton, of Norfolk, (my godmother) when Lord Rochester took her on the Stage; where for some Time they could make nothing of her____She could neither sing, nor dance, no, not in a Country-Dance.*

Beauty and potential talent are in the eye of the beholder, and the eyes of John Wilmot, 2nd Earl of Rochester were firmly fixed on this young woman. Rochester, libertine, poet, reprobate, and at that time married with two young children, made it his business to approach Mrs Barry, offering to train her to greatness.

Rochester was confident that she could become a great actress and entered into a wager with his friends:

> …But the Earl of *Rochester*, to shew them he had a Judgment superiour, entered into a Wager, that by proper Instructions, in less than six Months, he would engage she should be the finest Player on the Stage. He was opposed by them all, and

tho' they knew him to be a Person of excellent Sense, yet they thought, on this Subject, he had started beyond the Bounds of his Judgment; and so many poignant Things were said to him on this Occasion, that they piqued him into a Resolution of taking such Pains with Mrs. *Barry*, as to convince them he was not mistaken.[2]

It was not long during her training until Rochester, a man of great sexual charm and promiscuity, became intimate with this charming young girl, and it is said *that he never loved any Person so sincerely as he did Mrs. Barry*. That might have been true at the time, but their passion for each other did not endure, with their affair relatively short-lived. The woman who I believe the earl truly loved was his ever-tolerant wife, the heiress Elizabeth Malet (1651-1681). She stood by him steadfastly to the bitter end, and their children too were much loved by both their parents.

Mrs Barry's tutor was a forceful taskmaster, and on occasion made her rehearse a part some thirty times, with many of those in stage costume. He initially chose roles for her such as the Little Gipsy in the comedy *The Rover; or, The Banish'd Cavaliers* by Aphra Behn, and Isabella, the Queen of Hungary in the tragedy *Mustapha* by the Earl of Orrery (1621-1679). However, it is believed her initial performance, in 1673, was that of Isabella at the Dorset Garden Theatre. At that performance, Charles II, James Duke of York (1633-1701) and his Italian wife, Mary of Modena, Duchess of York (1658-1718) were present in the audience. It is said that the duchess was so impressed with Elizabeth's acting that she presented the actress with her wedding suit, and also took lessons in English from her. When Mary eventually became queen to James II, she afterwards gave Elizabeth her coronation robes when the actress played Queen Elizabeth I in *The Unhappy Favourite; or, The Earl of Essex*, a tragedy by Restoration playwright John Banks (c.1650-1706).

Perceptive Rochester won his wager, Elizabeth *did* become a celebrated actress and the most famous tragedienne of her day. Their affair lasted but a few years, but a child, Elizabeth, was born of this liaison in late 1677, at a time when their ardour for each other had somewhat waned.

Daughter Elizabeth 'little Barry', became a bone of contention for her father, he of all people not liking Mrs Barry's supposedly promiscuous lifestyle. He felt that she was not a fit mother for his daughter; *the child is of the soft sex I love*. Rochester then abducted the child, not a course of action alien to him, he having many years before abducted, at Charing Cross, his future wife, Elizabeth, in an effort to win her. This daring act greatly angered the king, for which Rochester paid the price of a few weeks' incarceration in the Tower. Being a favourite of the king at that time, Rochester was soon released:

> MADAM,
>
> I Am far from delighting in the *Grief* I have given you, by taking away the *Child*; and you, who made it so absolutely necessary for me to do so, must take that Excuse from me, for all the ill Nature of it: On the other side, pray be assur'd, I love *Betty* so well, that you need not apprehend any *Neglect* from those I employ; and I hope very shortly to restore her to you a finer *Girl* than ever. In the mean time you wou'd do well to think of the *Advice* I gave you, for how little shew soever my *Prudence* makes in my own *Affairs*, in yours it will prove very successful, if you please to follow it; and since *Discretion* is the thing alone you are like to want, pray study to get it.[3]

This was not the most kindly letter to receive from a former lover. The year was 1679 and Rochester's health was declining fast, so 'little Barry' was soon returned to her mother's care. Her father died the following year at High Lodge, Woodstock, a reported penitent. In his will, he left *to an Infant Child by the Name of Elizabeth Clerke Fourtie pounds Annuitie to commence from the day of my decease, and to continue during her life.* I have never truly believed that this Elizabeth Clerke was *their* daughter, as there would be no logical reason whatsoever why she should have been named Clerke. Research has revealed in later documents, that Barry's daughter is clearly named as Elizabeth Barry, who sadly died c.1689 at the age of twelve, an event much lamented by her mother.

Chapter Four

The Famous Mrs Barry

Elizabeth Barry's stage career endured for thirty-seven years, and for those times of male domination that was some feat. Her command of the stage was unparalleled at the time; even her fellow actresses knew their place and were very rarely tempted to try their luck in the roles she had made her own.

She had begun to tread the boards as a member of the Duke's Company at the Dorset Garden Theatre in 1673, two years after it opened under the management of Thomas Betterton.

Betterton was born in Tuttle Street, Westminster. His father was an under-cook to King Charles I. When young Betterton was old enough, his father apprenticed him to Mr John Rhodes (fl.1624-1665), a bookseller at the sign of the Bible in Charing Cross. Coincidently his other apprentice at that time was Mr Edward Kynaston. It so happened that Rhodes had formerly been Wardrobe Keeper to the King's Company of comedians in Blackfriars. In 1660, on the return to London of General George Monck, 1st Duke of Albemarle (1608-1670), Rhodes obtained from him a licence to set up his own company of players at the Cockpit in Drury Lane. With his two apprentices having the aspirations of becoming actors, Rhodes employed them at his new venture, with Thomas Betterton taking male roles, making his first appearance on stage that same year at the age of twenty-five, while Edward Kynaston took women's roles. Thus began the careers of those celebrated actors.

Two years later, in 1662, Thomas Betterton married actress and singer, Mary Saunderson, widow, on Christmas Eve in the parish of Islington, he of Westminster and she of St Giles, Cripplegate, Middlesex. They had a happy marriage that lasted for forty-eight years.

When Sir William Davenant obtained a patent from Charles II for the Duke's Company, he wisely employed Betterton and others of Rhodes' players for himself. In 1662 he set up his playhouse in Lincoln's Inn Fields.

After Davenant's death in 1668, a new theatre was built under the supervision of the remaining Davenant family, it being managed by their leading actor, Thomas Betterton. The funds for its construction were raised by the company's shareholders. They amounted to some nine thousand pounds, well over a million in today's currency. By November 1671, the theatre was complete and the Duke's Company moved in. The site was leased for thirty-nine years at an annual rent of one hundred and thirty pounds.

The new theatre was constructed on the grounds of Dorset House, the former home of the Sackvilles, Earls of Dorset, which had been destroyed in the Great Fire of London. The house was never replaced, and in its stead were built tenements. The theatre's position near Dorset stairs in Whitefriars, adjacent to the river Thames, allowed its theatregoers to travel there safely by boat, thus avoiding 'Alsatia', a name given to the Whitefriars area, which spanned from the Whitefriars monastery to the south of the west end of Fleet Street adjacent to the Temple, and which was once a refuge for culprits of crime.

When premiered, *The Squire of Alsatia*, a play written in 1688 by Poet Laureate and playwright Thomas Shadwell (c.1642-1692), had a remarkable success, running for thirteen days. Shadwell wrote in his dedication to the Earl of Dorset; *...no Comedy, for these many years, having fill'd the Theatre so long together: And I had the great Honour to find so many Friends, that the House was never so full since it was built, as upon the Third day of this Play: and vast numbers went away, that could not be admitted...*

Amusingly, inside the print copy of the play was a handy glossary, just in case you ever had the need to parley in Whitefriars!

An Explanation of the Cant.

Alsatia. White-fryers.
Prig, Prigster. Pert Coxcombe.
Bubble, Caraven. The Cheated.
Sealer. One that give Bonds and Judgments for Goods and Money.
A Put. One who is easily wheedled and cheated.
Coale, Ready, Rhino, Darby. Ready money.
Rhinocerical. Full of money.
Megs. Guineas.
Smelts. Half-Guineas.
Decus. A Crown piece.
George. A Half-Crown.
Hog. A Shilling.
Sice. Six pence.
Scout. A Watch.
Tattler. An Alarm, or Striking Watch.

Famble. A Ring.

Porker, Tilter. A Sword.

A Rumm Nab. A good Beaver.

Rigging. Cloaths.

Blowing, Natural, Convenient, Tackle, Buttock, Pure Purest pure. Several Names for a Mistress, or rather a Whore.

To Equip. To furnish one.

A Bolter of White-fryers. One that does but peep out of *White-fryers*, and retire again like a Rabbit out of his hole.

To lugg out. To draw a Sword.

To Scamper, to rub, to scowre. To run away.

Bowsy. Drunk.

Clear. Very Drunk.

Smoaky. Jealous.

Sharp. Subtle.

A Sharper. A Cheat.

A Tattmonger. A Cheat at Dice.

Tatts. False Dice.

The Doctor. A particular false Die, which will run but two or three Chancers.

Prog. Meat.[1]

Tragically, on the evening of 25 January 1672, the King's Company theatre, known as the Theatre Royal in Bridges Street, caught fire. The fire had started below the stage, but fortunately, the performance had been finished for some time, with the audience and players safely out of the building. Half the theatre was burned down. Its scenery and wardrobes were also destroyed together with many houses close by. This catastrophe forced the King's Company to use the Lincoln's Inn playhouse during the necessary building of their new theatre on the existing site. It opened in 1674 and was renamed the Theatre Royal in Drury Lane. After the company's removal, the building was converted back to a tennis court and remained so for a further twenty years until, in 1695, Betterton's Company converted the building once more into a theatre.

It appears from the following extract that two of the players of the King's Theatre became somewhat annoyed by the success of the new Dorset Garden Company, with a certain amount of animosity brewing. The outcome of these disputes was the reaching of an agreement, with a Memorandum drawn up between the parties awarding two of the king's leading actors, Charles Hart (1625-1683) and Edward Kynaston, a share of the Dorset Garden Company's profits. A proviso of the agreement was that Hart and Kynaston could continue with this arrangement provided neither of them would under any circumstances perform at the King's Theatre. This memorandum appeared to be an amicable one with all parties gaining, Hart and Kynaston making money, and the Dorset Garden playhouse gaining two prominent actors:

> But notwithstanding all the Industry of the Patentee and Managers, it seems the *King's House* then carry'd the vogue of the Town; and the *Lincolns-Inn Fields* House being not so commodious, the Players and other Adventurers built a much more magnificent Theatre in *Dorset Gardens*; and fitted it for all the Machines and Decorations the Skill of those times could afford. This likewise proving less effectual than they hop'd, other Arts were employ'd, and the Political Maxim of *Divide and Govern* being put in Practice, the Feuds and Animosities of the King's Company were so well improv'd, as to produce an Union betwixt the two Patents. To bring this Design about, the following Agreement was sign'd by the Parties hereafter mention'd.

> *Memorandum, Octob.* 14. 1681.

> It was then agreed upon between Dr. *Charles Davenant, Thomas Betterton*, Gent. and *William Smith*, Gent. of the one Part, and *Charles Hart*, Gent. and *Edward Kynaston*, Gent. on the other Part,—That the said *Charles Davenant, Thomas Betterton*, and *William Smith*, do pay, or cause to be paid, out of the Profits of Acting, unto *Charles Hart* and *Edward Kynaston*, five Shillings a-piece for every Day there shall be any Tragedies, or Comedies, or other Representations acted at the *Duke*'s Theatre in *Salisbury Court*, or where-ever the Company shall act during the respective Lives of the said *Charles Hart*, and *Edward Kynaston*, excepting the Days the young Men or young Women play for their own Profit only; but this Agreement to cease, if the said *Charles Hart* or *Edward Kynaston* shall at any time play among, or effectually assist the King's Company of Actors; and for as long as this is pay'd, they both covenant and promise not to play at the King's Theatre.

If Mr. *Kynaston* shall hereafter be free to act at the Duke's Theatre, this Agreement with him, as to his Pension, shall also cease.

In Consideration of this Pension, Mr. *Hart* and Mr. *Kynaston* do promise to make over, within a Month after the Sealing of this, unto *Charles Davenant, Thomas Betterton*, and *William Smith*, all the Right, Title, and Claim which they or either of them may have to any Plays, Books, Cloths, and Scenes in the King's Play-house.

Mr. *Hart* and Mr. *Kynaston* do both also promise within a Month after the Sealing hereof, to make over to the said *Charles Davenant, Thomas Betterton*, and *William Smith*, all the Title which they each of them have two Six and Three Pence a-piece for every Day there shall be any Playing at the King's Theatre.

Mr. *Hart* and Mr. *Kynaston* do both also promise to promote with all their Power and Interest an Agreement between both Play-houses; and Mr. *Kynaston* for himself promises to endeavour as much as he can to get free, that he may act at the *Duke*'s Play-house, but he is not obliged to play unless he have ten Shillings *per* day allow'd for his Acting, and his Pension then to cease.

Mr. *Hart* and Mr. *Kynaston* promise to go to Law with Mr. *Killigrew* to have these Articles perform'd, and are to be at the Expense of the Suit.

In Witness of this Agreement, all the Parties have hereunto set their Hands, this 14th of *October*, 1681.[2]

After her initial training by Lord Rochester, Elizabeth Barry, through hard work and determination, became a very accomplished actress.

One particular play staged at Dorset Garden Theatre on 11 March 1676, during the time of Elizabeth's love affair with Rochester, was the comedy *The Man of Mode; or, Sir Fopling Flutter*, by Sir 'gentle' George Etherege (*c.1636-c.1692*). The protagonist in the play was the rakish character Dorimant who on this day was played by Thomas Betterton, with Mrs Barry acting the role of Mrs Loveit, in love with Dorimant. Etherege may have based *The Man of Mode* on his friend Rochester. Although there is no actual evidence for this, many in the audience at the time must have been thinking on those lines. Apparently, Rochester was not in the audience, he at that time being absent from the town, but it seems that John Dennis was in attendance, and in the following extract recalls his thoughts in *A Defence of Sir Fopling Flutter*:

> Now I remember very well, that upon the first acting this Comedy, it was generally believed to be an agreeable Representation of the Persons of Condition of both Sexes, both in Court and Town, and that all the World was charm'd with *Dorimont*, and that it was unanimously agreed, that he had in him several of the Qualities of *Wilmot* Earl of *Rochester*, as, his Wit, his Spirit, his amorous Temper, the Charms that he had for the fair Sex, his Falshood, and his Inconstancy, the agreeable Manner of his chiding his Servants, which the late Bishop of *Salisbury* takes Notice of in his Life, and lastly, his repeating, on every Occasion, the Verses of *Waller*, for whom that noble Lord had a very particular Esteem,...[3]

No doubt Mrs Barry would have been most able to play her part with the utmost realism, being at that time Wilmot's mistress. However, their relationship was waning a little through much of her lover's time being spent away from the town. By late 1677, after the birth of their daughter, their love for each other had hit rock bottom, never to be rekindled, whereas Elizabeth's fame as an actress was certainly in the ascendant.

Mrs Barry was renowned as the finest tragedienne of her day, an accolade which stemmed from her leading roles as Monimia in the tragedy *The Orphan; or, The Unhappy Marriage* and as Belvidera in the tragedy *Venice Preserved; or, A Plot Discover'd*, both of these plays by love-lorn Otway; and as Isabella in the tragicomedy *The Fatal Marriage; or, The Innocent Adultery*, a play by dramatist Thomas Southerne (1660-1746).

It has been suggested that *The Orphan*, whose premiere took place on 1 February 1680 at the Dorset Garden Theatre, could have been inspired by Otway's unrequited love for Mrs Barry.

The prompter John Downes had this to say of her performances in the three plays:

> ...gain'd her the Name of Famous Mrs. Barry, both at Court and City; for when ever She Acted any of these three Parts [Monimia, Belvidera in *Venice Preserved*, and Isabella in *The Fatal Marriage*], she forc'd Tears from the Eyes of her

Auditory, especially those who have any Sense of Pity for the Distress't.[4]

In Betterton's *The History of the English Stage*, he extols Mrs Barry's outstanding performances, and includes his advice to actors:

> …How often have I heard Mrs. *Barry* say, that she never spoke these words in the *Orphan*, – *Ah! poor CASTALIO* !--- without weeping. Nay, I have frequently observed her to change her Countenance several Times as the Discourse of *others* on the *Stage* have affected her in the Part she acted. This is being thoroughly concerned, this is to know one's Part, this is to express the Passions in the Countenance and Gesture.
>
> The stage ought to be the *Seat* of *Passion* in its various Kinds, and therefore the *Actors* ought to be thoroughly acquainted with the whole Nature of the Affections, and Habits of the Mind, or else they will never be able to express them justly in their Looks and Gestures, as well as in the Tone of their Voice, and Manner of Utterance. They must know them in their various Mixtures, as they are differently blended together in the different Characters they represent; and then that excellent Rule, in the *Essay on Poetry*, will be of equal Use to the *Poet* and the *Player*,
>
> —*Who* must look *Within* to find
> Those *secret* Turns of *Nature* in the *Mind*;
> Without this *Part* in vain would be *Whole*,
> And but a *Body* All, without a Soul.
>
> BUCK.[5]

By June 1680, Elizabeth's former lover, Rochester, lay dying at High Lodge, Woodstock, lovingly nursed by his mother and wife, both labouring with heavy hearts. Meanwhile, at Dorset Garden on the first of that month, Mrs Barry was again mesmerising her audience as Corina, the whore, in a play *The Revenge; or, A Match at Newgate*, believed to be by Aphra Behn.

Mrs Barry's former lover and father of her child died peacefully on 26 July 1680 at High Lodge, after weeks of unbearable torment and pain:

> …And on *Monday* about Two of the Clock in the Morning, he died, without any *Convulsion*, or so much as a groan.[6]

Aphra Behn was a friend of Rochester's and she greatly mourned his loss, later penning a poignant poem to his memory titled *On the Death of the Late Earl of Rochester*.

The poem begins:

> Mourn, mourn, ye Muses, all your loss deplore,
> The young, the noble Strephon is no more.
> Yes, yes, he fled quick as departing light,
> And ne'er shall rise from Death's eternal night,
> So rich a prize the Stygian gods ne'er bore,
> Such wit, such beauty, never graced their shore.
> He was but lent this duller world t' improve
> In all the charms of poetry, and love;
> Both were his gift, which freely he bestowed,
> And like a god, dealt to the wond'ring crowd.
> Scorning the little vanity of fame,
> Spight of himself attained a glorious name.
> But oh! in vain was all his peevish pride,
> The sun as soon might his vast luster hide,
> As piercing, pointed, and more lasting bright,
> As suffering no vicissitudes of night...

And ends with:

> ...Large was his fame, but short his glorious race,
> Like young Lucretius lived and died apace.
> So early roses fade, so over all
> They cast their fragrant scents, then softly fall,
> While all the scattered perfumed leaves declare,
> How lovely 'twas when whole, how sweet, how fair.
> Had he been to the Roman Empire known,
> When great Augustus filled the peaceful throne;
> Had he the noble wond'rous poet seen,
> And known his genius, and surveyed his mien,
> (When wits, and heroes graced divine abodes),
> He had increased the number of their gods;
> The royal judge had temples rear'd to's name,
> And made him as immortal as his fame;
> In love and verse his Ovid he'ad out-done,
> And all his laurels, and his Julia won.

Mourn, mourn, unhappy world, his loss deplore,
The great, the charming Strephon is no more.

Rochester was buried in the Lee family vault at All Saints Church, Spelsbury in Oxfordshire. There is no memorial to him; just a simple brass plate affixed to his coffin, with the words *John Earle of Rochester 1680.*

Centuries later, an historic event occurred at the church:

John Wilmot, 2nd Earl of Rochester.
"so great a man and so great a sinner."

Over a quarter of a century ago, the then vicar of Spelsbury accompanied by church officials, decided to finally settle a rumour current among the local population for centuries, that a certain tomb in the church held riches. They descended into the vault where the coffin rested. The coffin plate was removed and the lid raised. The first thing they saw was a small casket which, when opened, clearly revealed it had contained viscera and which gave off a strong scent of the herbs in which they had been packed more than three centuries before. There was no sign of treasure. Instead the searchers found themselves gazing upon the mortal remains of one of the most complex, talented, wayward and controversial figures of the seventeenth century. He was John Wilmot, the second Earl of Rochester, a notorious rake yet a poet so gifted that his lyric and satirical verses are today included in anthologies of the works of the greatest poets in our language.[7]

With a total of some twenty-six performances at Dorset Garden Theatre, under the old management, Mrs Barry then became a member of the newly formed United Company.

Chapter Five

Not a Very United Company

By 1682, the King's and Duke's companies had merged to form the United Company staging their performances at the Theatre Royal, Drury Lane. This new venue was managed by the Duke's Company leaders. Thirteen years later however, circumstances were to take a very different turn.

Mrs Barry's first performance as a member of the United Company took place on 28 November 1682. The play was *The Duke of Guise*, a collaboration of John Dryden and clergyman's son and dramatist Nathaniel Lee (c.1653-1692). This was an all-male cast, apart from two of the roles; the Queen Mother was acted by Lady Mary Slingsby (d.1693) who had become the wife of Sir Charles Slingsby, 2nd Baronet, after the death in 1680 of her first husband, actor John Lee, while Mrs Barry took the role of Marmoutier.

History relates that the clergyman's son, following a disastrous attempt at acting, had a promising start as a dramatist but, drawn to pleasure, he became hedonistic in the company of the likes of Rochester and his debauched friends. After a time, Nathaniel Lee grew more and more disreputable, causing his patrons to neglect him. By 1684, the effect of his excesses unhinged his mind and the poor man was incarcerated in the hellish Bedlam Hospital at Moorfields. After spending five long years there, it is believed he exclaimed *They called me mad, and I called them mad, and damn them, they outvoted me.* Just three years after his welcome release from the hospital, with no apparent mending of his ways, Lee, aged thirty-nine, died in a drunken fit and was buried at St Clement Danes on 6 May.

Also in the performance of *The Duke of Guise* was actor Edward Kynaston playing the king, one of many masculine roles he was compelled to adapt to after the introduction of female players. Up until that revolutionary time, Kynaston had acted in many female roles owing to his good looks which made him a convincing woman. The famous diarist Samuel Pepys called him *the loveliest lady that ever I saw in my life, only her voice [is] not very good.*

There is an amusing anecdote regarding Kynaston and Charles II in *An Apology for the Life of Colley Cibber*, 1740, by actor-manager, playwright and Poet Laureate, Colley Cibber (1671-1757):

THO' as I have before observ'd, Women were not admitted to the Stage, 'till the Return of King *Charles*, yet it could not be so suddenly supply'd with them, but that there was still a Necessity, for some time, to put the handsomest young Men into Petticoats; which *Kynaston* was then said to have worn, with Success; particularly in the Part of *Evadne*, in the *Maid's Tragedy*, which I have heard him speak of; and which calls to my Mind a ridiculous Distress that arose from these sort of Shifts, which the Stage was then put to— The King coming a little before his usual time to a Tragedy, found the Actors not ready to begin, when his Majesty not chusing to have as much Patience as his good Subjects, sent to them, to know the Meaning of it; upon which the Master of the Company came to the Box, and rightly judging, that the best Excuse for their Default, would be the true one, fairly told his Majesty, that the Queen was not *shav'd* yet: The King, whose good Humour lov'd to laugh at a Jest, as well as to make one, accepted the Excuse, which serv'd to divert him, till the male Queen cou'd be effeminated. In a word, *Kynaston*, at that time was so beautiful a Youth, that the Ladies of Quality prided themselves in taking him with them in their Coaches, to *Hyde-Park*, in his Theatrical Habit, after the Play; which in those Days, they might have sufficient time to do, because Plays then, were us'd to begin at four a-Clock; The Hour that People of the same Rank, are now going to Dinner—Of this Truth, I had the Curiosity to enquire, and had it confirmed from his own Mouth, in his advanced Age: And indeed, to the last of him, his handsomeness was very little abated; en died wealthyv'n as past sixty, his Teeth were all found, white, and even, as one would wish to see, in a reigning Toast of twenty...[1]

Nonetheless, as much as the ladies enjoyed Kynaston's company, the actor did, according to Pepys, unfortunately fall foul of dramatist, politician and known profligate Sir Charles Sedley, 5th Baronet (1639-1701). The diarist, in February 1669, made the comment ...*and away with my wife by coach to the King's playhouse, thinking to have seen The Heyresse, first acted on Saturday last; but when we came thither, we find no play there __ Kinaston, that did act a part there in abuse to Sir Charles Sidly, being last night exceedingly dry-beaten with sticks by two or three that assaulted him __ so as he is mightily bruised, and forced to keep his bed...* It had come to pass that Kynaston was strolling in St. James's Park attired in the clothes in which he had impersonated Sedley on the stage. Apparently, Sedley had told the thugs to pretend that they thought Kynaston was Sedley himself and they were getting even for an insult to them received from Sedley. Whatever the truth of this shameful incident, poor Kynaston surely did not deserve such harsh treatment for merely impersonating the likes of an arrogant baronet.

It also seems that even one of Kynaston's descendants was not proud of having a famous *actor* among his ancestors:

> …Kynaston died wealthy; he bred his only son a mercer, who lived in Covent-garden; father and son were buried in that parish. The Reverend Mr. Kynaston, the grandson, I have seen; but this gentleman thought it no honour to be the descendant of a player, and would not communicate any anecdotes of his ancestor…[2]

On 1 February 1684, the United Company put on a performance at Court of *Valentinian*, a play originally written by Jacobean playwright John Fletcher and later adapted by John Wilmot, 2nd Earl of Rochester. In this production, Mrs Barry took the part of Lucina, wife to Maximus. Knowing that this version of the play had been written by her now-dead ex-lover, it must have surely brought back strong memories of their once passionate affair, albeit *little Barry* must have been a daily reminder of that too.

The play's Preface concerning the Author and his Writings is an astonishing twenty-four pages in length and apparently written by the earl's friend and diplomat, Robert Wolseley (c.1648-1697). Here is a short extract from the Preface which clearly demonstrates Wolseley's admiration for Rochester's genius:

> *He had a Wit that was accompanied with an unaffected greatness of Mind, and a natural Love to Justice and Truth; a Wit that was in perpetual War with Knavery, and ever attacking those kind of Vices most, whose malignity was like to be most diffusive, such as tended more immediately to the prejudice of publick Bodies, and were of a common Nusance to the happiness of humane kind. Never was his Pen drawn but on the side of good Sence, and usually imploy'd like the Arms of the ancient Heroes, to stop the progress of arbitrary Oppression, and beat down the Bruitishness of headstrong Will; to do his King and Countrey Justice upon such publick State-Thieves, as wou'd*

beggar a Kingdom to enrich themselves, who abusing the
Confidence, and undeserving the Favour of a gracious Prince,
will not be asham'd to maintain the cheating of their Master,
by the robbing and starving of their fellow Servants, and under
the best Form of Government in the World blush not to live
upon the spoyl of others, till by their impudent Violations of
Right, they grow like Beasts of Prey, Hostes humani Generis.
These were the Vermin whom [to his eternal Honour] his Pen
was continually pricking and goading. A Pen, if not so happy
in the Success, as generous in the Aim, as either the sword of
Theseus, *or the Club of* Hercules; *nor was it less sharp than*
that, or less weighty than this. If he did not take so much care
of himself as he ought, he had the Humanity however to wish
well to others, and I think I may truly affirm, he did the World
as much good by a right application of Satyre, as he hurt
himself by a wrong pursuit of Pleasure.

Mrs Barry also recited one of three prologues written especially for the
play, which consisted of some lines no doubt familiar to her; *As sharply*
could he wound, as sweetly engage; As soft his Love, and as divine his Rage
and He charm'd the tenderest Virgins to delight:

Prologue intended for *VALENTINIAN,*
    to be spoken by Mrs. Barrey.

NOW would you have me rail, swell, and look big,
Like rampant Tory *over couchant* Whig.
As spit-fire Bullies swagger, swear, and roar,
And brandish Bilbo, when the fray is o're.
Must we huff on when we're oppos'd by none?
But Poets are most fierce on those wh're down.
Shall I jeer Popish Plots that once did fright us,
And with most bitter Bobs taunt little Titus?
Or with sharp Style, on sneaking Trimmers *fall,*
Who civilly themselves Prudential *call?*
Yet Witlings to true Wits as soon may rise,
As a prudential Man can ere be wise.
No, even the worst of all yet I will spare,
The nauseous Floater, changeable as Air,
A nasty thing, which on the surface rides,

Backward and forward with all turns of Tides.
An Audience I will not so coursely use;
'Tis the lewd way of every common Muse.
Let Grubstreet-*Pens such mean Diversion find,*
But we have Subjects of a nobler kind.
We of legitimate Poets sing the praise,
No kin to th' spurious Issue of these days.
But such as with desert their Laurels gain'd,
And by true Wit immortal Names obtain'd.
*Two like Wit-*Consuls *rul'd the former Age,*
With Love, and Honour graced that flourishing Stage,
And t'every Passion did the Mind engage.
They sweetness first into our Language brought,
They all the Secrets of man's Nature sought,
And lasting Wonders they have in conjunction wrought.

Now joyns a third, a Genius *as sublime,*
As ever flourish'd in Rome's *happiest time.*
As sharply could he wound, as sweetly engage,
As soft his Love, and as divine his Rage.
He charm'd the tenderest Virgins to delight,
And with his Style did fiercest Blockheads fright.
Some beauties here I see____
Though now demure, have felt his pow'rful Charms,
And languish'd in the circle of his Arms.
But for ye Fops, his Satyr reach'd ye all,
Under his Lash your whole vast Herd did fall.
Oh fatal loss! that mighty Spirit's gone!
Alas! his too great heat went out too soon!
So fatal is it vastly to excel;
Thus young, thus mourn'd, his lov'd Lucretius *fell.*

And now ye little Sparks who infest the Pit,
Learn all the Reverence due to sacred Wit,
Disturb not with your empty noise each Bench,
Nor break your bawdy Jests to th' Orange-Wench;
Nor in that Scene of Fops, the Gallery,
Vent your No-wit, and spurious Raillery;
That noisie Place, where meet all sort of Tools,
Your huge fat Lovers, and consumptive Fools,
Half Wits, and Gamesters, and gay Fops, whose Tasks

Are daily to invade the dangerous Masks;
And all you little Brood of Poetasters,
Amend and learn to write from these your Masters.

And Elizabeth had the honour of reciting the Epilogue too:

Epilogue.
Written by a Person of Quality.

'TIS well the Scene is laid remote from hence,
'Twould bring in question else our Author's sence.
Two monstrous things; produc'd for this our Age,
And no where to be seen but on the Stage.
A woman ravisht, and a Great man wise,
Nay honest too, without the least disguise.
Another Character deserves great blame,
A Cuckold daring to revenge his shame.
Surly, ill-natur'd Roman, *wanting wit,*
Angry when all true Englishman *submit,*
Witness the Horns of the well-headed Pit.
Tell me ye fair ones, pray now tell me, why
For such a fault as this to bid me dye.
Should Husbands thus command, and Wives obey,
'Twould spoil our Audience for the next new Play,
Too many wanting who are here to day.
For I suppose if ere that hapned to yee,
'Twas force prevailed, yee said he would undo yee.
Struggling, cried out, but all alas in vain,
Like me yee underwent the killing pain.
Did you not pity me, lament each groan,
When left with the wild Emperor *alone?*
I know in thought yee kindly bore a part,
Each had her Valentinian *in her heart.*

Between November 1682 and April 1694, Elizabeth Barry acted in some twenty-four plays with the United Company, beginning with *The Duke of Guise* and ending her time under the disagreeable management of Christopher Rich (1657-1714) as Mrs Loveley in *The Married Beau; or, The Curious Impertinent*, by dramatist John Crowne (1641-1712).

During the 1688 season with them, Mrs Barry fell ill on stage at the premiere of Crowne's *Darius King of Persia*, in the month of April, whilst playing the part of Barzana, a beautiful princess of the Royal blood. In the printed play, the author commented on this unusual event in his dedication:

> …A misfortune fell upon this Play, that might very well dizzy the Judgments of my Audience. Just before the Play began, Mrs. *Barry* was struck with a very violent Fever, that took all Spirit from her, by consequence from the Play; the Scenes She acted fell dead from her; and in the 4th Act her distemper grew so much upon her, She cou'd go on no farther, but all her part in that Act was wholly cut out, and neither Spoke nor Read;…[3]

Poor Elizabeth was obviously very seriously ill, and did not return to acting until some eighteen months later in the autumn of 1689. Her sudden illness might well have been caused by the death of her beloved daughter. Stress and anxiety would have been very great indeed for the actress during her daughter's serious ill health. Compound that with demanding stage performances and you have a disastrous recipe for a sudden nervous breakdown.

The event was even noted by poet, playwright, and politician, George Granville, 1st Baron Lansdowne (1666-1735), a title he didn't gain until 1712, who was obviously present at the premiere, as on 5 May he wrote to Sir William Leveson with this comment; *she was forced to be carried off, and instead of dying in jest was in danger of doing it in earnest.*

It is quite unbelievable too that such callous lines, by an anonymous author, could have been written in the same year:

> To the most Virtuous and most devoted Overkind, Notorious Madm Barry:
>
> Retyre thou Miser from thy Shop the
> Stage
> Retyrement will befit they Sins and Age:
> The Vitious Treasure they base ways have
> gain'd,
> Which for thy Daughters sake was still
> obtain'd,
> Give to some Pious Use, or thou'lt be
> damn'd.[4]

Eventually, things became somewhat disunited at the United Company, and big changes were afoot.

Chapter Six

Nice and Settled at Lincoln's Inn Fields

By 1693, lawyer and theatrical manager Christopher Rich took over the helm of the United Company. His methods of management were not liked by many of the players, being thought *as sly a Tyrant as ever was at the Head of a Theatre*, and caused a split of the senior players the year after. Fifteen of those players, including Elizabeth Barry, Thomas Betterton, and Anne Bracegirdle formed their own company, the Actors' Company at Lincoln's Inn Fields, with Elizabeth one of the patent-holders. Their new theatre opened in 1695 with a performance of *Love for Love*, a very successful comedy that ran for thirteen days, by playwright and poet William Congreve (1670-1729). The star-studded cast included; Thomas Betterton, John Bowman (1651-1739), Cave Underhill (*1634-c.1710*), Thomas Doggett (c.1640-1721), and Anne Bracegirdle, with Elizabeth Barry acting the role of Mrs Frail, sister to Mrs Foresight, a woman of the town.

The now famous phrase *Kiss and Tell* was coined in 1695, in *Love for Love; O fie, Miss, you must not kiss and tell*. Other phrases that have stood the test of time were coined in *The Mourning Bride*, also by Congreve; *Musick has charms to soothe a savage breast* and *Heav'n has no rage, like love to hatred turn'd, Nor hell a fury, like a woman scorned*, the latter now paraphrased as *Hell hath no fury like a woman scorned*.

The Poetical Register; or, The Lives and Characters of the English Dramatick Poets...1719, had this to say of the play:

> *Love for Love*; a Comedy, acted at the Theatre in Little *Lincoln's-Inn-Fields*, by his Majesty's Servants, 1695. Dedicated to the Right Honourable *Charles* Earl of *Dorset* and *Middlesex*. This Play was acted with very great Applause, at the opening of the New House. There is abundance of Wit in it, and a great deal of fine and diverting Humour; the Characters are justly distinguish'd and the Manners well mark'd. Some of the nicer Criticks find fault with the unravelling of the Plot, and the Conduct of *Angelica* in it: But in spite of Envy, this Play must be allowe'd to be one of the best of our modern Comedies.[1]

53

Lincoln's Inn Fields Theatre, off Portugal Street, also known as Betterton's Company, was granted a licence on 25 March 1695 by King William III to perform there.

The original building was constructed in 1656 as a court for 'real' tennis, but later was converted to a theatre, its shape being ideal for that purpose. It was the brainchild of Sir William Davenant, who obtained a lease on the tennis court in 1660, and purchased some adjacent land in order to expand the building. His new theatre opened on 28 June 1661, and a most innovative playhouse it was too. It was the first theatre in London to use moveable scenery, and the first to build a proscenium arch creating a window around the scenery and performers. This new style theatre must have seemed quite spectacular to the audience, not to say to the players themselves.

Mrs Barry stayed with Betterton's Company from 1695 to 1705, with her performances there totalling at least fifty, as detailed in *The London Stage* database. It's quite astonishing to find that all fifty plays were individual, with barely any repeats. A thespian's life was not an easy one; just imagine having to learn all those separate roles, the scripts of which, to us in the twenty-first century, seem confusingly archaic and certainly don't roll off the tongue readily.

Here are some of the opening lines to the comedy *The Man of Mode; or, Sir Fopling Flutter* where Dorimant is musing on his note for Mrs Loveit:

> ...What a dull insipid thing is a Billet doux written in cold blood, after the heat, of, the business is over? It is a Tax upon good-nature, which I have here been labouring to pay, and have done it; but with as much regret, as ever Fanatick paid the Royal Aid, or Church-Duties. 'Twill have the same Fate I know that all my Notes to her have had of late, 'Twill not be thought kind enough. Faith Women are i'the right, when they jealously examine our Letters, for in them we always first discover our decay of passion...[2]

One particular play staged at Lincoln's Inn Fields on 1 January 1698, was *Heroic Love*, by George Granville. Elizabeth's role in this new tragedy was that of Ghruseis. The play's prologue was written by Henry St. John (1652-1742), then esquire but who acceded to the title of 4th Baronet on his father's death in 1708. Later still, in 1716, he was awarded a peerage as 1st Viscount St. John, allowing him a seat in the House of Lords.

In the print of *Heroic Love*, there is a wonderful dedication to Mr Granville on his play from John Dryden:

To
Mr. *GRANVILLE*,
On his excellent Tragedy, called, HEROIC LOVE.

AUSPICIOUS poet, wert thou not my friend,
How could I envy, what I must commend!
But since 'tis nature's law in love and wit,
That youth should reign, and with'ring age submit,
With less regret, those laurels I resign,
Which, dying on my brows, revive on thine.
With better grace and ancient chief may yield
The long contended honours of the field,
Than venture all his fortune at a cast,
And fight like Hannibal, to lose at last.
Young princes obstinate to win the prize,
Tho' yearly beaten, yearly yet they rise:
Old monarchs tho' successful, still in doubt,
Catch at a peace; and wisely turn devout.
Thine be the laurel then; thy blooming age
Can best, if any can, support the stage,
Which so declines, that shortly we may see
Players and plays reduc'd to second infancy.
Sharp to the world, but thoughtless of renown,
They plot not on the stage, but on the town,
And in despair, their empty pit to fill,
Set up some foreign monster in a bill:
Thus they jog on; still tricking, never thriving;
And murd'ring plays, which they miscall reviving.
Our sense is nonsense, thro' their pipes convey'd;
Scarce can a poet know the play he made;
'Tis so disguis'd in death: nor thinks 'Tis he
That suffers in the mangled tragedy.
Thus Itys first was kill'd, and after dress'd
For his own fire the chief invited guest.
I say not this of thy successful scenes;
Where thine was all the glory, theirs the gains:
With length of time, much judgment and more toil,
Not ill they acted, what they could not spoil:
* Their setting-sun still shoots a glimm'ring ray,
Like ancient Rome, majestic in decay:

And better gleanings their worn soil can boast,
§ Than the crab-vintage of the neighb'ring coast.
This difference, yet the judging world will see;
Thou copiest Homer, and they copy thee.

JOHN DRYDEN.

* Mr. Betterton's company in Lincolns-inn fields.
§ Drury Lane Play-house.[3]

Henry St. John's Prologue to *Heroic Love*:

PROLOGUE.

By the right honourable HENRY ST. JOHNS, Esq;

HOW hard's the poet's tast, in these our days,
Who such dull palates is condemn'd to please,
As damn all sense, and only fustian praise?
Charm'd with heroic nonsense, lofty strains,
Not with the writers, but the players pains,
And by the actors lungs, judge of the poet's brains.
Let scribling judges, who your pleasures serve,
Live by your smiles, or by your anger starve,
To please you in your vain fantastic way,
Renounce their judgment, to secure their pay:
By written laws, our author would be try'd,
And write as if Athenians should decide,
With Horace and the Stagyrite for guide.
Applause is welcome, but too dearly bought,
Should we give up one rule, those mighty masters taught.
Yet some, methinks, I here and there descry,
Who may with ancient Rome and Athens vie;
To whose tribunal we submit with joy:
To them, and only them; for not to wrong ye
'Twould be a shame to please the most among ye.
Chiefly the softer sex he hopes to move,
Those tender judges of heroic love:
To that bright circle he resigns his cause,
And if they smile, he asks no more applause.[4]

It is thought that there might have been an intrigue between St. John and Mrs Barry. Could the year 1698 have been the start of their possible love affair?

One has to surmise from Mrs Barry's choice of lovers that she might have been sometimes attracted to men of a certain unprincipled character. It is believed others of her paramours, along with John Wilmot, 2nd Earl of Rochester, were Sir George Etherege, Charles Dering (1657-1719), and Henry Goring (1646-1685). Goring was tragically killed by Dering in Mrs Barry's dressing room, believed to be at Drury Lane. Dering and Goring, at the time of the dressing room fracas, were both under the influence of drink. Dering was subsequently arrested for murder, but soon was free on bail. The outcome of the Coroner's inquest was the lesser verdict of manslaughter, then so often the case with the privileged wealthy.

Apparently, this was not the first time hothead Charles Dering had caused an affray at the theatre. On 2 May 1682, the *Impartial Protestant Mercury* reported that on 27 April 1682: *Mr. Ch[arles] De[ering], son to Sir. Edw. D., and Mr. V[aughan], quarrelled in the Duke's play-house, and presently mounted the stage and fought, and Mr. D. was very dangerously wounded, and Mr. V. secured, lest it should prove mortal.*

Henry St. John's reputation doesn't fare much better, he being involved in a murder at the Globe Tavern in Fleet Street in 1684. It appears that following the acquittal of St. Ives MP, Edward Nosworthy (1637-1701), the jury, whose foreman was Sir William Estcourt (1654-1684), MP for Malmesbury, entered the tavern to celebrate. During that time a brawl broke out between Henry St. John and Francis Stonehouse (1654-1738), involving a trivial argument in regard to *a discourse about leaping horses.* Somehow, poor Estcourt was run through by the swords of both St. John and his cousin Edmund Webb (c.1639-1705). Both men were found guilty of murder and condemned to death. However, they secured pardons, at that time not an unusual event for men of wealth and influence. Webb obtained his, apparently, through a comment made by Judge George Jeffreys, 1st Baron Jeffreys (1645-1689), later known notoriously as the *Hanging Judge.* Webb was also favoured, since he was a gentleman usher in the household of Prince George of Denmark and Norway, Duke of Cumberland (1653-1708). St. John's mother obtained her son's reprieve at a reported sum of sixteen thousand pounds! The barefaced St. John, in just a few weeks following his pardon, won the parliamentary election for Wootton Bassett and was duly appointed.

One wonders that if Mrs Barry had had an affair with Henry St. John, then not only had John Wilmot the son of Anne, Countess of Rochester

(1614-1696) been Barry's lover, but Anne's nephew may have been Barry's lover too! This surely would have been too much for the redoubtable Anne to stomach.

During the rest of the 1698 season at Lincoln's Inn Fields, Mrs Barry acted in a further four plays, the last of those on 1 November that year. The play was John Dennis's opera *Rinaldo and Armida*, with Elizabeth as Armida, and Rinaldo played by the ageing stalwart Betterton; he was sixty-three at this time.

There is held in the Horace Howard Furness Memorial Library, in the University of Pennsylvania, a rare letter of Mrs Barry's to Rochester's daughter Mallet Wilmot, Lady Lisburne (1676-1709). Their friendship continued for years after Rochester's demise, and in the letter, Elizabeth mentions the success of the play, after a perceived dismal time; *as for the Little affairs of our house I never knew a worse Winter only we have had pretty good success in the Opera of Rinaldo and Armida*. The letter is written in a clear hand, with remarkably good spelling, so no doubt Lady Davenant's educating of Elizabeth had made its mark. So often the spelling in women's writing at this time was very poor indeed. Even the letters of the likes of Anne, Countess of Rochester were of a similarly inadequate ilk.

The late M. A. Shaaber's transcription of the letter from Mrs Barry to *The Right Honorable the Lady Lisburne att her house att Troscod in Cardiganshire*, 1699:

> Madam
>
> The pleasure I received in hearing from your Ladyship is impossible to be expressed and were my time as much in my power as my inclination I shou'd be perpetually making use of the Honor your Ladyship has done me in permitting me to write to you I obeyed your Ladyships commands to Mr Batterton and Mrs Bracegirdle who returned their humble service and thanks for soe great a favour; publick news is uncertain but I presume to give your Ladyship an account of a marriage and christening in your family my Lord Baltomer's son was a tuesday last married to my Lord Litchfield Eldest Daughter and my Lady Wharton is brought to bed of a son who is by my Lady Orford the Duke of Shrewsbury & my Lord Chancellour on Friday next to be made a Christian by the name of Phillip as for the Little affairs of our house I never knew a worse [v°] Winter only we have had pretty good success in the Opera of Rinaldo and Armida Where the poet made me command the Sea the

earth and Air but had I really that Authority I cou'd with joy forsake it all to wait on your Ladyship in your retirment which your Ladyships great goodness gives me hopes wou'd not be unwellcome to you I am with all submission

Madam	
I beg Leave	Your Ladyships
to present my	
humble Service	
to my Lord and wish	Most Obliged
him and your Ladyship	and humble serv^t
Many happy new years	

Lon: jan: ye 5th	
This moment Alexander	
is bespoke to entertain ye	
Bride I mentioned &	
all their guest to-morrow	Eliza: Barry

The superscription reads:
ffor
The Right Honorable the
Lady Lisburne att her
House att Troscod in
Cardiganshire

Salope post

Mongomery bagg[5]

Mrs Barry continued at Lincoln's Inn Fields for a further seven years, covering some twenty-six more performances, with her last one there on 22 February 1705 being *The Gamester*, she playing the apt role of Lady Wealthy. The play, a comedy by Susanna Centlivre (c.1669-1723), was held as a benefit play for the author. Centlivre was a poet and actress, professionally known as Susanna Carroll, and believed to be the most successful female playwright of the eighteenth century, having written a total of nineteen plays.

Chapter Seven

Fame Brings Its Price

Mrs Barry's fame brought her great adoration from many quarters, but it also hailed vile satirical verse from others. She had, it seems, gained a reputation of sexual promiscuity. Such reputation no doubt gleaned in view of her medley of supposed lovers.

Elizabeth was not alone in being lampooned, as she and many of the female actresses at that time were looked upon as women of easy virtue, whether they were or otherwise. But for one reason or another, Elizabeth seemed to be particularly targeted. Throughout her life she had taken lovers but, given the licentious times of the Restoration Court, this was not an unusual trait. There were no doubt many *mercenary, prostituted dames!*

To give a flavour, here are a delightful few lines on Mrs Barry in an anonymous poem *A Satire on the Players*:

> …There's one, Heav'n bless us! by her cursed pride,
> Thinks from the world her brutish lust to hide;
> But will that pass in her, whose only sense,
> Does lie in whoring, cheats, and impudence!?
> One that is pox all o'er, *Barry* her name,
> That mercenary, prostituted dame;
> Whose nauseous a----like *Tony's tap* does run:
> Unpity'd fool, that can't her ulcer shun!
> Tho' like a *Hackney* jade, just tir'd before,
> And all her little fulsome stock run o're;
> Tho' faces are distorted with meer pain,
> So that wry mouth ne'er since came right again:
> Yet ten times more she'd bear for slavish gain…[1]

Adding insult to injury this next one, which is only part of a poem *On Three Late Marriages*, written in early 1682, takes some beating:

> But slattern Betty Barry next appears,
> Whom every fop upon the stage admires,

But when he sees her off he hangs his ears.
With mouth and cunt, though both awry before,
Her cursed affectation makes 'em more.
At thirty-eight a very hopeful whore,
The only one o'th'trade that's not profuse,
A policy was taught her by the Jews.
Though still the highest bidder she will choose,
Which makes her all the captain's love forget,
And nauseous St. Johns to her arms admit;
Her fifty shillings a week has raised her price.
Besides her other charming qualities,
As dewlaps hanging down her tawny thighs
And ever moistened with congenial glue,
Just like the bull that fierce Almanzor slew
Besides an odoriferous perfume,
Which yet, like strength of cordials, may o'ercome.
So, with the gums of all Arabia blessed,
The Phoenix lies dissolving in its nest,
But the predominant sense that strikes the brain
Are the divine effluences of her grain.
And have you got at last a husband? Then
What jubilees will be at Surrenden!
If thou art married, Charles, and truly grieved,
As Barry fain would have it be believed,
For thy own sake this life and follies end;
Thy New Year's gift was sent thee by a friend.[2]

There is a further piece, *Satire On Bent[in]g*, penned in March 1689, to be found in *Wilson's Court Satires* along with his specific note on the text, *The copy text is "Satyr 1688/9," in Bodleian MS. Firth, c. 15, p. 311. A version in "A Choyce Collection," p. 299, lacks the last fifty-seven lines, on Barry.*

This offensive piece of work has some history to it, which I will elaborate on later. Whoever this author was, to make mockery of a young girl's death was surely the lowest form of satirical prose imaginable:

Tis Barry, the illustrious of her kind,
Whose charity the poor could never find.
Rochester taught her first how to be lewd,
Fathered a cheddar child as his own brood;

And had he lived to Hesty's fifteen year,
He'd fucked his girl t'have been a grandfather,
But dying left it to his niece's care.
She likewise dies and leaves three thousand pound
To dower the girl provided she be sound.
T. Wharton is to have her maidenhead,
And if not sound, the dowry's forfeited.
If he to gain the sum should pox her now,
And swear before the judge he found her so,
The mother would (if she were him) all know.
Oh Barry, Barry, speedily repent,
Or else be doubly damned by my consent.
Bring forth thy mighty magazine of lust,
And in thy vile account be sure, be just.
As thou expectst to waste thy crimes away,
The trophies of thy countless fuckings lay
Sincerely at the shrine of Modena,
With a strict catalogue of every sin,
If paper can be found to put 'em in.
That wonder-working dame and none but she
Can intercede for such a bitch as thee.
Thy Jewish presents, howsoe'er they're prized,
Give 'em the duchess, 'tis well advised;
They'll [stink?] of trading with the circumcized.
Unlucky Whitmore's presents, all that pride,
The locket too that changed the day [he] died,
The citizens' rich silks and their fine linen,
The necessaries which thou ne'er wert seen in,
But shoes and stockings which thou ne'er went clean in.
Bring Goring's medals, all the wealth he gave
To purchase of a punk a shameful grave,
Which, though foreseen, himself he could not save.
Bring too the name of every occupation,
Each bidding fair, according to his station,
A list of every sect thou'st swived with, of each nation;
And if the duchess can thy pardon gain,
I'd not despair, though I'd my father slain.[3]

And had he lived to Hesty's fifteen year... But dying left it to his niece's care... She likewise dies and leaves three thousand pound. These particular lines refer to Rochester and Barry's daughter, Elizabeth Barry, *little Barry*. The author of them was unbelievably well versed in the private lives of Barry, Rochester and his beloved niece Anne Lee (1659-1685) who was the first wife of nobleman and politician Thomas Wharton, 1st Marquess of Wharton (1648-1715). The whole business of Anne's bequest to Barry's daughter caused terrible ructions within the family, including lengthy correspondence on the subject. Here is an extract of a letter written on 23 November 1689, after the death of Anne Lee in October of that year. The letter is regarding an Indenture dated 4 May 1685, and is written by 'honest' John Cary Esq (c.1601-1702), faithful friend and steward, of Rochester's mother, Anne, Countess of Rochester, to her grandson Edward Henry Lee, 1st Earl of Lichfield (1663-1716). Cary, who had once seen the deed, was doing his best to relay its contents to the earl. The letter is very involved, but this particular paragraph shows the reasons for the family's utter resentment of the Indenture.

> ...And all the Manors and lands therein particularly named in the County of Wilts to her self for life and after that a lease of 500 years is made to Mr. Bradbury my son Harry Cary & Mr. Thomas Booker for the raising & paying out of the rents & profits three thousand pounds to little Barry and divers Annuities & legacies to other persons but not 6^d to my remembrance to any of her owne relatives...[4]

The relevant piece in the Indenture referred to in Cary's letter:

> ...And upon this further Trust & confidence that they the said George Bradbury Francis Henry Carey & Thomas Baxter their Executors or Admin^{rs} by and out of the said Rents Issues & profitts or by Leases or Mortgages of any part or parts of the aforesaid Mannors Messuages Lands Tenements Hereditaments and p^{re}mises so before limitted to them for Five Hundred years do & shall raise advance and pay unto Elizabeth Barry naturall Daughter of John late Earle of Rochester if she shall happen to live to attaine to the age of One & Twenty years the full sum of Three thousand pounds of lawfull money of England...[5]

Even the passing of time did not diminish Elizabeth's supposed bad reputation. Centuries later, the Victorian poet, author and critic, Sir Edmund

William Gosse CB (1849-1928), drew on Elizabeth's earlier scurrilous critics:

> Mrs. Barry was an ignoble, calculating woman; no generous act, even of frailty, is recorded of her. Whether or not, in rivalry with Mrs. Gwyn, she set her cap at royalty, she had a well-balanced sense of her own value, and smiled at nothing lower than an earl...[6]

Critic and playwright John Dennis (1658-1734) was exceedingly praising of Mrs Barry; *that incomparable Actress changing like Nature which she represents, from Passion to Passion, from Extream to Extream, with piercing Force and with easy Grace.* And a glowing endorsement to the remarkable actress from Thomas Betterton, the leading actor of his day, suggests that *she often so greatly exerted her art in an indifferent character, that her acting had given success to plays that would disgust the most patient reader.*

The playwright Delarivier Manley (c.1663-1724), penned admiration for Elizabeth when the actress played Princess Homais in Manley's she-tragedy, *The Royal Mischief* (1696):

> ...I do not doubt when the ladies have given themselves the trouble of reading and comparing it with others, they'll find the prejudice against our sex and not refuse me the satisfaction of entertaining them, nor themselves the pleasure of Mrs. Barry, who by all that saw her is concluded to have exceeded that perfection which before she was justly thought to have arrived at. My obligations to her were the greater, since against her own approbation, she excelled and made the part of an ill woman, not only entertaining, but admirable.[7]

In The Epilogue, *Shakespeares Ghost*, spoken by John Baptista Verbruggen (d.1708), in the play *Measure For Measure; or, Beauty The Best Advocate*, there is expressed a wonderful sentiment; *And long may Barry Live to Charm the Age.* The drama, originally by William Shakespeare, had been much altered by Charles Gildon (c.1665-1724):

> Enough your Cruelty Alive I knew;
> And must I Dead be Persecuted too?
> Injur'd so much of late upon the *Stage*,

My *Ghost* can bear no more; but comes to Rage.
My *Plays*, by *Scriblers*, Mangl'd I have seen;
By Lifeless *Actors* Murder'd on the *Scene*.
Fat *Falstaff* here, with Pleasure, I beheld,
Toss off his Bottle, and his *Truncheon* weild:
Such as I meant him, such the *Knight* appear'd;
He Bragg'd like *Falstaff*, and, like *Falstaff*, fear'd.
But when, on yonder *Stage*, the Knave was shewn
Ev'n by my Self, the Picture scarce was known.
Themselves, and not the Man I drew, they *Play'd*;
And Five *Dull Sots*, of One poor Coxcomb, made.
Hell! that on you such Tricks as these shou'd pass,
Or I be made the Burden of an *Ass!*
Oh! if *Machbeth*, or *Hamlet* ever pleas'd,
Or *Desdemona* e'r your Passions rais'd;
If *Brutus*, or the Bleeding *Caesar* e'r
Inspir'd your Pity, or provok'd your Fear,
Let me no more endure such Mighty Wrongs,
By *Scriblers* Folly, or by *Actors* Lungs.
So, late may *Betterton* for sake the *Stage*,
And long may *Barry* Live to Charm the *Age*.
May a New *Otway* Rise, and Learn to Move
The *Men* with *Terror*, and the *Fair* with *Love!*
Again, may *Congreve*, try the *Commic* Strain;
And *Wycherly* Revive his Ancient *Vein*:
Else may your Pleasure prove your greatest Curse;
And those who now *Write dully*, still *Write worse*.[8]

And still with Gildon:

> Gildon in his Comparison between the two Stages in 1702
> makes Sullen say of Mrs. Barry— "What think you of the
> renowned Cleopatra?"
>
> *Critick.* By that nickname, so unfortunate to poor Antony,
> as the other has been to many an honest country Gentleman,
> I should guess whom you mean.
>
> *Sullen.* You take me right.
>
> *Critick.* In her time she has been the spirit of action every
> way; nature made her for the delight of mankind; and till nature
> began to decay in her, all the town shared her bounty.

Ramble. I do think that person the finest woman in the world upon the stage, and the ugliest woman off on't.

Sullen. Age and intemperance are the fatal enemies of beauty; she's guilty of both; she has been a rioter in her time; but the edge of her appetite is long ago taken off; she still charms (as you say) upon the stage; and even off I don't think so rudely of her as you do: 'Tis true, time has turned up some of her furrows, but not to such a degree.

Ramble. To the degree of loathsomeness upon my faith; but on the stage, I am willing to let her still pass for an heroine.

Critick. And still off on't too, if all be true that is said of her.[9]

Leaving the best till last, Colley Cibber, who knew Elizabeth over many years, was under no illusion as to her greatness, which he alluded to in his personal and amusing memoir, *An Apology for the Life of Colley Cibber*:

Mrs. *Barry* was then in possession of almost all the chief Parts in Tragedy: With what Skill she gave Life to them, you will judge from the Words of *Dryden*, in his Preface to *Cleomenes*, where he says,

Mrs. Barry, *always excellent, has in this Tragedy excell'd herself, and gain'd a Reputation, beyond any Woman I have ever seen on the Theatre.*

Mrs. *Barry*, in Characters of Greatness, had a Presence of elevated Dignity, her Mien and Motion superb, and gracefully majestick; her Voice full, clear, and strong, so that no Violence of Passion could be too much for her: And when Distress, or Tenderness possess'd her, she subsided into the most affecting Melody, and Softness. In the Art of exciting Pity, she had a Power beyond all the Actresses I have yet seen, or what your Imagination can conceive. Of the former of these two great Excellencies, she gave the most delightful Proofs in almost all the Heroic Plays of *Dryden* and *Lee*; and of the latter, in the softer Passions of *Otway's Monimia* and *Belvidera*. In Scenes of Anger, Defiance, or Resentment, while she was impetuous, and terrible, she pour'd out the Sentiment with an enchanting Harmony; and it was this particular Excellence, for which *Dryden* made her the above-recited Compliment, upon her acting *Cassandra* in his *Cleomenes*. But here, I am apt to think his Partiality for that Character, may have tempted his Judgment to let it pass for her Master-piece; when he could not but know, there were several other Characters in which her Action might have given her a fairer Pretence to the Praise he has bestow'd on her, for *Cassandra*; for, in no Part of that, is there the least ground for Compassion, as in *Monimia*; nor equal cause for Admiration, as in the nobler Love of *Cleopatra*, or the tempestuous Jealousy of *Roxana*...[10]

According to Cibber, Mrs Barry... *was the first Person whose Merit was distinguish'd by the Indulgence of having an annual Benefit-Play, which was granted to her alone, if I mistake not, first in King James's time,...* These benefits would have boosted her income, as the actress would be awarded the playhouse's evening's takings, less its general expenses. Benefit performances were very lucrative and could gift the recipient upwards of fifty pounds!

Elizabeth's popularity, no doubt, would have caused friction in the form of rival jealousy. Documented in *The History of the English Stage*, is one particularly memorable event during a performance of *The Rival Queens; or, The Death of Alexander the Great*, by dramatist Nathaniel Lee. This was a very apt title considering what ensued. In this play, Elizabeth's character was that of Roxana, with fellow actress Elizabeth Bowtell (Boutell) (c.1650-1715) playing Statira. The disagreement between the two actresses seemed quite trivial, but the outcome could have been deadly serious:

> It happened these Two Persons before they appeared to the Audience, unfortunately had some Dispute about a *Veil* which Mrs. *Boutel* by the Partiality of the Property-Man obtained; this offending the haughty *Roxana*, they had warm Disputes behind the Scenes, which spirited the Rivals with such a natural Resentment to each other, they were so violent in performing their Parts, and acted with such Vivacity, that *Statira* on hearing the King was nigh, *begs the Gods to help her for that Moment*; on which *Roxana* hastening the designed Blow, struck with such Force, that tho' the Point of the Dagger was blunted, it made way through Mrs. *Boutel*'s Stayes, and entered about a Quarter of an Inch in the Flesh.

This Accident made a great Bustle in the House, and alarmed the Town; many different Stories were told; some affirmed, Mrs. *Barry* was jealous of Mrs. *Boutel* and Lord *Rochester*, which made them suppose she did it with Design to destroy her; but by all that could be discovered on the strictest Examination of both parties, it was only the *Veil* these two Ladies contended for, and Mrs. *Barry* being warmed with Anger, in her Part, she struck the Dagger with less Caution, than at other times.[11]

Though this whole incident might have brought tears to Mrs Boutell, Mrs Barry's excellent performance in the play definitely brought tears from her attentive audience:

Tho' I have mentioned several Passages of this Play in which Mrs. *Barry* shined, I cannot conclude without taking notice that tho' before our Eyes we had just seen *Roxana* with such Malice murder an innocent Person, because better beloved than herself; yet, after *Statira* is dead, and *Roxana* is following *Alexander* on her Knees, Mrs. *Barry* made this Complaint in so Pathetic a Manner, as drew Tears from the greatest Part of the Audience,

O! speak not such harsh Words, my Royal Master:
But take, dear Sir, O! Take me into Grace;
By the dear Babe, the Burden of my Womb,
That weighs me down when I would follow faster.
My Knees are weary, and my Force is spent;
O! do not frown, but clear that angry Brow;
Your Eyes will blast me, and your Words are Bolts
That strike me dead: the little Wretch I bear,
Leaps frighted at your Wrath, and dies within me.[12]

One thing Barry and Boutell did have in common, apart from a possible Rochester connection, is that they were both at the mercy of the lampooners, as the following lines written about 1678 will reveal:

Betty Bowtall is true to whom shee
        p^{e}tend
Then happy is hee whom shee Chuses
        for freind

Shee faine would hang out widdows
      peak for a signe
But ther's noe need of Bush where there
      is so good wine[13]

And in the anonymous *The Session of Ladies, April 1688* these delightful lines were penned of both Boutell and Barry:

There was chestnut-maned Boutell, whom all the Town fucks,
Lord Lumley's cast player, the famed Mrs. Cox,
And chaste Mrs. Barry, I'th'midst of a flux,
To make him a present of chancre and pox.[14]

Chapter Eight

Mrs Barry's Latter Stage Years

By late October 1705, Mrs Barry had moved with Betterton's Company to a new venue built by architect and dramatist Sir John Vanbrugh (1664-1726) to be known as the Queen's Theatre, Haymarket. Playwright and poet William Congreve was also part of the new venture, which included the formation of an actors' co-operative with Thomas Betterton at its helm:

> At the opening of the eighteenth century Vanbrugh was a well-established dramatist on the threshold of a career as an architect. The three principal theatres in London were the Theatre Royal, Drury Lane, presided over by Christopher Rich, the theatre in Dorset Gardens, already nearing extinction, and the theatre at Lincoln's Inn Fields, where Thomas Betterton had performed in *The Provok'd Wife* in 1697. Betterton's company was in disorder, and 'To recover them, therefore, to their due Estimation, a new Project was form'd of building them a stately Theatre in the *Hay-Market*, by *Sir John Vanbrugh*, for which he raised a Subscription of thirty Persons of Quality, at one hundred Pounds each, in Consideration whereof every Subscriber, for his own Life, was to be admitted to whatever Entertainments should be publickly perform'd there, without farther Payment for his Entrance'. These subscribers were probably members of the Kit-Cat Club; the only subscriber whose name is known is John Hervey, first Earl of Bristol.
>
> The ground ultimately acquired by Vanbrugh comprised a rectangle measuring 132 feet from north to south along the west side of the Haymarket and 145 feet in depth east to west; the west side backed on to Market Lane. The middle of this rectangle was an open yard (known in Vanbrugh's time as Phoenix Yard and later in the century as King's Yard) which was approached through a covered gateway from the Haymarket. The buildings occupying the site in 1703 included the Phoenix

inn, stables, coach-houses and a number of small houses, including five or six which fronted on to the Haymarket and backed on to the yard.[1]

John Vanbrugh, knighted in 1714 by King George I (1660-1727), was the son of Giles Vanbrugh, a London cloth merchant who had descended from Flemish-Protestant merchants after they had settled in London in the sixteenth and seventeenth centuries, with some rising to become minor courtiers and landowning gentry.

A man of many talents, Vanbrugh worked undercover in relation to the invasion (The Glorious Revolution) of 1688 by William of Orange, later King William III, but in this guise, he was arrested, remaining in prison in France for four and a half years. On his release, returning to England, he spent a short time in the Navy. An ardent Whig, Vanbrugh became a member of the famous London Kit-Cat Club whose members held strong political and literary associations.

Yet Vanbrugh is known more famously as a successful playwright and gifted architect, his most famous undertaking being Blenheim Palace which during its construction caused him considerable aggravation from the formidable but brilliant Sarah Churchill, Duchess of Marlborough (1660-1744). Their bitter arguments eventually culminated in Vanbrugh's banishment from the site.

Not surprisingly, the first play to be premiered at the new theatre was *The Confederacy*, a comedy by Vanbrugh, who must have had a great sense of humour considering some of the splendid characters' names in the play, such as Gripe and Moneytrap, *two rich money scriveners*; Dick, *a gamester*; Brass, *Dick's companion*; Clip, *a goldsmith*; Flippanta, *a maid*; Mrs Amlet, *a seller of all sorts of private affairs to the ladies* and Mrs Cloggit, *Amlet's neighbour*. Along with many of Betterton's top players, Mrs Barry acted the part of Clarissa, *wife to Gripe, an expensive luxurious Woman, a great Admirer of Quality*, and she also recited the Epilogue:

EPILOGUE,

Spoken by Mrs. *Barry*.

I'VE heard wise Men in Politicks lay down
What Feats by little England *might be done,*
Were all agreed, and all would act as one,
Ye Wives a useful Hint from this might take.

71

The heavy, old, despotick Kingdom shake,
And make your Matrimonial Monsieurs quake.
Our Heads are feeble, and we're cramp'd by Laws;
Our Hands are weak, and not too strong our Cause:
Yet would those Heads and Hands, such as they are,
In firm Confed'racy resolve on War,
You'd find your Tyrants_____ _____what I've found my Dear.
What only Two united can produce
You've seen to-night, a Sample for your Use:
Single, we found we nothing could obtain;
We join our Force____and we subdu'd our Men.
Believe me (my dear Sex) they are not brave;
Try each your Man, you'll quickly find your Slave.
I know they'll make Campaigns, risk Blood and Life;
But this is a more terrifying Strife;
They'll stand a Shot, who'll tremble at a Wife.
Beat then your Drums, and your shrill Trumpets sound,
Let all your Visits of your Feats resound,
And Deeds of War in Cups of Tea go round:
The Stars are with you, Fate is in your Hand,
In twelve Months time you've vanquish'd half the Land;
Be wise, and keep 'em under good Command.
This Year will to your Glory long been known,
And deathless Ballads hand your Triumphs down;
Your late Achievements ever will remain,
For tho' you cannot boast of many slain,
Your Pris'ners shew, you've made a brave Campaign.[2]

Mrs Barry was by now a woman of substantial means; not only an actress but someone with a good business sense. Between performances of Francis Beaumont (1584-1616) and Fletcher's *The Maid's Tragedy* and Cibber's *The Careless Husband* at the Queen's Theatre on 2 and 7 November 1706, Mrs Barry became the new lessee of Town Mills, Newbury in Berkshire, on the fourth of that month. Cibber's play, a comedy, was first performed on 7 December 1704, and in a letter from William Congreve to his Irish friend Joseph Keally (1673-1713), written two days later presumably after seeing the play at the Theatre Royal, Drury Lane, he had this to say:

…Rowe writ a foolish farce called the Biter, which was damned. Cibber has produced a play, consisting of fine gentlemen and fine conversation altogether; which the ridiculous town for the most part likes: but there are some that know better…[3]

The original Town Mills lease is today held by St George's Chapel Archives & Chapter Library. The deed itself has some amount of age damage with parts illegible. However, an excellent description of the lease has been documented by them and begins *Lease by the Dean and Canons of Windsor to Elizabeth Barry of St Martin's in the Fields, Middx.* The lease consists of *water mills with land belonging thereto; a further plot of land and a tenement in Bartholomew Street, Newbury, then in occupation…* At least we know from this deed that, at that date, Mrs Barry was living in the parish of St Martin-in-the-Fields. Elizabeth held the benefit of this lease until her death in 1713, she having bequeathed the lease in her will to Gabriel Ballam, Gent. (1627-1715).

Although a little off-piste from Mrs Barry's stage career, I feel it worth some explanation about the character of Gabriel Ballam and the sort of friends he was connected with.

Was Gabriel Ballam the last of Mrs Barry's lovers? A question, I believe, that can never be truly answered. He was fifteen years her junior, and that might have been the attraction between the two of them, she enjoying the company of a young wit and he seeking the friendship of, or more intimate relationship with, a mature woman with a degree of fame on and off the stage.

Gabriel was baptised on 6 February 1672/3 at St Saviour, Southwark. He was the second son of four born to Jonadab and Patience Ballam who were married on 6 November 1664 at St Olave's Church, Southwark. Gabriel's father established his own successful grocery business in Southwark and later became a member of the Grocers' Company.

Born into wealth, little appears to be known of the occupation, if any, of Gabriel, but from evidence he appears to have been a man of leisure and acquainted with contemporary poets, playwrights and dramatists. A frequenter of the famous Will's Coffee House in Covent Garden, which was founded by William Unwin, Gabriel appeared to be one of its witty patrons, with John Dryden the centre of attraction for their gatherings. Such a circle of playwright and dramatist friends could point to Gabriel's initial friendship with Mrs Barry.

My conjecture on Gabriel possibly being Mrs Barry's lover stems from remarks in certain letters written to and from him c.1698, when Mrs Barry was still a player on the stage. Correspondence between Ballam and his friend Anthony Smith M.A. of Cambridge, who died at Newport Pagnell in Buckinghamshire in 1721 aged forty-nine, shows that they were in discussion regarding the censorious *Short View of the Immorality and Profaneness of the English Stage* 1698. This work was by Jeremy Collier (1650-1726), theatre critic, non-juror bishop and theologian, which leads to the thought that Gabriel was a keen patron of the playhouse:

> To Mr. Gabriel Ballam: *To be left at* Will's *Coffee-house* in Covent-garden.

> *Sir,*
> Tho' I have been under the Scene of Silence, yet now, I appear to pay my Promise to him that can forgive: To make an Apology, is Effeminate; or to tell Business was the Cause, is Threadbare: And therefore, I confess I have committed a Soloecism in Friendship; and send this Sheet to do Penance. To furnish you with News, I cannot; and to tell you *Cambridge* Jests, that's Foreign; since they, like their Learning, are confin'd only to their own Meridian: To tell you their Disputes in Divinity, is altogether as strange, since that's out of your Sphere, and consequently must Affront, rather than oblige you: but to add something for your Two Pence, *Collier's* Book is greedily swallow'd, and all your little carping, envious Answers, are, like their Authors, scandalous. D——— is the most rejected, since his Book answers not his Title, nor his Title Mr. Collier's. Mr. *V*_____*ook* is not yet descanted on, since its Arrival is not of a Day. I can't furnish you with more Lines now, since I am going to be Cap'd Master of Arts; therefore beg your Excuse till I arrive at *Newport-Pagnel*, whither I gang on *Thursday.*

> > Your Assured Friend,
> > *Anthony Smith*[4]

Gabriel's witty reply to Smith's letter:

> *To Mr.* Anthony Smith, *M.A.*

> *Sir,*
> Your learned *Cambridge* Epistle I receiv'd with no common Satisfaction; for truly, Sir, it carries that Air of a Philosophy-

Lecture, that I cannot fancy any thing less, than that you have honoured me with some Part of your Exercise that Cap'd you with your New Title of Master of Arts. I confess, you happy University-Gentlemen, with your seven Years Labour amongst Books and Letters, arrived to the Crowning your Heads with that Honourable Cap; and then, in half a dozen Years more, amongst Men and Manners here in *London*, you fill them with brains to: For indeed you Politick Architects of Literature, wisely Roof first and then Floor, Finish, and Furnish afterwards

I assure you, Sir, you have no occasion of doing Penance in a Sheet, as you call your Letter; and I less of giving you your own dear Collier's Blessing, viz. ABSOLUTION. And now I talk of that famous Author, whose Book you tell me is so greedily swallow'd amongst you, I am afraid your *Cambridge* Swallow is better than your Digestion, and that Mr. *Collier* slips down with you like an Eel through a Cormorant; for otherwise, if you would give your selves the leisure of chewing upon it, you would hardly find it so palatable a Piece: For really, Sir, I am afraid his Sophistry is as much out of your learn'd Sphere, as your Divinity (you are pleas'd to say) is out of mine, else you would not be such over-passionate Admirers of that Greatest of Carpers, and have such very humble Thoughts of the little, envious (and therefore scandalous Ones) his Answerers; but possible, your *Cambridge* Opinion of that Stage-Critick, may, like the rest of your Learning, be confin'd, as you call it, to your own Meridian, and then you cannot do yourselves, nor the World more Justice, than to keep them both amongst you, especially if your Opinion and Learning are both of a Piece.

I am,
Your most humble Servant,
Gabriel Ballam.

P.S. Mr. Congreve's *Answer is come out, wherein he proves Mr.* Collier *to be a very honest Man, by his false and imperfect Citations, and his becoming Assurance, in Charging him with his own Nonsense: All this is very plain, and fully proved, with mild, yet forceable Arguments. As to Mr.* Dennis, *I must be silent, for I have not yet read him.*[5]

The following letter to Gabriel, although not dated, probably written c.1699, was from critic and dramatist John Dennis. Dennis was one of the leading figures on the London literary scene though he eventually fell out with many of his contemporary greats, withdrawing from city life in 1704. The reason for thinking that Dennis's letter might have been penned in 1699 is regarding his references to the *Play-house* and *Italians Voice*, as during that year his play/opera *Rinaldo and Armida* was performed at Lincoln's Inn Fields and printed in the same year; a strange choice for Dennis as he was one of the most damning critics of opera of his day.

Dennis's letter to Gabriel Ballam, with particular reference to Gabriel's mistress at the playhouse:

To Mr. Gabriel——

Dear——
Though it seems hast a mind to pass for a Wit, by the very same means that *Æsop's Jack-Daw* thought fit to set up for a *Beaux*. (By the way I must tell you, that the Transformation of Beau to Wit, has something more of the Miracle in it, than the change of *Jack-Daw* to *Beau*) Yes, *B*——, with borrow'd Plumes hast thou imp'd thy Wings. But I took more particular notice of a couple, that were plucked from a certain Bird of Night; which if we give Credit to *W*—— the Owner is a very filthy obscene Animal; from which ominous Creature, may Heav'n defend us Mortals, that is, we in the Country here, call him *Bell*, but the Gods, that is, those in *Covent-Garden*, have named him *Break-a-day*. But it is time to begin to speak plain English, for you, if I am not mistaken, pretend to know other language: But then, as you have writ for the Witty Club, the Witty Club may understand for you. I look upon your last to be the Act and Deed of them all. And you shall henceforward be Secretary to them, as *Julian* was to their Mistresses. Tho' I must tell you by the way, that the Affection which some of them show for the Muses, is not unlike that merry Passion, which put the little French parson into an amorous Fit for the Queen. Return them all Thanks, in my Name, for the Honour they have done me, in offering to admit me, in my Absence, a Member of their Noble Society. But, *Domine, non sum Dignas:* However, I think my self obliged to make them as

extraordinary a compliment, as the *Morocco* Ambassador would have thought himself engaged to return the University of *Oxford*, if in the midst of their extream Civility, they had offered to make him *D.D.* But to speak to that part of your Letter which concerns yourself: I do not wonder, that you go to the Play-house only for the sake of your Mistress; but methinks, at the Music-meeting the Italians Voice might have Charms for you. But as you go thither too, you say, only for the sake of your Mistress, I will believe, to oblige you, that she does not go for the Eunuch's. Now I go to your Comedy here, purely for the Comedy sake, which is a Politic Country Club; and partly for the Musick sake I go to our Musick-meeting, which is a pack of shrill-mouth'd Beagles for Trebles, and a pack of deepmouth'd Bumpkins for Bases. And whenever our Consort begins, half the Men in *Bucks*, in spite of their Souls, are our Audience. Once more I salute the Witty Club; tell them, that they little deserve that Name, if they have not more Wit, than to take any thing ill I have said. Assure them, that I know how to respect their good Qualities, and that I shall endeavour to set off their Bad, which is a Friend's Part.

> *I am,*
> *Dear* _____,
> *Yours, &c.*

Postscript,

In your first Letter you gave me notice of some Gentlemen who designed to write to me. The Post before that, I had a very Witty Letter from one of them: it is no hard matter to guess that it was from Mr. *Wycherly*. But *Ch——* Wit, if he sent any, either went astray, or came short. Who should wonder at either[6]

The dramatist William Wycherley (1641-1716), on writing to Mr John Dennis on 1 December 1694, had this to say of Dennis's absence, with a mention of Gabriel Ballam in the postscript:

...nor is *Wills* the Wits Coffee-House any more, since you left it, whose Society for want of yours is grown as Melancholly, that is as dull as when you left 'em a Nights, to their own Mother-Wit, their Puns, Couplets, or Quibbles...

Postscript.

...For News, *W*—lives Soberly, *Ch*—goes to bed Early; *D'Vrfy* sings now like a Poet, that is, without being ask'd: And all the Poets or Wits-at Wills, since your departure, speak well of the Absent. *Bal*—says his ill Looks proceed rather for want of your Company, than for having had that of this Mistress...[7]

After Dryden's death in 1700, it is believed Wills Coffee House was never the same again as Richard Steele comments in the *Tatler* on 8 April 1709. *This place is very much altered since Mr. Dryden frequented it; where you used to see songs, epigrams, and satires in the hands of every man you met, you have now only a pack of cards; and instead of the cavils about the turn of the expression, the elegance of the style, and the like, the learned now dispute only about the truth of the game.*

Here is Gabriel's reply to Dennis's letter, with further references to a lady of his acquaintance of *very great quality*, together with mention of a mistress *who has lately had 'em*, i.e. the smallpox.

Mr. Gabriel B——'s *Answer to Mr.* John D——; *to be left at* Will's *Coffee-house.*

Yesterday I receiv'd a Letter from you, where you suspect the Rabble to other hand in my Letter; but you may assure your self it is not so, for I writ both mine in my Closet, and no body has seen 'em but your self; I do not say this to value myself upon two frivolous Letters, but that I would not have you suspect the Rabble of so much Dullness: indeed both yours I have shown to the Rabble (as you call 'em) or rather the Witty Club; and I have shown 'em to some of the Grave Club, and to some who are neither of the * Rabble nor grave Club, but both; and upon my word, they like 'em as well as I do. Since I writ to you, I have happen'd upon an Intreague with a Woman of very great Quality, (there's a Subject for your next Letter) which makes me up so much, that I have hardly time to eat: so you must not expect so just an Answer to your Letter (by reason of the length) as I would have done, had I been at liberty; so I hope you will excuse me: Our Correspondence hitherto methinks, looks as if we were seasoning a Sallad between us: I am for softning it with Oil, and you are still souring it with vinegar. (But pardon me) reflecting upon your last, if I dress the remaining part of my Letter according to your own Pallat. You hit me in the Teeth of having but one Language, which I am very well contented with, for I fear more Tongues than one would make me vain like other Folks, and so much Knowledge as you have, distract me; but if I can make a shift to write a Letter with indifferent Sense and good Breeding, (a thing harder to come by, than Latin or Greek,) I shall ne'er have occasion to doubt whether the Rabble's Wit shall take anything ill of me, whenever I shall write to 'em; which I am sure they do not of you, because they hold that Satyr (in its strictest Sense) is the incurable Disease of your Mind; tho' an essential Part of the witty and learned Mr. D——, and becomes you just as well as the Marks of the Small-Pox does a certain Mistress of mine, who has lately had 'em, which tho' it does not set her off at all, yet I am resolved to fancy her as much as before, because she cannot help her Blemishes.

I am yours, &c.[8]

I am not purporting to say categorically that the mistress referred to in Gabriel's letter is Mrs Barry, having found no particular reference to her ever having had *the smallpox*. However, with her leaving to Gabriel one of her greatest assets, the Town Mills, it would appear a strongly supported surmise. And with Gabriel being the first legatee named in her will, he was obviously at the forefront of her mind during her fatal illness.

Elizabeth continued her life on the stage at the Queen's Theatre for a further four years, working until the age of fifty-two years.

In one special performance, this time at the Theatre Royal, Drury Lane, on 7 April 1709, she, along with her friend Anne Bracegirdle and others, acted in the play *Love For Love* in support of their dear old friend Betterton's benefit night, he himself acting the part of Valentine. No person was to be admitted but by printed ticket at half a guinea each. No actor then deserved more, and he gained mightily by the sale of tickets. The Epilogue was spoken by Mrs Barry, she having dear old Betterton on her right hand, between herself and Mrs Bracegirdle:

EPILOGUE *spoken by Mrs.* Barry, *at the Theatre-Royal in* Drury-Lane, April *the 7th*, 1709, *at her Playing in* LOVE for LOVE *with Mrs.* Bracegirdle, *for the Benefit of Mr.* Betterton.

AS some brave Knight, who once with Spear and Shield
Had fought Renown in many a well-fought Field;

But now no more with sacred Fame inspir'd,
Was to a peaceful Hermitage retir'd:
There, if by Chance disast'rous Tales he hears,
Of Matrons Wrongs, and captive Virgins Tears,
He feels soft Pity urge his gen'rous Breast,
And vows once more to succour the Distress'd.
Buckl'd in Mail, he sallies on the Plain,
And turns him to the Feats of Arms again.
So we, two former Leagues of Friendship true,
Have bid once more our peaceful Homes adieu,
To aid *old Thomas,* and to pleasure you.
Like errant Damsels, boldly we engage,
Arm'd as you see, for the defenceless Stage.
Time was, when this good Man no help did lack,
And scorn'd that any She should hold his Back;
But now, so Age and Frailty have ordain'd,
By* two at once he's forc'd to be sustain'd,
You see what failing Nature brings Man to;
And yet let none insult, for ought we know,
She may not wear so well with some of you.
Tho' old, you find his Strength is not clean past,
But true as Steel he's Mettle to the last.

Mrs. Barry *and Mrs.* Bracegirdle *clasped him round the waste.*

If better he perform'd in Days of Yore,
Yet now he gives you all that's in his Pow'r;
What can the youngest of you all do more?
What he has been, tho' present Praise be dumb,
Shall haply be a Theme in Times to come,
As now we talk of ROSCIUS and of *Rome.*
Had you withheld your Favors on this Night,
Old SHAKESPEAR'S Ghost had ris'n to do him Right.
With Indignation had you seen him frown
Upon a worthless, witless, tasteless Town;
Griev'd and repining, you had heard him say,
Why are the Muses Labors Cast away?
Why did I write what only he could play?
But since, like Friends to Wit, thus throng'd you meet.

DIEV ET MON DROIT.

The Second Charles, Heire of yᵉ Royall Martyr,
who, for Religion and his Subiects Charter,
spent the best Blood.yᵉ uniust Sword ere dy'de,
since the rude Souldier pierc'd our Sauiours side:
who such a Father hadʃt; art such a Son;
redeeme thy people and assume thy Crone.

I.C.

Sir William Davenant, poet and playwright. *The Works of Sir William Davenant*, frontispiece, London, 1673. (wikimedia commons, public domain)

Thomas Killigrew, dramatist. (wikimedia commons, public domain)

Edward Kynaston, actor.
(wikimedia commons, public
domain)

Elizabeth Barry, actress.
After Sir Godfrey Kneller.
(wikimedia commons,
public domain)

John Wilmot, 2ⁿᵈ Earl of Rochester. Anonymous, c.1600 and 1699. (wikimedia commons, public domain)

THE

Man of Mode,

OR,

Sʀ Fopling Flutter.

A

COMEDY.

Acted at the *Duke's Theatre.*

By *George Etherege* Efq;.

LICENSED,

June 3.
1676.

Roger L'Eſtrange.

LONDON,

Printed by *J. Macock*, for *Henry Herringman*, at the Sign of the *Blew Anchor* in the Lower Walk of the *New Exchange*, 1676.

George Etherege's Restoration comedy, *The Man of Mode; or, Sir Fopling Flutter*, 1676. (wikimedia commons, public domain)

Above left: Thomas Otway, dramatist, by John Riley c.1680-85. (wikimedia commons, public domain)

Above right: Anne Bracegirdle, actress. (wikimedia commons, public domain)

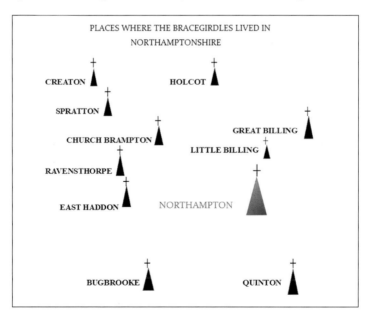

PLACES WHERE THE BRACEGIRDLES LIVED IN
NORTHAMPTONSHIRE

CREATON

HOLCOT

SPRATTON

GREAT BILLING

CHURCH BRAMPTON

LITTLE BILLING

RAVENSTHORPE

EAST HADDON

NORTHAMPTON

BUGBROOKE

QUINTON

Pictorial map of Northamptonshire parishes where the Bracegirdle families lived. (Susan Margaret Cooper)

William Congreve Esq., 1733, John Faber the Younger, ca.1695-1756. (Yale Center for British Art, Paul Mellon Collection, B1977.14.9862. https://collections.britishart.yale.edu/)

Leeds Civic Trust blue plaque on the birthplace of William Congreve, in Bardsey. (wikimedia commons, public domain)

Lincoln's Inn Theatre, Portugal Street. (wikimedia commons, public domain)

Above left: Thomas Betterton in a scene from William Shakespeare's Hamlet, in which the Ghost of Hamlet's Father confronts him in his mother's chamber. 1709. (wikimedia commons, public domain)

Above right: Mary Saunderson, actress. (wikimedia commons, public domain)

THE DUKE'S THEATRE, DORSET-GARDENS.

This Theatre was built by Sir Christopher Wren, and first opened by the Duke of York's Company, on their removal from the Play-house in Little Lincoln-Inn fields, the 9th Nov 1671.— Betterton, stage manager; with Kynaston, Hart, Terry-Leigh, Lady Slingsby, Mrs Betterton, and other principal actors, performed here until the union of the Duke and the King's Companies in 1682, and performances were continued occasionally until 1697.— The whole building was demolished about April 1709 and the present offices of the New River Company have been erected on the site of the Theatre.

London Published July 1 1814 by J. Wilson & C Red Lion Passage .

Above: The Duke's Theatre, Dorset Gardens. (wikimedia commons, public domain)

Left: Inside the Dorset Garden Theatre: part of the forestage with doors and balconies on both sides, the proscenium arch with the music box above it and one of the scenes for Elkanah Settle's *The Empress of Morocco*, performed in 1673. Settle's play included numerous spectacular stage effects. (wikimedia commons, public domain)

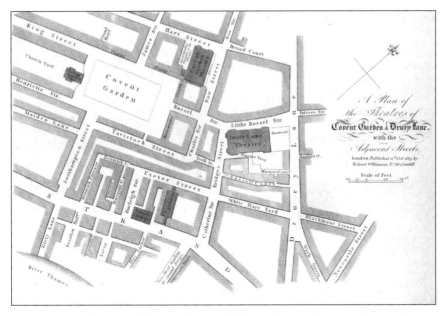

A Plan of the Theatre of Covent Garden & Drury Lane with the Adjacent Streets.
1813. (wikimedia commons, public domain)

Drury Lane Theatre. 1674. (wikimedia commons, public domain)

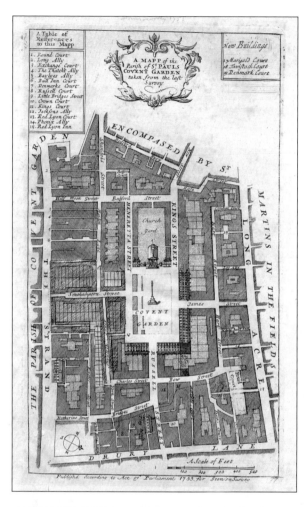

Left: Map of the area surrounding St Paul's Covent Garden, and the market, as far as Drury Lane to the east, Long Acre to the North and the Strand to the south; with the addition of Broad Court; illustration to vol II of the sixth edition of Stow's 'Survey of London'. 1720. (wikimedia commons, public domain)

Below: Blue Plaque to Anne Oldfield at 60 Grosvenor Street, Mayfair, London. (wikimedia commons, public domain)

Above left: Portrait of Samuel Pepys, by Robert White, after Sir Godfrey Kneller. 1690. (wikimedia commons, public domain)

Above right: John Fletcher, 1729. Print made by George Vertue, 1684–1756, (Yale Center for British Art; Yale University Art Gallery Collection, B1998.14.530 https://collections.britishart.yale.edu/)

Right: John Dryden, 1743, by Jacobus Houbraken, 1698–1780, (Yale Center for British Art; Yale University Art Gallery Collection, B1998.14.591. https://collections.britishart.yale.edu/)

Sir John Vanbrugh, 1733
John Faber the Younger,
ca.1695-1756, (Yale Center
for British Art, Paul Mellon
Collection, B1977.14.12655.
https://collections.britishart.
yale.edu/)

Aphra Behn, ca.1670.
Sir Peter Lely. (Yale
Center for British Art,
Bequest of Arthur D.
Schlechter, B2002.15
https://collections.
britishart.yale.edu/)

Above left: Susanna Centlivre, poet, actress and playwright. Early 18th Century engraved print (wikimedia commons, public domain)

Above right: William Shakespeare. Engraver: Samuel Cousins. Artist: After (?) John Taylor (British, died 1651). 1849. (Courtesy of Metropolitan Museum of Art, NYC, under Creative Commons CC0 1.0, www.metmuseum.org)

St. Mary's Church depicted in the 18th century, as Mrs. Barry would have known it before its rebuilding in 1866. Image from *Records and Recollections of Acton,* Henry Mitchell. 1913.

St Giles Church, Northampton. (wikimedia commons, public domain)

Henrietta Godolphin, 2nd Duchess of Marlborough. (wikimedia commons, public domain)

Thomas D'Urfey (Tom Durfey), poet and playwright, by Gerard Vandergucht. 1700. (wikimedia commons, public domain)

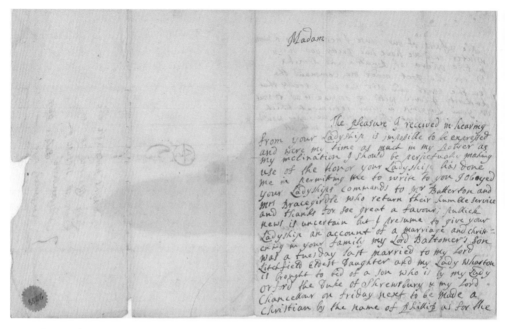

Letter from Mrs. Barry to The Right Honourable the Lady Lisburne. With kind permission from the University of Pennsylvania. Kislak Center for Special Collections – Manuscripts. Ms. Coll. 617. (Furness Autograph Collection)

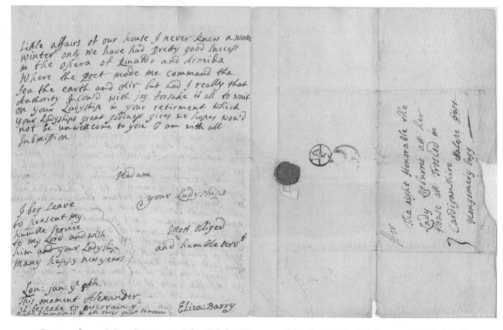

Letter from Mrs. Barry to The Right Honourable the Lady Lisburne. With kind permission from the University of Pennsylvania. Kislak Center for Special Collections – Manuscripts. Ms. Coll. 617. (Furness Autograph Collection)

Go on and make the gene'ous Work compleat;
Be true to Merit, and still own his Cause,
Find something for him more than bare Applause,
In just Remembrance of your Pleasures past,
Be kind, and give him a Discharge at last,
In Peace and Ease Life's Remnant let him wear,
And hang his consecrated Buskin* there.

    *Pointing to the Top of the Stage.

The first number of *The Tatler* had this to say of Betterton's benefit:

Will's Coffee-house, April 8.

On Thursday last was acted, the benefit of Mr. Betterton, the celebrated comedy called Love for Love. Those excellent players, Mrs. Barry, Mrs. Bracegirdle, and Mr. Dogget, though not at present concerned in the house, acted on that occasion. There was not been known so great concourse of persons of distinction as at that time; the stage itself was covered with gentlemen and ladies, and when the curtain was drawn, it discovered even their very splendid audience. This unusual encouragement, which was given to play the advantage of so great an actor, gives an undeniable instance, that the true relish for manly entertainments rational pleasures is not wholly lost. All the parts were acted to perfection: the actors were careful of their courage, and no one was guilty of the affectation to insert witticisms of his own; but in due respect was had to the audience, for encouraging this accomplished player. It is not now doubted but plays will revive, and take their usual place in the opinion of persons of wit and merit, notwithstanding their late apostacy in favour of dress and sound. This place is very much altered since Mr. Dryden frequented it; where you used to see songs, epigrams, and satires, in the hands of every man you met, you have now only a pack of cards; and instead of the cavils about the turn of the expression, elegance of style, and the like, the learned now dispute only about the truth of the game. But however the company is altered, all have shown a great respect for Mr. Betterton: and the very gaming part of this house have been so touched with a sense of the uncertainty of human affairs (which alter with themselves every moment) that in this gentleman they pitied Mark Antony of Rome, Hamlet of Denmark Mithridates of Pontus, Theodosius of Greece, and Henry the Eighth of England. It is well known, he has been in the condition of each of those illustrious personages for several hours together, and behaved himself in those high stations, in all the changes of the scene, with suitable dignity. For these reasons, we intend to repeat this late favour to him on a proper occasion, lest he, who can instruct us so well in personating feigned sorrows, should be lost to us by suffering under the real ones. The town is at present in very great expectation of seeing a comedy now in rehearsal, which is the twenty-fifth production of my honoured friend Mr. Thomas D'Urfey; who, besides his great abilities in the dramatic, has a peculiar talent in the lyric way of writing, and that with a manner wholly new and unknown to the ancient Greeks and Romans, wherein he is but faintly intimidated in the translations of the modern Italian operas.[9]

What a wonderful night that would have been, to see two of the most celebrated actresses of their day supporting 'literally' the Restoration's leading actor and theatre manager who was then aged seventy-four. What a stalwart old Betterton was!

After the success of that benefit, a further one was staged for the illustrious Betterton on 13 April 1710, with a performance of *The Maid's Tragedy*, the old actor as Melantius and Mrs Barry once again playing the part of Evadne.

In Cibber's *Apology*, he states that poor Betterton had *been suddenly seiz'd by the Gout, he submitted, by extraordinary Applications, to have his Foot so far reliev'd that he might be able to walk on the Stage in a Slipper, rather than wholly disappoint his Auditors*. The consequence of this drastic measure to relieve his painful distemper together with the exertion on that day's performance was to take its toll on the brave, aged actor; he died a few days later on the twenty-eighth and was buried in Westminster Abbey.

His widow grieved the loss of her beloved husband very much and was reported to have *lost her reason* for a time. However, she continued to act for the next two years, receiving a traditional widows' benefit play on 4 June 1711. Mary then made her will on 10 March 1712 and, dying soon after, was buried beside her husband on 13 April:

In the Cloysters are buried the following Persons, for whom there are no Monuments or Gravestones viz.

...Mr. Thomas Brown, the Poet, buried in the East Walk, near the Poetical Mrs. Aphra Behn.

Mr. Thomas Betterton, the Actor, near them, and upon his Coffin, Mrs. Mary Betterton, his Wife...[10]

There is no denying that Mary's loss of her dear husband caused her much sorrow, although it has been remarked that at Betterton's death he was very indigent, which no doubt added to his widow's misery, even though she had been granted a yearly pension by Queen Anne (1665-1714). But it appears that at his demise, he was in possession of a large collection of portraits, executed in crayons, which were disposed of at a sale of his goods. Also among the items was a picture of William Shakespeare, the famous playwright, poet, and actor, which it is believed was purchased by Mrs Barry, although some modern-day research seems to question this. Albeit, I think it is still worth transcribing a piece on the portrait written in 1827:

That this picture was once in the possession of Sir William D'Avenant, is highly probable; but it is much more likely to have been *purchased* by him from some of the players, after the theatres were shut up by authority, and the veterans of the stage were reduced to great distress, than to have been bequeathed to him by the person who painted it, in whose custody it is improbable that it should have remained. Sir William D'Avenant appears to have died insolvent. There is no will of his in the Prerogative Office; but administration of his effects was granted to John Otway, his *principal creditor*, in May, 1668. After his death, Betterton, the àctor, bought it, probably at a public sale of his effects. While it was in Betterton's possession, it was engraved by Vander Gucht, for Mr. Row's edition of Shakespeare, in 1709. Betterton made no will, and died very indigent. He had a large collection of portraits of actors, in crayons, which were bought at the sale of his goods, by Bullfinch, the Printseller, who sold them to one Mr. Sykes. The portrait of Shakespeare was purchased by Mrs. Barry, the actress, who sold it afterwards for forty guineas to Mr. Robert Keck. In 1719, while it was in Mr. Keck's possession, and engraving was made from it by Vertue: a large half sheet, Mr. Nichol, of Colney Hatch, Middlesex, marrying the heiress of the Keck family, this picture devolved to him; and while in his possession, it was, in 1747 engraved by Houbraken, for Birch's *Illustrious Heads*. By the marriage of the Duke of Chandos with the daughter of Mr. Nicoll, it became his Grace's property.[11]

Even at the end of her life, Mary's love and devotion for Mrs Barry and Mrs Bracegirdle never waned, she leaving them twenty shillings apiece for rings. It's noted that the actor Thomas Doggett received the same too. Although Mary had apparently been left fairly poor at her husband's death, she generously made several bequests to be paid out of her arrears of pension to family and friends. This annual pension from Queen Anne was quite substantial, in the sum of one hundred pounds, but it is believed that none of it was paid until after her death. It appears that the queen was tainted, like her uncle Charles II, in promising but not delivering. Nonetheless, the bequests in the widow's will added up to eighty-five pounds, today's equivalent of some eight thousand nine hundred pounds!:

> **In the Name of God Amen** The Tenth Day of March 1711 I Mary Betterton of the Parish of S^t. Martin in the Feilds in the County of Middlesex Widow being weak in Body but (praised be God) of sound mind and understanding Do make my last Will and Testament as followeth First I bequeath my Soul into the hands of God trusting through the merits of my dear Saviour Jesus Christ to inherit eternall Life with him my Body I desire may be buried at the discretion of my Executrix hereafter named As to what worldly substance God hath been pleased to bestow on me I give and dispose thereof as followeth I give to M^{rs}. Susannah Long M^{rs}. Marg^t. Robinson and my Sister M^{rs}. Mary Head each of them Twenty pounds apeice to be paid as soon as Effects come to my Executrixes hands to be paid out of the arrears of my Pention which the Queen hath been graciously pleased to grant me Item I give to my Nephew M^r. John Williamson my Neices M^{rs}. Mary Kelly and M^{rs}. Anne Harrison each of them Five pounds to be also paid out of my said Arrears Item I give and bequeath unto my Freinds M^{rs}. Bracegirdle M^{rs}. Barry M^{rs}. Dent M^{rs}. Anne Betterton my Neice Flint M^r. Doggett M^r. Wills Doctor Robinson and his Lady and their Daughter the said M^{rs}. Marg^t. Robinson each

of them Twenty shillings to buy them Rings in memory of me and to be paid out of the said arrears of my said pention as aforesaid Item I give unto my Neice M^{rs}. Frances Williamson Wife of the said M^{r}. John Williamson my dear Husbands Picture and all the rest and residue of my Goods chattels and Estate whatsoever of which I shall dye possessed or intitled unto And I make her sole Executrix of this my Will I hereby revoke all Wills by me formerly made And in Witness that this is my last Will I have hereunto sett my hand and Seal the Day and year above written Mary Betterton. Sealed Signed published and declared by the said Testatrix to be her last Will in the presence of Adrian Moore the mark of Martha Jaque[12]

Mary Betterton was a very respected woman and actress of her day. Colley Cibber praised her most highly in his *Apology*:

> Mrs. *Betterton*, tho' far advanc'd in Years, was so great a Mistress of Nature, that even Mrs *Barry*, who acted the Lady *Macbeth* after her, could not in that Part, with all her superior Strength, and Melody of Voice, throw out those quick and careless Strokes of Terror, from the Disorder of a guilty Mind, which the other gave us, with a Facility in her Manner, that render'd them at once tremendous, and delightful. Time could not impair her Skill, tho' he had brought her Person to decay. She was, to the last, the Admiration of all true Judges of Nature, and Lovers of *Shakespear*, in whose Plays she chiefly excell'd, and without a Rival. When she quitted the Stage, several good Actresses were the better for her Instruction. She was a Woman of an unblemish'd, and sober Life; and had the Honour to teach Queen *Anne*, when Princess, the Part of *Semandra* in *Mithridates*, which she acted at Court in King *Charles*'s time. After the Death of Mr. *Betterton*, her Husband, that Princess, when Queen, order'd her a Pension for Life, but she liv'd not to receive more than the first half Year of it.[13]

Mrs Barry's last performance at the Queen's Theatre was on 14 April 1710, the day after Betterton's swan-song. The play was *The Spanish Friar; or, The Double Discovery*, by Dryden. Aptly, as Mrs Barry had been the celebrated queen of the London stage for over thirty years, her final role at curtain down was that of Leonora, Queen of Aragon.

Chapter Nine

A Welcome Retirement
But a Tragic Death

Mrs Barry retired, with the applause still ringing in her ears, to the then quiet, rural village of Acton. The place had become a very popular country retreat from the City of London for those of wealth, with some having houses built there for country leisure. The discovery at that time of mineral springs at Acton Wells also made it a very pleasant place to reside. Nevertheless, in later years, owing to the vogue for Tunbridge Wells and Bath, Acton's popularity began to decline:

> Acton was held to be blessed with very sweet air in 1706 and the rector accordingly urged a friend, in verse, to move there. The fashion for medicinal waters brought a brief period of fame, with the exploitation of the wells at Old Oak common, when East Acton and Friars Place were said to be thronged with summer visitors, who had brought about improvement in the houses there.[1]

Sadly, Elizabeth's idyllic retirement was short-lived. She deserved so much more, after toiling for so long entertaining the masses. But one likes to think that the remaining three years of her life, spent in the *sweet air* of Acton, were pleasurable for her, she enjoying the company of her few close friends, whom she fondly acknowledged in her will.

In a report of Mrs Barry's death in *Volume III of Dramatic Miscellanies* by Thomas Davies, London, 1784, it is said; *Cibber relates, in his Apology, that Mrs. Barry died, of a fever, in the latter part of Queen Anne's reign; and judges, by this expression, in her last delirium_____ 'Ha! Ha! and so they make us lords by dozens! _____ that it was about the time when twelve peers were created at once. The date of her epitaph, at Acton, is fixed two years after this extraordinary promotion. An actress, who was in London when Mrs. Barry died, assured me, many years since, that her death was owing to the bite of a favourite lap-dog, who, unknown to her, had been seized with madness. We can assume from this statement, if true, that poor*

Mrs Barry died from rabies, *a viral disease that causes inflammation of the brain in humans and other mammals*; with reference to *in her last delirium* it would seem this was the likely scenario.

Poor Elizabeth must have died in much pain, fever and delirium. Be that as it may, during the horrors of her distemper and knowing for sure her death was imminent, she had wit enough to make a will and bequeath her wealth. With the absence of any known family, Barry's close and varied friends were her chosen beneficiaries.

The following is a transcription of Mrs Barry's will, showing who were her legatees receiving money, real and personal estate, and her estate at Newbury largely consisting of the mills:

> **In the Name of God Amen** I Elizabeth Barry Spinster being sick in body but of sound mind and memory praised be God for the same doe make and ordaine this my last will and Testament Imprimis I committ my Soul into the hands of Almighty God and my Body to the Earth to be decently buried and as for my estate I give and dispose as follows Item I give to Mr Gabriel Ballam Gent my Estate at Newbury consisting of mills. I give to Mrs Cary Twenty pounds. I give to Mrs Bracegirdle and Mrs Phubs Twenty pounds each Item I will that Two hundred pounds shall be to save Mrs Bracegirdle harmless from any Debt of the Play-House Item I give to Mrs Hawker wife of Thomas Hawker Painter Twenty pounds Item I give the residue and remainder of my whole Estate whatsoever both Reall and personall (after my Debts paid) to John Custis Gent formerly Page to the Prince and Abigal Stackhouse Spinster whom I make Executors of this my last Will to be divided equally between them Hereby Revoking all former wills by me made In wittness whereof I have hereunto sett my hand and seal this fourth day of November Anno Dmi. One thousand seven hundred and Thirteen. E. Barry. Signed Sealed Published and Declared to be the last Will and Testament of Eliz: Barry in the presence of Anne Hodge, the mark of Katherine Miller. Rich: Barrow[2]

Also attached to her will is the following, which surprisingly occurred some thirty-four years after her death:

> On the first day of March in the year of our Lord 1747 administration (with the will annexed) of the goods chattles and credits of Elizabeth Barry late of the parish of St. Mary

le Savoy in the county of Middlesex spinster deceased left unadministered by John Custis and Abigail Overton formerly Stackhouse (wife of Philip Overton) the Executors and residuary Legatees named in the said Will now also respectively deceased was granted to Mary Sayer formerly Overton (wife of James Sayer) the Administratrix of the Goods of the said Abigail Overton formerly Stackhouse deceased whilst living the surviving Executrix and residuary legatee named in the said will being first sworn duly to administer.[3]

A remarkable chance discovery revealed a further Rochester/Barry connection pertaining to one of the witnesses to Mrs Barry's will, Richard Barrow (1674-1723). He had also witnessed Mrs Barry's lease of the Newbury Mills, dated 1706, so he seemed to have been a close friend of Elizabeth's for several years. Richard Barrow, formerly gentleman of Hereford but later of King Street, St. James's in London, made a will in 1723 and in it he states:

> ...whereas I have had severall dealings and Transactions with my most worthy Lady and Mistress the right Honourable Elizabeth Countess of Sandwich and for the preventing all manner of difference and disputes with a Lady from whom I have had so many Obligations I will that my Executor hereafter named Shall give her a general Discharge upon Condition that she likewise does the same but I hope that when it may be a Convenient time that she will pay at such payment as she pleases to my Sister Elizabeth Murphy the two hundred pounds that M[r] Baron Page was to have paid me Item I will that my Executor do deliver unto the said Countess all her Boxes and Cases that are in my Lodgings...[4]

The Right Honourable Elizabeth, Countess of Sandwich (1674-1757) was one of the daughters of John Wilmot, 2nd Earl of Rochester, Elizabeth Barry's one-time lover. At the time of Richard's will, in 1723, Countess Sandwich was forty-nine years old. She had been, it appears, unhappily married for some time, seemingly due to her husband, Edward Montagu, 3rd Earl of Sandwich's purported insanity. He died in 1729 at the age of fifty-nine. The earl had wed Elizabeth in 1689 and they had two children; a daughter, Elizabeth, who died in infancy and a son, Edward Richard

Montagu, Viscount Hinchingbrooke, born in 1692, who died at the young age of thirty in 1722. Might the countess's hapless marriage have brought a particular closeness with the widowed Richard Barrow?

And a further interesting discovery in Richard's will, *Item I desire the honour of her Grace the Duchess of Hamilton to accept of Mrs Barrys picture which my Executor will waite on her Grace with.* This Duchess was Lady Anne Cochrane (1707-1724), the daughter of John Cochrane, 4th Earl of Dundonald (1686-1720) and his wife Anne Murray (1697-1710). Anne Cochrane was the first wife of James Hamilton, 5th Duke of Hamilton (1703-1743) and was only six years old at the time of Barry's death. Was *Mrs Barrys picture*, then in the possession of Barrow, the original by Sir Godfrey Kneller, 1st Baronet (1646-1723)? Or is there another portrait of Barry that has yet to come to light?

Elizabeth's entry in the original parish register reads; *Mrs. Eliz: Barry was Buryed in the Pish Church of Acton in the South oyle under ye End of Madam Lambe Pew being att ye uper End between ye two Pillers she was Buryed the 12th day of Novmber 1713.* Madam Lambe refers to Anne Lambe who was the wife of Henry Lambe, Citizen and Goldsmith of London, both residents of Acton. Henry died in July 1712 and was buried at St Mary's Church there on the ninth. Anne passed away sixteen years after Henry and was interred in the vault beside her late husband in St Mary's on 3 August 1728.

There is also to be found a poignant poem to Elizabeth Barry, by one of the Harding brothers, either Silvester or Edward, in their publication of 1795 *The Biographical Mirrour*, in the chapter headed *Memoirs of Mrs. Barry*:

> To which the compiler of these anecdotes takes the liberty to subjoin a few lines.
>
> The scene is clos'd, the curtain dropt,
> And famous Barry's part is o'er:
> The music of that tongue is stopt,
> Which sooth'd and charm'd us heretofore!
> Veil'd are those eyes, once piercing bright;
> Those rose-lips faded, late so red;
> That once-fine form, unfit for sight,
> Laid low, to mingle with its bed!
> Yet, tho' from earth's vain stage by Death now driv'n,
> An Angel's part we trust she'll act in heav'n![5]

There is an interesting letter, written by playwright and poet William Congreve referred to in *The Complete Works of William Congreve*, edited by Montague Summers. Vol. 1. The Nonesuch Press. 1923. p. 101, regarding a picture of the 2nd Earl of Rochester that was in the possession of Mrs Barry. Although this letter is not dated it must have been written shortly after her death in 1713:

> Sr
>
> if you see Mr: Custis to night pray know of him if it be possible for me to have a picture of Ld Rochester which was Mrs. Barrys. I think it is a head. I think it is not as a painting any very great mater, however I have a very particular reason why. I would have it at any reasonable rate at least the refusal of it, if this can be don he will very much oblige his &
>
> > yr:
> > very humble servant
> > Wm CONGREVE
>
> fryday even:

That one piece of evidence surely belies her supposed indifference to the man, before and after his death in 1680, and proves to some extent that her fondness for Rochester endured for many years after their short affair began in the early 1670s.

As to Anne Bracegirdle receiving the vast sum of two hundred pounds from her dear friend, today's equivalent of some twenty thousand pounds, such a sum would have undoubtedly kept her *harmless from any debt of the Play-House*! This seems a rather strange term, considering Mrs Bracegirdle retired from the stage in 1707. Did it mean that 'Bracy' owed an amount of money to the playhouse, which she was finding difficult to pay off? Or simply that she might have held shares in the company, and that Elizabeth's bequest would guarantee her against its possible collapse?

Mrs Elizabeth Barry was certainly a great celebrity of her day, and was revered by many for her acting prowess but, as can be seen, she had acquired many friends and acquaintances, not just in the world of theatre. These friends of hers were from all walks of life including: those of the Court; titled folk of eminent families; artists, writers, poets and dramatists; and ordinary people too.

To have known and befriended such a wide variety of people, Elizabeth must have been an intelligent and amiable person.

Her freedom and independence, on and off the stage, might have been a reason for her never marrying, although I can imagine she would have had plenty of offers. And who knows, in her years of retirement, had she lived long enough, she might well have taken the opportunity of a companion husband in her dotage. But I feel that would never have been her style, she having lived such a celebrated life of fame as a single, independent woman.

And probably given time, with which tragically she had not been blessed, she might, during her residence in Acton's sweet air, have written her memoirs. And what a bestseller that would have been, then and now. One can only imagine the fascinating contents such a work would have held, from her presumed humble beginnings in her role as a lady's maid, to her celebrated roles on the stage, to her purported string of lovers and her supposedly mercenary reputation so maliciously and undeservedly penned by ruthless satirists.

But what other things might we have read in such memoirs? I believe we would have learned of Mrs Barry's good education, for she could no doubt read and write as well as anyone. She had the gift to memorise the lines of all the many characters she performed, which would have been no easy task. Could she, in her later years as a woman of some wealth and good taste possessing fine clothes and a well-furnished house, have entertained people of quality and refinement including wits, dramatists, poets, artists and musicians? Or rather, being in the media so to speak, would she have enjoyed solace away from the crowded theatre, with a handful of special friends where she could relax in their company? Her retirement to Acton would seem to suggest the latter.

We could speculate forever on what would and could have been, had the gifted Mrs Elizabeth Barry survived into real old age and outlived many of her contemporaries.

One thing is certain… that Mrs Elizabeth Barry and her actress friend, Mrs Anne Bracegirdle were very good friends, holding great respect for each other throughout their careers and long after. They each had similar backgrounds; families experiencing hard times with the consequence of the children needing to find their own way in the world. Was this the mutual catalyst that prompted Elizabeth and Anne's affection for each other?

This leads me on conveniently to the life of Mrs Anne Bracegirdle.

PART TWO

Mrs Anne Bracegirdle
(1671–1748)

Chapter Ten

Unlocking Anne's Ancestry

It is common with a great many English forenames and surnames that their spelling developed many variations over time. Bracegirdle is no exception and can be found as Bracegerdle, Brasgirdle, Brasegirdle, Bretchgirdle, Brastgerdle and in many other forms. In the case of Anne's youngest brother, baptised Hamlett on 31 July 1674, this uncommon forename is found variously as Hamnet and as Hamnit with other Bracegirdle records. The same applies to the name Justinian in its various forms in this narrative. Acknowledging these variations was relevant to unlocking the true ancestral line of the famous actress.

Anne Bracegirdle was baptised at St Giles Church, Northampton on 15 November 1671, a town noted for its shoemaking then and now. The town stands just eleven miles as the crow flies from the site of the famous battle of Naseby; a bloody, decisive battle during the first English Civil War, fought on 14 June 1645 with an overwhelming defeat of the Royalists. But, with the coming of the Restoration in 1660, Anne's world was far removed from that of the usurper Cromwell.

When Anne was four years old, in September 1675, she and her family would witness a catastrophic event, when a great fire swept through the town centre of Northampton, destroying all in its wake. Sparks from an open fire on St Mary's Street, together with a strong westerly wind, caused six hours of dreadful devastation, with some seven hundred of the town's buildings destroyed including the ancient All Saints Church. There were only one hundred and fifty buildings left standing, leaving three-quarters of the town totally destroyed. By some miracle, only eleven people died, but it left some seven hundred families homeless.

Northampton's citizens were determined to have their town back and the rebuilding of its centre began after they raised the colossal sum of twenty-five thousand pounds. A generous donation by King Charles II of one thousand tons of timber from the Salcey Forest was gratefully received and, on the rebuilding of All Saints Church, a statue of the king was erected on its portico parapet in 1712.

One who was very concerned about the fire and its aftermath was Welsh Anglican priest and writer Edward Pearse (c.1630-1694). After studying at

Oxford, he was ordained in 1659 after which he served in various parishes in Northamptonshire including Northampton, Duston, Aldwincle and lastly Cottesbrooke where he was later buried in the chancel in 1694.

After the fire, he wrote a very lengthy letter to a friend in London on the fire's devastation caused to the town. Here are a few excerpts from the letter:

SIR,

IF I had not expected a true and full Account of the beginning and Progress of the dreadful Fire at Northampton, as also of the Losses, State, and Relief of that distressed People, from a faithful and able hand, I should have laboured to have prepared this, such as it is, sooner for your satisfaction. I do not pretend to inform you with every Circumstance and Accident, that's not to be looked for; Because I know none that had so much leisure from their own or other Mens Concenments, as to observe and trace the Motions of that terrible Element, which was that day carried up and down upon the Wings of a strong and violent Wind. And indeed, I find in mine own diligent enquiry, even of understanding Men, that it is as impossible for a Man who imploys all his endeavours to save his own Goods and Life in one part of a Street, to tell me when and in what House the Fire brake out in another place distant from him, as it is for a Soldier, whose Life is engaged in a narrow particular Station, to relate what was out of his sight, done in every Wing, in every Regiment, Troop or Company, much more in every Rank and File of the whole Army, at once engaged and spread over all the Field, as this Fire was spread over the Body, and all parts of the Town. The All-seeing Eye of the Lord of these mighty Hosts of Fire and Wind, can give an exact and perfect Story of every particular Action of that fatal Day. No one Man can, nor many Men apart, because they were not in every place, nor observed all things, but as each one gives in his Observation; which must be gathered together to make a Story, so it must be taken up. And this I assure you, that I gathered these following passages, as well as I was able, and from persons as able to inform me, and as distinctly related, as can be expected from persons under the disorders of Care, Fear, and Amazement at the same time.

That I may represent Northampton in its Ruines, it may not be amiss to present the Figure and Scituation of it as it stood and flourished; because some may peruse these lines, that knew it not, and the better conceive the course of the Fire, which I shall shew you, and the great alteration of it, from a Beautiful Town, to Pitts and Rubbish. Northampton might well contend with the best Inland-City or Town, that is not seated upon a Navigable River, for sweet and wholsom Air, pleasantness of Scituation, plenty and cheapness of Corn and Butchers Meat, good ancient Buildings, dry and commodious Cellarages broad and cleanly Streets, a spacious Market-Hill, fine and profitable Gardens and Orchards, within the Walls (while it was Beautified and honoured with their standing.) The Prospect of it was very delightful from Queens-Cross, which stands upon a Hill in London-Road, within a Mile distance from it. You come down from that Cross to a Bottom, called Gotton-end, and from thence, passing a fair Stone-Bridg over the River Nen or Nine, you entred the Town on a flat, till you come within the South-Gate, and thence keeping the Northern-Road, you went out at the North-Gate, overcoming three Ascents.... .

...Hundreds of Inhabitants were turned out of their Houses, upon a little or no Warning at all. To some the Sovereign Lord would not grant so much as leave to remove their Goods off his Ground; not so much as a Bed to lie on, or a Garment to shift them, not a Stool to sit on, nor a Dish to eat in.... .

...Sir, I know you can understand without my telling you, that this miserable People were loth to leave their convenient and comfortable Dwellings, but more loth to lose their Wares and Goods; but they were forced to leave the one to a Fire that would have them; and at last forced to leave both House, and Shop, and Goods, to save their Lives. Give me leave to try, if I can make you sensible of their Condition, in a Dull and Misty and Cold representation of it: For a lively Image I cannot draw, because my Bosom cannot hold their Passions, nor my Pen weep out their Tears. No words can report the Cries, Fears, Dangers, Distractions, Carefulness, and Amazedness of Young and Old, that doleful Day. Oh! the Roaring of Fire and Wind, what a Thunder in the Air! What Clouds of Smoak! What tearing cracks of Timber! Ancient Couples, Beams and Walls keeping close to one another, till forced to part, suffering themselves to be burnt Inch by Inch before they could be separated!...

...the Citizens will lose their Customers, the Countryman will lose his Market, and the Landlord must fall his Rent, if Northampton be not relieved: yea more, many a Man must go further to seek for an honest Man to teach his Child a Trade; and many a one will want a service, that cannot well be kept and maintained at home... .

...The Mayor sent Messengers with Letters to intreat the Noble-Men and Gentlemen in the Town-Hall, to take their distressed condition into Consideration. There appeared the Saturday following the dreadful Fire, the Right Honourable the Earl of Northampton; Recorder of the Town: three Lords; Sir Richard Rainsford, one of the Judges of the Kings-Bench. Seven or eight Baronets and Knights, and many Justices of the Peace and Gentlemen. The Meeting was principally managed by the Earl. The Result of all their Discourses, was a Subscription to two Papers, to this purpose.

We the Noble-Men and Gentlemen do promise to pay the several sums set down over against, our Names, &c. The one was towards the Re-building of the Town, and the other was for the payment of Dr. Conant's Salary (which was 100 l. per Annum) and for the Relief of the Poor, and other uses of the Town... .

And now, Sir, because I said I will conclude, I will instead of making an Apologie for my self, Why so late? Why so long? Or to others why so short? Or why I? I will only say, that I have some feeling of the Sufferings of my worthy and dear Acquaintance, pray it may rise higher and better, that I hope your Interest and Endeavours may do good, that I have endeavoured to make their deplorable Condition to speak for them, and that I owe you a far greater Service, when you shall command it, if I can perform it. For I am

Sir,
Your most Obliged Servant. E. P.
FINIS.[1]

It seems from the above that Northampton was a very prosperous and pleasant town before the dreadful conflagration. Whether the fire was the cause of Anne's father's *problematic dealings of surety to friends*, history is not clear, but either way the fire's devastation brought upon the Bracegirdle family and all those other families of the town was catastrophic, with so many losing everything they'd owned after a lifetime of hard-earned trade.

Anne was born of a respectable family, her father Justinian Bracegirdle a gentleman. She was also related to Oxford scholars, men of the cloth, landowners and a Northampton mercer. Her life was almost certainly not destined for the stage, but destiny saw it differently.

The parish register publication of banns and marriage of Anne's father Justinian and her mother Martha Furnis at the Church of All Saints, Northampton, in February 1656 is shown below. The page is headed *Publication and Marriages Joseph Sargeant being Maior January 1656 John Spicer Justis*:

> The system of Parochial registration having fallen more or less into abeyance owing to the frequent change of ministers during the civil war* and under the commonwealth an Act was passed in August 1653 on marriage and registration. "By this legislation the clergy were obliged to give up their register books to laymen who were to be called the 'parish register'. The new officials were to be chosen by the householders on or before September 22nd 1653, and after being sworn and approved by the local magistrate the appointments were to be entered in the register books. The parish register had to keep a record of all publications of banns, marriages, births and burials, and was paid 12d. for every certificate of banns and entry of marriage and 4d. for every entry of birth and burial..."
>
> The Act already mentioned relating to marriages and registration enjoined that no marriages were in future to be considered valid unless the knot had been tied by a civil magistrate...
>
> The same act allowed the publication of banns either in the "public meeting place commonly called the church or chapel", or in the Market Place on market day. The following are instances of the latter:-
>
> Feb, 1656-7 – Justinian Brastgerdle of Creaton, Gent and Mⁱˢ Martha Furnis of Sibbertart [Sibbertoft] have been 3 severall Market dayes in 3 severall weeakes published and ended 14 day.

May 1659 – Henry Buckerfeilde of Sulgrave, Gent. And Elizabeth West of Cricke was at our Market place ther published 23 day.

* The vicar of Kibworth, Leicestershire, made the following entry in his register:- "Know all men that the reason why little or nothing is registered from the year 1641 until the year 1649 was the Civil Wars between King Charles and his Parliament, which put all into a confusion till then and neither minister nor people could quietly stay at home for one party or the other."[2]

Several children were born of this union before Anne's baptism in 1671. There were Martha 22 July 1659 and Frances 15 July 1660, both baptised at St James, Gretton in Northamptonshire. A further five of her siblings were baptised at St Giles, Northampton; Elizabeth, 22 March 1665; Honnor, 21 August 1668; Justinian, 22 August 1670; John, 21 March 1673 and Hamlett, 31 July 1674.[3]

In 1664, eight years after their marriage, Justinian was, by purchase, admitted Freeman of Northampton and is named on the admissions roll for that year. It is clear from this that Justinian and his family had settled in Northampton which is also evidenced by their children's baptisms from 1665 onwards.

Over the years, Mrs Bracegirdle was well-known for her benevolence as Anthony Aston writing in the eighteenth century attests: *She was when on the Stage, diurnally charitable, going often into Clare Market, and giving Money to the poor unemploy'd Basket-women, insomuch that she could not pass that Neighbourhood without the thankful Acclamations of People of all Degrees; so that if any Person had affronted her, they would have been in Danger of being killed directly.*

This benevolence seems in fact to follow an inherent tradition practised by several of her Northamptonshire ancestors; in particular, that of the Cheshire born Justinian Bracegirdle who was rector of St Andrew's in Great Billing, Northamptonshire and who died in October 1625.

Rector Bracegirdle combined the roles of God's servant and shrewd businessman, ensuring him a place in heaven. He was most pious and charitable to his flock of parishioners as can clearly be seen from the engraved brass plaque set in the floor of the church:

JVSTINIAN BRASGIRDLE VNDER NEATH THIS STONE
HATH LEFT HIS PAWNE OF RESVRRECTION
WHO FOVRE AND FIFTY WINTERS DID AFFORDE

THIS FLOCK THE PASTVRE OF GODS HEAVELY WORD
AND ALL HIS LIFE TIME DID IMPLOY HIS CARE
SOE TO GROWE RICH TO MAKE THE POORE HIS
   HEYRE
BEING CHARITYES FAYTHFVLL STEWERT HE
   IMPARTS
TWELVE HVNDRED POVNDS TO NOVRISH OXEFORD
   ARTES
THEN IF OVR GOD TO THEM OPE HEAVEN DOORE
THAT GIVE BVT DROPS OF WATER TO THE POORE
 SVRE HIS WISE SOVLE LAID VP A TREASVRE THERE
THAT NERE SHAL RVST WHO NOW BOVGHT HEAVEN
   SO DEARE
WHEN FAYTH AND GOOD WORKES HAVE SO LONG
   CONTENDED
THAT FAITH IS ALMOST DEAD AND GOOD WORKES
   ENDED
OBIJT OCTOB XXV 1625

The charitable amount of *Twelve hvndred povnds to novrish Oxeford artes* was from the Glebe lands at Mears Ashby, Northamptonshire and this legacy continues to the present day. It is known as The Justinian Bracegirdle Exhibition Foundation and awards grants to students attending Oxford University.

Not all though were enamoured of the charitable Justinian, with a Bill of Complaint ensuing in the Star Chamber regarding an event of riotous persons disputing over tithes of corn. Later attention was turned to the judges and officers of the Ecclesiastical Court in libellous verse, of which a few lines alluded to Rector Justinian Bracegirdle:

A girdle of Brasse from Billing Great
Is third of this Judiciall Court,
A stuttering foole I thinke he is,
And never goodness goes about.
Yf I had time to tell yow all
Of that he doth in everie place,
I should his falts make manifest
And much he doltshippe should disgrace.[4]

From one benevolent ancestor of Anne Bracegirdle to another; James Bracegirdle, gentleman of Church Brampton in Northamptonshire. James married at the age of twenty-seven, in 1626, but he died aged just thirty-five in 1634. He died without issue but in his will, dated 24 March 1633/4, he was most charitable to the poor of Northampton and also with annual payments to other parishes. Many of his family members, including his wife Anne Bracegirdle (nee Wade), benefited greatly from his will too:

Bracegirdle's Charity

James Bracegirdle, by a will dated 24th March 1633, gave to the poor people of the parish of All Saints, in Northampton, the yearly sum of 20s., and to the poor people of the parish of Saint Sepulchre, in Northampton, the like yearly sum of 20s., to be paid out of the annual sum of 31 *l.* 5s., issuing out of the lands or inclosed grounds of Thomas Reeve, in Bugbrook, to be distributed on Saint Thomas's-day yearly, at the discretion of the churchwardens and overseers of the poor of each of the said parishes, and among the poorest sort of people.

The above-mentioned annuity of £31*l* 5s. is payable out of an estate at Bugbrook belonging to Henry Cadwallader Adams, esq., and there is received annually by the churchwardens of All Saints and of Saint Sepulchre respectively the sum of 16s., 4s. being deducted from each annuity for land-tax. The money received is distributed by the churchwardens among the poor.[5]

From the above, it is quite clear how Anne's benevolent nature became inherent, she learning from an early age that kindness and generosity were the Bracegirdles' forte.

Chapter Eleven

The Play House, Anne's New Home

In 1680, at the age of nine, a young girl found herself upon the stage, playing the part of a Page in Thomas Otway's tragedy, *The Orphan; or, The Unhappy Marriage*, at the Duke's Theatre in Dorset Gardens, London. She held a natural beauty, with white teeth, an unusual asset for those times, a fresh blushing complexion and, with dark hair and eyes, she won the hearts of her audience. The girl in question was Anne Bracegirdle, whose father suffered great monetary loss through problematic dealings of surety to friends. Thus, finding himself in dire circumstances, he reluctantly felt compelled to place his young daughter with the actor Thomas Betterton and his wife Mary who were then both living and working at the theatre.

In Betterton's *The History of the English Stage*, 1741, the following was said of Anne Bracegirdle:

> WE are, in this Place, obliged, in Justice to her Merit, to introduce, a Lady now living, Mrs. *Anne Bracegirdle*. She was the Daughter of *Justinian Bracegirdle* of *Northamptonshire*, Esq; where she was born.
>
> It is not any Matter of our Enquiry by what Means a Gentlewoman of so good an Extraction came upon the Stage, since the best Families have been liable to the greatest Misfortunes, amongst which was that of her Father, in being bound, and suffering for Others. But it may be some kind of Alleviation to say, that in the Scene, wherein Providence had consigned her Fate, she had the good Fortune to be well placed, when an Infant, under the Care of Mr. *Betterton* and his Wife, whose Tenderness she always acknowledges to have been Paternal; Nature formed her for the Stage, and it was to the Admiration of all Spectators that she performed the Page in The *Orphan*, at the Duke's Theatre in *Dorset-Garden*…

For Anne's parents to have chosen the Bettertons, in similar circumstance to that of young Mrs Barry, appears somewhat puzzling, although it is believed

102

that Anne and Elizabeth were not the only young girls the Bettertons took under their wing. Even though the couple were respectably married and of excellent character, they were, it must be said, in a precarious occupation; it was one where, in particular, actresses were employed in risky surroundings, since although female players were remunerated in their own right, they were nevertheless looked upon frequently as women of easy virtue.

The necessity of adoption resulted in an acting vocation for young Anne as, under the Bettertons' care and guidance, she rose from child player to be one of London's most respected Restoration actresses. She was admired equally with other notable actresses such as; Elizabeth Boutell, Elizabeth Barry, Eleanor 'Nell' Gwyn, Anne Oldfield, and also her devoted custodian the formidable Mary Saunderson Betterton. Thus emerged the brilliant career of Mrs Anne Bracegirdle.

Following her debut at the age of nine, during her time in the theatre, Anne took on many parts created by leading contemporary playwrights such as William Mountfort (c.1664-1692), Thomas Shadwell, William Congreve, Aphra Behn, and John Vanbrugh.

At the age of seventeen, in 1688, Anne made her debut at the Theatre Royal, Drury Lane. This was six years after the merger of the Duke's and King's theatres. She played Antelina, daughter of Ghinotto, in *The Injured Lovers; or, The Ambitious Father,* a tragedy by actor and playwright William Mountfort. Anne's now close friend Mrs Barry was also in the cast as The Princess Oryala, in love with Rheusanes. On reading the Prologue to the play, written and recited by Mountfort, one cannot help but think of the dreadful disaster that would later befall this promising young actor:

> JO Haynes's *Fate is now become my Share,*
> *For I'm a* Poet, Married, *and a* Player:
> *The greatest of these* Curses *is the* First;
> *As for the latter* Two, *I know the* worst;
> *But how you mean to deal with me to Day,*
> *Or how you'l* Massacre *my harmless Play,*
> *I must confess distracts me every* Way:
> *For I've not only* Criticks *in the Pit.*
> *But even in the upper Gallery they sit,*
> *Knaves that will run down Mr.* Mountforts's *Wit;*
> *I'm the unlucky'st* Dogg *that ever Writ.*
> *Some Care then must be taken, that may save*
> *This* Dear, *my First Begotten, from the Grave:*
> *Some Friends Advise, like Brother* Ben *declare,*

By God 'tis Good, *deny't the Slave that dare.*
Were I but sure 'twould Take, *I'd do my best;*
But to be kick'd, you know, would spoil the Jest.
However I must still my Play maintain,
Damn *it who will,* Damn me, *I'll write again;*
Clap down each Thought, nay, more than I can think,
Ruin my Family in Pen *and* Ink.
And tho' my Heart should burst to see your Spite,
True Talboy *to the last I'll Cry and Write,*
That's Certain.
Or since I am beset so by my Foes,
I beg your Favours, Friends, Brother Beaux;
Join with the Ladies, to whose Power I bow,
Where I see Gentleness on every Brow;
To whose acuser Judgments I submit,
O! Save me from the Surlies *of the Pit:*
Those Nauseous Wretches which have not the tast
Of Wit or Gallantry, if nicely drest.
I never writ till Love *first touch'd my Brain,*
And surely Love *will now* Loves *Cause Maintain,*
Besides my Natural Love *to write again.*
Yet as you Please, Ruin *or* Pity *bear,*
Sir Courtly *fears no Enemy so Fair:*
Execute as you please your Tyrant-Will,
His Character's, Your humble Servant still.

The evil catastrophe that happened to poor Mountfort did concern his actress friend Anne Bracegirdle. The fateful event took place on the night of 9 December 1692, in Howard Street, Strand. Just a week earlier on the second, Mountfort had given a great performance as Alexander in *The Rival Queens; or, The Death of Alexander the Great.* What a seemingly dreadful omen this play was for the talented Mountfort.

It transpires that a Captain Richard Hill, believed to be aged eighteen or twenty at the time, held a great passion for Mrs Bracegirdle, to the point of offering her his hand but he was refused. Not deterred by this refusal, he had a mind to abduct her, and even borrowed some night-linen from Mrs Radd, the landlady, whose house he lodged in at Buckingham Court. It is possible that he engaged his friend Charles Mohun, 4th Baron Mohun (c.1675-1712) to assist him in the capture, as Mohun was close by at the time. Hill was certainly serious about the attempted abduction, he stationing a coach near the Horseshoe Tavern in Drury Lane along with six soldiers who would attempt to force poor Anne into the coach and carry her off. All this had been planned to coincide with the actress returning from a Mr Page in Princes Street, off Drury Lane, with whom she had stopped that evening, to her lodging at Mrs Dorothy Brown's in the same street. As Anne walked down Drury Lane that evening, accompanied by her mother, brother and her friend Mr Page, one of Hill's soldiers grabbed the actress in an attempt to force her into the coach. Gallant Mr Page intervened but Hill drew his sword and struck Page on the head. The inevitable screams of horror from the ladies drew the attention of others in the street, leaving Hill no alternative but to tell the soldiers to let her go.

Hill's friend Mohun had been seated in the coach the whole time. At that moment he stepped out and, together with Hill, insisted that they would see Anne safely home. Mr Page, who was not seriously hurt, then accompanied Hill, Mohun and Anne to aid her security. With Anne safely returned home, Hill and Mohun loitered in the street, sending for a bottle of wine from the nearby Horseshoe Tavern in Drury Lane. Anne was naturally very concerned to know if Mountfort was safe, being aware of Hill's jealousy of his friendship with her, and the captain's bad intentions towards her friend. Anne sent her maid to Mountfort's house, but she returned saying he was not there. Anne became more alarmed, knowing that Captain Hill and Charles Mohun were still in the street, and had been drinking.

Mountfort then appeared on the scene addressing Mohun who embraced him tenderly, apologising for Hill's behaviour who, it was said, was standing in the middle of the street when Mountfort approached him. But, according to an eyewitness, Hill in fact walked up behind Mountfort, hitting him on the ear and asking him to draw his sword. A fight ensued in which Mountfort fell to the ground with a mortal wound to the right of his stomach near a rib. Later, severely injured and in agony, lying on the floor in his house, Mountfort told Mr Page that the coward Hill had run him through before he could draw his own sword. Poor victim, Mountfort, died the following day and was buried in the vault of St Clement Danes in the Strand. It was reported that there were a thousand people who attended his funeral, and legend has it that the church's bell cracked when tolled that day.

Captain Hill escaped and was reported to have fled to the Isle of Wight and later to Scotland, but Baron Mohun surrendered himself to the authorities. He was put on trial for murder as an accessory before the fact but, as one might expect, the majority of his peers found him not guilty. Also added to this, before his death, Mountfort had declared Mohun *offered me no violence*.

Nonetheless, trouble-maker and rake Charles Mohun did get his comeuppance later, when he and James Douglas, 4th Duke of Hamilton and 1st Duke of Brandon KG KT (1658-1712), fought a duel over a disputed inheritance. This illegal event took place in Hyde Park in London, on 15 November 1712, when both men were mortally wounded.

Referring to Macaulay's voluminous work, *The History of England*, first published in 1848, I think we could all agree on his comments regarding the deplorable, unanimous acquittal of Mohun:

> ...Had the issue been tried by Holt and twelve plain men at the Old Bailey, there can be no doubt that a verdict of Guilty would have been returned. The Peers, however, by sixty nine votes to fourteen, acquitted their accused brother. One great nobleman was so brutal and stupid as to say, "After all the fellow was but a player; and players are rogues." All the newsletters, all the coffeehouse orators, complained that the blood of the poor was shed with impunity by the great. Wits remarked that the only fair thing about the trial was the show of ladies in the galleries. Letters and journals are still extant in which men of all shares of opinion, Whigs, Tories, Nonjurors, condemn the partiality of the tribunal. It was not to be expected that, while the memory of this scandal was fresh in the public mind, the Commons would be induced to give any new advantage to accused peers.[1]

But whether we could agree on Macaulay's impression of Mrs Bracegirdle would be debatable:

> The most popular actress of the time was Anne Bracegirdle. There were on the stage many women of more faultless beauty, but none whose features and deportment had such power to fascinate the senses and the hearts of men. The sight of her bright black eyes and of her rich brown cheek sufficed to put the most turbulent audience into good humour. It was said of her that in the crowded theatre she had as many lovers as she had male spectators. Yet no lover, however rich, however high in rank, had prevailed on her to be his mistress. Those who are acquainted with the parts which she was in the habit of playing, and with the epilogues which it was her especial business to recite, will not easily give her credit for any

extraordinary measure of virtue or of delicacy. She seems to
have been a cold, vain, and interested coquette, who perfectly
understood how much the influence of her charms was
increased by the fame of a severity which cost her nothing,
and who could venture to flirt with a succession of admirers,
in the just confidence that no flame which she might kindle in
them would thaw her own ice...[2]

In the opera, *The World in the Moon*, 1697, by poet and playwright Elkanah
Settle (1648-1724), there is a piece of dialogue between Stanmore and
Wildblood with reference to the virtuous Anne Bracegirdle:

Stan.   But why do you tell me you never stay out a Play,
        when you know I have seen you perking behind the
        Scenes, from the first Musick to the last Candle, to
        clear Stage; nay, and to a clear Dressing-room, the
        very last Man bourn.

Wild.   Behind the Scenes! Ay, there the Case is altered.
        There Ned, I have nothing to say to the Play, but the
        Players —Oh! I could dance Attendance, and dangle
        at the Train of a High Feather, and a Stage Princess
        (especially that Phoenix amongst 'em under the
        reputation of a Virginity) as contentedly and with
        as much mortal Resignation for three whole Hours
        together, as I could lye a whole Night by her.

In *Six Plays Written by Mr. Mountfort*, Volume I, 1720, there is a further
version of the events of that lamentable day:

HIS Fame encreas'd on the THEATRE 'Till the Time of his
unhappy Misfortune, concerted by Mr. *Hill*, and the late
Lord *Mohun*; the melancholly Circumstances whereof are
so well known, that they need not be repeated: But 'Tis very
remarkable, that the Night after he was kill'd he was to have
Acted the Part of *Busy* D'*Amboys*, in Mr. *Chapman*'s PLAY,
bearing that Title; wherein he was to be Shot through the Back
in the Catastrophe, and his own Murder was accomplish'd by a
Wound in that Part with a Sword; so that the same Tragedy, at
least with very little Variation, was actually effected on himself,
which he was only intended to represent on the THEATRE.

THE Period of this unfortunate Accident, was as I have been inform'd, about the Year 1696. in the Prime of his Years, not exceeding the Age of 35. His Death was very much lamented in General; but it had so great an Affect on Dear Companion, Mr. LEE the Comedian, that he did not survive him above the space of a Week.

HE was Buried in the Vault of St. *Clement Danes* in the Strand, Mr. *Purcell* performing the Funeral Anthem; a great many Gentlemen attended his Obsequies, as the last Office they could do for one whom they Lov'd and Esteem'd. He was Married to a Daughter of Mr. *Percival* the Player, by whom he left two Daughters; one whereof is an excellent Actress, but she has lately quitted the Stage.

Chapter Twelve

Fresh-faced Anne Bracegirdle, the Darling of the Stage

Following that terrifying incident with Hill and Mohun, it is a wonder that Anne continued as an actress. Although her outward appearance was one of a genteel young woman, she must have possessed nerves of steel, and duly became the darling of the stage.

Her first appearance following the incident was on 16 February 1693, in *The Maid's last Prayer; or, Any rather than Fail*, a comedy by the Irish dramatist Thomas Southerne. Anne played Lady Trickitt, with Mrs Barry as Lady Malepert and with Mountfort's widow taking the role of Lady Susan Malepert. No doubt needs must, no matter how bereaved Susanna Mountfort (nee Percival) was. She had herself to feed as well as her two daughters; two-year-old Susanna, and Mary christened at St Clement Danes on 27 April 1693. Edward, their only son, was born in 1691 and died an infant that year. A daughter, Elizabeth, was born in March 1692 and sadly died eight days later.

Being a young widow with two children was not a good situation to be in, and the security of a wage-earning husband would have been desirable. Consequently, on 31 January 1694, Susanna married London actor, John Baptista Verbruggen, who she had known for a few years. It is recorded that a child from their marriage was born on 16 May 1703 and baptised on the twenty-seventh with the name Lewis. The poor mother died after the birth, sometime in July/August 1703, from complications and tragically the infant was buried on 2 October following. Five years later, John died and was buried in St Martin-in-the-Fields on 12 March 1707/8.

Following *The Maid's last Prayer*, a performance on 1 March 1693 of Congreve's *The Old Bachelor* was staged for the first time, with great success. The music for the play was composed by Henry Purcell (1659-1695), one of England's greatest composers. He was to die just two years later, on 21 November, at the young age of thirty-six, his burial taking place in Westminster Abbey. There are two versions of the possible cause of his death. One is that his wife locked him out of his home after he returned late from the theatre, he catching a night chill. The other, which is more plausible, is that he died from tuberculosis.

In *The Old Bachelor*, Mrs Bracegirdle played Araminta, with Mrs Barry as Laetitia. The proof of their popularity at this time was that Anne recited the Prologue and Elizabeth the Epilogue:

PROLOGUE,

Spoken by Mrs. *Bracegirdle.*

HOW this vile World is chang'd! In former Days,
Prologues, were serious speeches, before Plays;
Grave, solemn Things, as Graces are to Feasts;
Where poets begg'd a Blessing from their Guests.
But now, no more like Suppliants we come;
A Play makes War, and Prologue is the Drum:
Arm'd with keen Satire and with pointed Wit,
We threaten you who do for Judges sit,
To save our Plays, or else we'll damn your Pit;
But for your Comfort, it falls out to Day,
We've a young Author and his first-born Play;
So, standing only on his good Behaviour,
He's very civil, and entreats your Favour.
Not but the Man has Malice, would he show it,
But on my Conscience he's a bashful Poet;
You think that strange___no matter, he'll out-grow it.
Well, I'm his Advocate___by me he prays you,
(I don't know whether I shall speak to please you)
He prays___O bless me! what shall I do now!
Hang me if I know what he prays, or how!
And 'twas the prettiest Prologue as he wrote it!
Well, the Deuce take me, if I han't forgot it.
O Lord, for Heav'n's sake excuse the Play,
Because, you know, if it be damn'd to Day,
I shall be hang'd for wanting what to say.

For my sake then___but I'm in such Confusion,
I cannot stay to hear your Resolution.

[Runs off.][1]

During her time at Drury Lane, Anne Bracegirdle performed some twenty-six plays, from 1688 to 1694, which is an average of four plays a season. Traditionally, the theatre season ran from mid-September until mid-June, with a few players performing in addition at the London annual fairs such as Bartholomew Fair in order to subsidise their wages during the three months summer closure. However, I doubt whether Elizabeth or Anne ever ventured into that realm, it generally being a somewhat dangerous place.

The *infamous* Bartholomew Fair was held on 3 September 1855 for the last time by order of the City authorities. It had been one of the highlights of the Londoners' calendar and was usually held in August. A charter had been granted in 1133 by Henry I (c.1068-1135) to Rahere, an Anglo-Norman priest, most famous for having founded the Priory of the Hospital of St. Bartholomew in 1123.

Originally a fair for the trading of cloth, held at Cloth Fair and Priory graveyard, by 1641 it had outgrown its original purpose and had spread over four parishes including Christ Church and St Sepulchre's. By that time, the entertainments on offer were sideshows, musicians, acrobats, puppet shows, the odd wild animal or two, and play booths. Most plays, or drolls as they were often known, were short performances of a comic nature to entertain the masses.

I have selected an excerpt from *The Newgate Calendar* which gives a flavour of the hazardous setting and goings-on at the Fair, certainly not a place for the genteel, law-abiding citizen:

> We could wish, seriously, to caution all young people against a habit of attending fairs. They constitute an assemblage of idle people, where are indiscriminately mixed thieves and pick-pockets, who go from fair to fair; loose women, strolling players, and vagabonds of every description, waiting to plunder the honest part of the people. Saint Bartholomew's fair, from its long continuance, is a school of vice which has initiated more youth into the habits of villainy than even Newgate itself....[2]

Another place for out of season players was across the Thames at Southwark Fair, held for three days in September on the seventh, eighth and ninth. Liberty to hold an annual fair there was granted by charter to the City of London by Edward IV (1442-1483), in 1462. Akin to Bartholomew Fair, it too grew so perilous to man and beast that it was eventually banned in 1763.

There is a delightful engraving of Southwark Fair by the talented painter William Hogarth (1697-1764). Depicting the mayhem, it shows in the background the tower of St George the Martyr in Borough High Street and portrays an historic mishmash of the riotous assembly of citizens at the fair. Banners of all sorts are displayed, one being a satire *The Stage Mutiny* by Hogarth himself, representing the actors' rebellion at the Drury Lane Theatre in 1733: There are people falling from a temporary stage as it collapses under them. A woman at the head of a crowd bangs a large drum slung against her hip. A rope dancer performs acrobatic feats high up on a line strung between two buildings. Actors and actresses perform on a stage under a large painting of the Horse of Troy, and on a platform to the right of them a Harlequin alongside a hobby-horse gestures to the throng, whilst on the right of the picture a man emerges riding a horse and brandishing a sword.

Mrs Bracegirdle's last performance at Drury Lane, when under the poor management of Rich, was on 30 April 1694, in *The Married Beau; or, The Curious Impertinent*, a comedy by dramatist John Crowne, with the scene set in Covent Garden. Anne played the part of Camilla, a virtuous, devout, reserved young beauty of small fortune. Mrs Barry played Mrs Lovely, a witty, beautiful coquette, that loves to be courted and admired but aims at no more; she's proud, and has great value for honour. Mountfort's widow, now remarried and acting under the stage name of Mrs Verbruggen, took the part of Lionell, Mrs Lovely's waiting-woman. She's young, handsome and amorous, only very desirous of a husband.

Chapter Thirteen

A Happy Company at Lincoln's Inn Fields

Anne Bracegirdle also moved to Lincoln's Inn Fields Theatre at the time of the Rich rift. As with Mrs Barry, Anne performed in the theatre's opening play, Congreve's *Love for Love*, she playing the role of Angelica, a part no doubt written especially for her by her dear friend.

Mrs Bracegirdle and William Congreve were very close friends for many years. The big question was *how* close. It was rumoured by contemporaries that her friendship with Congreve might have been more than just platonic, he regularly visiting her until his death in 1729. There were even allegations that they might have married, though this seems very unlikely. Nonetheless, Congreve *did* take Henrietta Godolphin, 2nd Duchess of Marlborough as his long term lover. It is purported they had a child, Lady Mary Godolphin, born 1723. In his will, dated 26 February 1725, he left his entire estate to the duchess, with only a comparatively nominal sum bequeathed to Anne Bracegirdle; *To Mrs Ann Bracegirdle of Howard Street two hundred pounds*. One wonders if this amount, as with Mrs Barry, was to save his friend *harmless from any Debt of the Play-House*.

William Congreve was born on an estate near Ledston in the West Riding of Yorkshire. His parents were Colonel William Congreve (1637-1708) and his wife, Mary (nee Browning) (c.1636-1715). In 1672, the family moved to London, and then to the Irish port of Youghal in County Cork. Son William's education began at Kilkenny College and then continued at Trinity College in Dublin. He later moved to London to study law at the Middle Temple. Preferring to become a man of letters, he felt a lawyer's life was not for him. He, like many of his contemporaries, became a member of the Whiggish Kit-Cat Club, where possibly his friendship with fellow dramatist Vanbrugh began. As a member of the Club, Congreve's political bias culminated in his being awarded government posts and a lucrative lifelong appointment as Secretary of Jamaica. Despite this, it is believed he never actually travelled to that tropical Caribbean island.

One of Congreve's works was *The Judgement of Paris*, an operatic libretto in which Mrs Bracegirdle took part and excelled as Venus.

The offer of *A Musick Prize* for the best composition for the opera was announced in the *London Gazette* on 18 March 1700. Prize money was to be one hundred guineas for the winner followed by fifty, thirty and twenty. The competitors were John Weldon (1676-1736), John Eccles (1668-1735), Daniel Purcell (c.1664-1717), believed to be either the younger brother or cousin of Henry Purcell, and Gottfried Finger (c.1655-1730) also known as Godfrey Finger, who was born in Olomouc, in the modern-day Czech Republic. Their works were performed individually over four days, then staged together in a grand final at Dorset Garden Theatre on 3 June 1703. Weldon was the triumphant winner, with Eccles as runner-up, while third prize went to Purcell and fourth to Finger.

In a letter dated 26 March 1701 to his friend Joseph Keally, Congreve sets out in detail the night Eccles' music was first performed at Dorset Garden Theatre:

> ...All your friends in this quarter are ever inquisitive about you, and nobody thinks your correspondence frequent enough. I wished particularly for you on Friday last, when Eccles his music for the prize was performed in Dorset Garden, and universally admired. Mr Finger's is to be to-morrow; and Russel and Weldon's follow in their turn. The latter two I believe will not be before Easter. After all have been heard severally, they are all to be heard in one day, in order to a decision; and if you come at all this spring, you may come time enough to hear that. Indeed, don't think any one place in the world can show such an assembly. The number of performers, besides the verse-singers, was 85. The front of the stage was all built into a concave with deal boards; all which was faced with tin, to increase and throw forwards the sound. It was all hung with sconces of wax-candles, besides the common branches of lights usual in the play-houses. The boxes and pit were all thrown into one; so that all sat in common: and the whole was crammed with beauties and beaux, not one scrub being admitted. The place where formerly the music used to play, between the pit and stage, was turned into White's chocolate-house; the whole family being transplanted thither with chocolate, cool'd drinks, ratafia, portico, &c. which every body that would called for, the whole expence of every

thing being defrayed by the subscribers. I think truly the whole thing better worth coming to see than the jubilee. And so I remain yours,

W. CONGREVE.

Our friend Venus performed to a miracle; so did Mrs Hodgson Juno, Mrs Boman was not quite so well approved in Pallas...[1]

Tragically, at the young age of forty, Congreve was suffering from eyesight troubles due to cataracts. This was a particularly sad situation for a man of letters, and one that the poor playwright and poet endured for many years. In a letter to Keally dated 9 November 1710 he complains about his troubling eyes:

...I live entirely at home, see nobody, nor converse in any manner.... Excuse me to Luther and yourself for not writing oftener; 'Tis very painful to my eyes...[2]

Two years later, on 6 May 1712, Congreve writes again to his friend Keally regarding his poor eyesight:

...I have an old conjuror who has been some time about my eyes, and I hope will be able to keep 'em from being worse; and who, if I had met with him seven years ago, could have quite cured me...[3]

The above confirms that poor Congreve had *already* been suffering from declining eyesight as early as 1705, when he was just thirty-five years old.

In September 1728, at the age of fifty-eight, he was involved in a carriage accident. He never recovered fully from his injuries and died on 19 January 1729 and was buried in Poets' Corner in Westminster Abbey.

I wonder what was the attraction for both Anne Bracegirdle and Henrietta Godolphin to Congreve? I like to think that he being born in Yorkshire and spending his youthful days in Ireland, Congreve's early Northern brogue blended with an Irish twist, together with his fine features, might have been irresistible to the ladies.

One year after the death of Congreve in 1729, there was published *Memoirs of the Life, Writings, and Amours of William Congreve Esq; Interspersed with Miscellaneous Essay, Letters, and Characters, Written by Him. Compiled from their respective Originals*, by Charles Wilson Esq.

This publication was advertised in the Daily Post on 29 April 1729 by Edmund Curll whose reputation was not the best; Dr John Arbuthnot (1667-1735), a Scottish physician, satirist and polymath, termed him *one of the new terrors of death*, from his constantly printing every eminent person's life and last will:

> *Whereas it has been advertis'd by* E. Curll, *that there is now in the Press, miscellaneous Essays and familiar Letters, by* William Congreve *Esq; to which will be prefix'd Memoirs of his Life, Writings and Amours, by* Charles Wilson *Esq; This is therefore to inform the Publick, that Mr.* Congreve's *Life,* &c. *will be publish'd with all possible speed from authentick Papers, by a good Hand sufficiently authorized. To which will be added, an Account of his Works already printed, as well as of his posthumous Writings, of which no other Person can have any Memoirs relating thereto.*[4]

When this advertisement came to the attention of Anne Bracegirdle, she was upset to say the least and was reported to have demanded *a sight of the book in MS*, but this was refused. Apparently, she then asked *by what authority Congreve's life was written, and what pieces contained in it were genuine?* And being told that there would be several of his essays, letters, etc. Anne answered, *Not one single sheet of paper, I dare say.*

On reading this memoir, there are only a few instances where Mrs Bracegirdle's name is mentioned, and all of these refer to her as an actress reciting prologues and epilogues. Whether or not Anne did in fact have something to hide regarding a possible past love affair with Congreve, Wilson's memoirs had certainly not revealed anything of that nature whatsoever. It does make one wonder, with Mrs Bracegirdle's demanding a preview of the manuscript, that she might have been very concerned as to any reference to *Amours*.

Wilson, the author, in his Preface had printed the following:

PREFACE.

A certain Lady, to whom Mr. Congreve bequeath'd a handsome Legacy, would be more prudent, if hereafter she would not be so fond of exposing her own Ignorance in the Republick of Letters; for her Inquisitiveness led her so far, as to fancy she had a Right to demand a site of these Papers, while they were under the Press which been justly *refus'd her, she then wanted to know by what Authority Mr.* Congreve*'s Life was written, and what Pieces were contain'd in it that were genuine? Upon being civilly told, there would be found several Essays, Letters and Characters of that Gentleman's writing, she with the most affected, contradictory, Dramatick-drawl, cry'd out,* Not one single Sheet of Paper I dare to swear.[5]

Congreve was not alone in his esteem for Anne. She was greatly admired for her goodness and integrity by many men, they often presenting her with gifts of affection, which she was reluctant to accept, though she did once receive eight hundred guineas from a long list of contributors. This story goes that Lord Halifax, overhearing praise of her virtuous nature by dukes and other nobles, exclaimed *you all commend her virtue, &c. but why do we not present this incomparable woman with something worthy her acceptance?* Halifax then deposited two hundred guineas, and the rest made it up to eight hundred.

There were many who pursued her as a potential lover and others offering their hand in marriage. In this, they were all to be disappointed as she remained, as it seems according to history, unmarried and virtuous throughout her life.

Surprisingly, there was contemporary vindictiveness in that Anne's rejection of marriage proposals and expensive gifts from men of quality and title was not deemed characteristic of a low-born innkeeper's daughter. Was it justified, for it appeared common knowledge that she was in fact the genteel daughter of a Northamptonshire gentleman? In fact, in a short summary in an indenture of 17 January 1669/70 there is mention of Justinian Bracegirdle of Northampton, innholder, and Martha his wife. Unfortunately, in this rare document, there is no citation of the name or location of the inn. Further papers were scrutinised but to no avail until stumbling across Nicholas Rowe (1674-1718). This dramatist, poet and writer was lovesick for Mrs Bracegirdle, but his attentions were unrequited, as was the case with many of her other admirers. Rowe's bitterness was declared in the resultant verse:

...and, at a later date, he took a mean revenge in some occasional verses, wherein he ironically advised the Earl of Scarsdale, another of her numerous admirers, to marry her, notwithstanding her lowly origin.

Do not, most fragrant Earl, disclaim
Thy bright, thy reputable flame,

To Bracegirdle the brown;
But publicly espouse the dame,
And say, G___d___the town,

Though thy dear's father kept an inn
At grisly head of Saracen
For carriers at Northampton;
Yet she might come of gentler kin
Than e'er that father dreamt on.

Of proffers large her choice had she,
Of jewels, plate, and land in fee,
Which she with scorn rejected:
And can a nymph so virtuous be
Of base-born blood suspected?[6]

The *grisly head of Saracen* which Rowe depicts was the Saracen's Head in Northampton. The inn stood in Abington Street close by the Market Square and is mentioned in *The Records of the Borough of Northampton 1898.*

It is therefore manifest that Mrs Bracegirdle was not only the daughter of Justinian Bracegirdle, gentleman of Northamptonshire but, if truth be told, that of a Northampton innkeeper too.

The disparaging verses above obviously did not mar the poetical career of Rowe, as his appointment as Poet Laureate to George I in 1715 bears witness.

With regard to *Of proffers large her choice had she*; this is possibly referring to Lord Lovelace, whom Anthony Aston says was *an engaging man who drest well.* Lovelace sent his servant every day to Anne's house to ask after her. The servant always returned with the same answer, *she was indifferent well, she humbly thanked his lordship.* Another of her admirers was a Lord Burlington, whose story was told many years later by Horace Walpole (1717-1797). One day, Burlington sent Anne a present of some fine old china together with a letter. Anne very astutely told the servant *he had made a mistake; that it was true the letter was for her, but the china for his lady, to whom he must carry it. Lord! The countess was so full of gratitude when her husband came home to dinner!*

Thomas Brown also did not seem enamoured of our virtuous actress and penned these derogatory remarks about both Congreve and her in a chapter *Amusement IV. The Play-House* printed in *The Third Volume of the Works of Mr. Tho. Brown*:

...Hey day! What have we here? A Dutchess and a Dutchman together, *Pepper* and *Vinegar* on my Conscience, only 'Tis a difficult time of the Year, and People that lye so close together are warm enough without any such Matters to heat 'em. But that *Poet* there that shews his Assiduity by following yonder Actress, is the most entertaining sort of an Animal imaginable. But 'Tis *the Way of the World*, to have an Esteem for the fair Sex, and she looks to a Miracle when she is acting a Part in one of his own Plays. Would not any one think it pity she should not have an Humble Servant, when that Mrs. *Abigail* there, who is one of her Attendants, can be brought to bed of a Living Child without any Manner of notice taken of her. Look upon him one more? I say, if she goes to her *Shift*, 'Tis Ten to One but he follows her, not that I would say for never so much, to take up her *Smock*; he dines with her almost ev'ry Day, yet she's a *Maid*; he rides out with her, and visits her in Publick and Private, yet, she's a *Maid*; if I had not a particular Respect for her, I should go near to say he lyes with her, yet she's a *Maid*. Now I leave the World to judge whether it be his or her Fault that she has so long kept her *Maidenhead*, since Gentlemen of his Profession have generally *a greater Respect for the Ladies than that comes to*.[7]

After a busy and successful first season at Lincoln's Inn Fields, Anne continued as a celebrated actress there for many years.

Mrs Bracegirdle must have possessed a fine singing voice, she duetting with the renowned actor John Bowman on several occasions. The first was on 1 June 1696 in a comedy *Love's a Jest* by French-born Pierre Antoine Motteux, known as Peter Anthony Motteux (1663-1718). Motteux was an author, playwright and translator, and became the editor and publisher of the first English magazine, *The Gentleman's Journal, or the Monthly Miscellany*. Motteux, a man who advocated equality of the sexes, re-titled his journal *The Lady's Journal* in 1693, devoting it to articles by and about women.

Here is the song that Mr Bowman and Mrs Bracegirdle duetted; he in the role of Airy, friend to Railmore, and she playing Christina, sister of Francelia:

DIALOGUE.

Man.   *Hark you, Madam, can't I move you?*
             why the Devil do you run?

> *Hav'n't I told you twice I love you?*
> > *come then, kiss me, or I'm gone.*

Wom. *Foh! I hate a Rakish Lover,*
> > *Do not discompose my Dress:*
> *Good familiar Spark, give over!*
> > *how on Quality you press!*

Man. *From the Countess to the Cit,*
> > *ev'ry Beauty for me dies:*
> *Demme, why should I submit*
> > *to doat on this Woman's Eyes!*

Wom. *Fifty Beaux expire for me,*
> > *ogling, sighing all the Day;*
> *Yet not one dares be so free,*
> > *tho they let me win at Play.*

Man. *Sure we Rakes can better move you;*
> > *see this Shape and Leg, my Dear!*
> *In one Minute more I'll love you*
> > *than those Fops can in a Year.*

Wom. *But your Love will soon be over.*
Man. *Then you'll get a fresher Lover.*
> *Come, to Bed! I long t'embrace.*

Wom. *Leave my Hand!*
Man. *—Then lend your Face!*
> *First the Hand, and then the Face,*
> *Then the Breast,*
> *And then the rest,*
> *Then the Breast, and then—*

Wom. *—The Face. [Gives him a slap 'othe Face.*
Man. *'s Death, I've a good mind to beat you;*
> *No; to vex you more, I'll go.*
> *Thus I puff you—I'll go say,*
> *I refus'd your Love to Day.*

Wom. *Then I'll say how I did treat you.*
Both   } Man. *None will believe you cou'd do so.*
Together } Wom. *All will believe I us'd you so.*[8]

The music for the plays and operas was usually supplied by the small number of twelve musicians, mostly violinists, who were placed up high in an orchestral loft above an elaborate proscenium. On either side of the music room's curtained window at the Dorset Garden Theatre were two figures, Thalia and Melpomene. To the right of them were painted a drum and a trumpet, and to the left a violin and music score. Below the musicians' loft, in the centre was the emblem of the Duke of York, the theatre's patron.

Generally, the musicians played from their lofty position between the acts. However, when a singer or dancer performed in the production, the musicians came down to the stage in accompaniment, sometimes as characters in the play mingling with the players.

In the last paragraph of his preface to the play, Motteux was in praise of Mr John Eccles, the composer of the song:

> Let me leave this ungrateful Subject to acknowledge my obligations to Mr. *John Eccles*, who not only set my three Dialogues to most charming Notes, but humour'd the Words to Admiration; we need not fear Music shou'd decline, while we have so fine a Genius to support and raise it.[9]

One could easily imagine the uproar of laughter from the audience that this comical duet between Anne and John in *Love's a Jest* would have induced. Particularly, their gestures during the lines *Then lend your Face! First the Hand, and then the Face, Then the Breast, And then the rest, Then the Breast, and then.*

The whole play must have been one hell of a hoot from beginning to end, if the Epilogue is anything to go by. The scene was set in Sir Thomas Gaywood's seat in Hertfordshire, from noon till night, with Acts I to IV taking place in various rooms, the garden, and on a walk:

THE

EPILOGUE.

Mr. Underhill.	*Now for the Epilogue.*
Mr. Bowen	*There's none I think!*
Mr. Underhill.	*Let down the Curtain then, and let's go drink.*

Enter Mr. Mynns, one of the Gypsies.

Gypsie. ————————*Hold!*
I must here tell Fortunes e're you stir;
For I'm a Gypsie, tho no Conjurer.
First, Criticks, here in pain you'll always sit,

And swear, all's as Damn'd stuff, as tho by you 'Twere writ.
You'll strive not to be pleas'd, and, while we're playing,
Asses will chat, or hiss instead of Braying.
Poor Masks, who layout half Crown to get Cully,
You'll often sit alone damn'd Melancholy.
You'll Paint like Hell; but yet you'll have some grace,
In this lewd Play-house, you'll ne're shew your Face.
You, Rakish Sparks, shell jogg from House to House,
Look big, shift Boxes, and not pay a Souse.
When drunk, you'll reel out with some tawdry Miss,
And, when at last sh' unmasks, to drink, and kiss,
She'll cool your Courage with her damn'd old Phiz.
Or, if you're kind, she'll prove a grateful Wench,
She'll get the Guinea, but you'll get the French.
Tho the price of some Flesh is out of Reason,
Whores will be cheap, but ticklish wear this Season.
Close Sparks, who in our Gall'ry lead lewd lives,
You'll pickup Masks, yet dread they'll prove your Wives.
And, you, their wives, will vow you go to pray,
When you're at this or at another Play.
You Upper-gall'ry Beaux, may hope to find
Masters wife as your selves, some Ladies kind,
And your Sons in the Coach, while you're behind.
You nice Gallants, (I dare not call you Beaux,
That's threadbare, like your Cast-off-wenches Cloths)
You'll still be Beaux, and, while you're lash'd in Plays,
Cry, Dem the Clapping Mob; *smile, and take snuff with grace.*
Still to pursue the Fairest you'll delight,
Tho you, like smoak, will but offend their sight.
To conquer hearts you'll to the Park repair,
And, while your Prince take Towns, you'll take the Air.
Bright Ladies, Fortune must your wishes Crown,
You Save, or damn us, as you smile or frown;
Save him that spar'd your Blushes here to day;
But Damn his next, if not a better Play![10]

At this performance, John Bowman was forty-five years old, and lived on to the great age of eighty-eight, whilst Anne was twenty-five and in her prime. According to *The History of the English Stage,* young John *was brought into the Duke's Theatre to Sing at Seven Years old.* After the death of the old stager on 23 March 1739, just a year after his retirement at the remarkable age of eighty-seven, *The London Daily Post and General Advertiser* published his obituary, on the twenty-sixth:

> Last week died, in the 88th Year of his Age, Mr Bowman, belonging to the Drury Lane Theatre, who had the honour to perform several times before King Charles II. It is remarkable of him, that he was the oldest Player, the oldest Singer, and the oldest Ringer in England. He was a Man of good Character, a facetious, agreeable Companion, and well respected.[11]

Following the success of *Love's a Jest*, Anne was again in the guise of actress and singer in a play set to music in the same year, on 14 November. It was another of Motteux's works with a love theme, entitled *The Loves of Mars and Venus*. Mrs Bracegirdle acted the part of Venus, a very apt role for her as the Roman goddess of love and beauty. The absence of Mrs Barry from the playlist was unusual. Perhaps she was not well at this time, or out of town on some personal business. However, Anne was in the cast and again duetted with Bowman in a song in Act III. The music and dialogue to it were by composer Gottfried Finger.

The song:

Mars.
Yield, my Dear, let full possessing
Crown my Love and Charm my Sence.
Venus.
No, I must oppose your pressing
With as gallant a Defence.
Mars.
When Love's Harvest shou'd be reaping,
Will you wast the time in Doubt?
Venus.
Ev'ry Town that's worth the keeping,
Keeps a while th' Invader out.
 Cheap Embraces quickly cloy;
 Easy Conquest seems a toy:
 But denying,
 Struggling, flying,
 Wanton playing,
 Wise delaying,

Raise us to a Sence of Joy.
              Mars and Venus.
Love's a Hawk and stoops apace:
We all hurry
For the Quarry,
Tho' the Sport ends with the Chace.

[*Exit* Venus *and* Mars *after her.*[12]

By February 1697, the Lincoln's Inn Fields Company had been busy rehearsing another of Congreve's brilliant plays, *The Mourning Bride*, a tragedy, which premiered that month, on Saturday the twentieth, and continued for twelve days thereafter. Mrs Bracegirdle played Almeria, the Princess of Granada. Her friend Elizabeth Barry was back on stage that day as Zara, a captive queen. The sixty-two-year-old stalwart, Betterton, was in the cast too as Osmyn, a noble prisoner, and recited the Prologue, Anne having the honour of reciting the Epilogue:

EPILOGUE,

Spoken by Mrs. *Bracegirdle.*

THE Tragedy thus done, I am, you know,
No more a Princess, but in statu quo:
And now as unconcern'd this Mourning wear,
As if indeed a Widow, or an Heir.
I've leisure, now, to mark your sev'ral Faces,
And know each Critick by his sour Grimaces.
To poison Plays, I see some where they sit,
Scatter'd, like Rats-bane, up and down the Pit;
While others watch like Parish-Searches, hir'd
To tell of what Disease the Play expir'd.
O with what joy they run, to spread the News
Of a damn'd poet, and departed Muse!
But if he 'scape, with what Regret they're seiz'd!
And how they're disappointed when they're pleas'd!
Criticks to Plays for the same End resort,
That Surgeons wait on Trials in a Court;
For Innocence condemn'd they've no Respect,
Provided they've a Body to dissect.

As Sussex *Men, that dwell upon the Shoar,*
Look out when Storms arise, and Billows roar,
Devoutly praying, with uplifted Hands,
That some well-laden Ship may strike the Sands;
To whose rich Cargo they may make Pretence,
And fatten on the Spoils of Providence:
So Criticks throng to see a New Play split,
And thrive and prosper on the Wrecks of Wit.
Small Hope our Poet from these Prospects draws;
And therefore to the Fair commends his Cause.
Your Tender Hearts to Mercy are Inclin'd,
With whom, he hopes, this Play will Favour find,
Which was an Off'ring to the Sex design'd.

FINIS.[13]

Poet and physician Sir Richard Blackmore (1654-1729), was full of praise for Congreve and the players' performance of *The Mourning Bride*:

The Mourning Bride, a Tragedy, Acted at the Theatre in *Little Lincolns-Inn-Fields*, by His Majesty's Servants, and Dedicated to her Royal Highness the Princess *ANN* of *Denmark*, 1697. This Play had the greatest Success, not only of all Mr. *Congreve's*, but indeed of all the Plays that ever I can remember on the English Stage, excepting none of the incomparable *Otway's*; and if what Dr. *Blackmore* says of it be true, it deserved even greater than it met with; for the learned Doctor in the Seventh Page of his Preface to *King Arthur*, says thus:

—Since the writing of this, I have seen a Tragedy called, *The Mourning Bride*, which I think my self obliged to take notice of in this place. This Poem has receiv'd, and in my Opinion very justly, universal Applause; being look'd on as the most perfect Tragedy that has been wrote in this Age. The Fable, as far as I can judge at first sight, is a very Artful and Masterly Contrivance; the *Characters* are well chosen, and well delineated; that of *Zara* is admirable. The Passions are well touch'd, and skillfully wrought up. The *Diction* Proper, Clear, Beautiful, Noble, and Diversified agreeably to the Variety of the Subject. Vice, as it ought to be, is punish'd; and oppress'd Innocence at last rewarded. Nature appears very happily imitated, excepting one or two doubtful Instances, thro' the whole Piece; in which there are no immodest Images, or Expressions; no wild, unnatural Rants, but some few Exceptions being allow'd, all things are Chast, Just, and Decent. This Tragedy, as I said before, has mightily Obtain'd, and that without the unnatural, and foolish Mixture of Farce and Buffoon'ry; without so much as a Song or a Dance to make it more agreeable. By this it appears, that as a sufficient Genius can recommend it self, and furnish out abundant Matter of Pleasure and Admiration, without the paultry Helps above named: So likewise, that the Tast of the Nation is not so far deprav'd, but that a Regular and Chast Play, will not only be forgiven, but highly applauded.[14]

Although Blackmore was a respected medical doctor and theologian, he was an object of satire regarding his poetry, particular with members of *The Scriblerus Club*. Such members included; Alexander Pope (1688-1744), John Gay (1685-1732), John Arbuthnot, Robert Harley, 1st Earl of Oxford and Earl Mortimer (1661-1724), Henry St. John, 1st Viscount Bolingbroke (1678-1751), Jonathan Swift, and Thomas Parnell (1679-1718). Nevertheless, all was not lost on the efforts of Blackmore's epic poetry. He did gain the respect of philosopher and physician John Locke (1632-1704) and of William Molyneux (1656-1698), writer on science, politics and natural philosophy who admired him. There was also praise from minister, prolific hymn writer, theologian and logician, Isaac Watts (1674-1748) and from Matthew Henry (1662-1714), minister and author.

At this juncture, may I indulge the reader as to the lengths Congreve went to in his dedication of *The Mourning Bride* to Her Royal Highness, Princess Anne, later Queen of Great Britain. Congreve was not alone in his blatant flattery; many contemporary dramatists and playwrights dedicated their works to men and women of high nobility in a similar vein. Although the piece is lengthy, it is a good example of the type of contrived seventeenth-century penning for gain:

TO
HER ROYAL HIGHNESS
THE
PRINCESS.

MADAM,

That high Station, which by Your Birth You hold above the People, exacts from every one, as a Duty, whatever Honours they are capable of paying to Your Royal Highness: But that more exalted Place, to which Your Virtues have rais'd You, above the rest of Princes, makes the Tribute of our admiration and Praise, rather a Choice more immediately preventing that Duty.

The Public Gratitude is ever founded on a Publick Benefit; and what is universally Bless'd, is always an universal Blessing. Thus from Your self we derive the Offerings which we bring; and that Incense which arises to Your Name only returns to its Original, and but naturally requires the Parent of its Being.

From hence it is that this Poem, constituted on a Moral, whose End is to recommend and to encourage Virtue, of consequence has recourse to Your Royal Higness's Patronage; aspiring to cast it self beneath Your Feet, and declining Approbation, 'Till You shall condescend to own it, and vouchsafe to shine upon it as on a Creature of your Influence.

'Tis from the Example of Princes that Virtue becomes a Fashion in the People; for even they who are averse to Instruction, will yet be fond of Imitation.

But there are Multitudes, who never can have Means nor Opportunities of so near an Access, as to partake of the Benefit of such Examples. And to these, Tragedy, which distinguishes it self from the Vulgar Poetry by the Dignity of its Characters, may be of Use and Information. For they who are at that distance from Original Greatness as to be depriv'd of the Happiness of Contemplating the Perfections and real Excellencies of your Royal Highness's Person in Your Court, may yet behold some small Sketches and Imagings of the Virtues of Your Mind, abstracted, and represented on the Theatre.

Thus Poets are instructed, and instruct; not alone by Precepts which persuade, but also by Examples which illustrate. Thus is Delight interwoven with Instruction, when not only Virtue is prescrib'd, but also represented.

But if we are delighted with the Liveliness of a feign'd Representation of Great and Good Persons and their Actions, how must we be charm'd with beholding the Persons themselves? If one or two excelling Qualities, barely touch'd in the single Action and small Compass of a Play, can warm an Audience, with a Concern and Regard even for the seeming Success and Prosperity of the Actor; with what Zeal must the Hearts of all be fill'd, for the continued and encreasing

Happiness of those, who are the true and living instances of Elevated and persisting Virtue? Even the Vicious themselves must have a secret Veneration for those peculiar Graces and Endowments, which are daily so eminently conspicuous in Your Royal Highness; and though repining, feel a pleasure, which in spite of Envy they per-force approve.

If in this Piece, humbly offer'd to Your Royal Highness, there shall appear the Resemblance of any one of those many Excellencies which You so promiscuously possess, to be drawn so as to merit Your least Approbation, it has the End and Accomplishment of its Design. And however imperfect it may be in the Whole, through the Inexperience or Incapacity of the Author, yet if there is so much as to convince Your Royal Highness, that a Play may be with Industry so dispos'd (in spight of the licentious Practice of the Modern Theatre) as to become sometimes an innocent, and not unprofitable Entertainment; it will abundantly gratifie the Ambition, and recompence the Endeavours of,

> *Your Royal Highness's*
> Most Obedient, and
> Most humbly Devoted Servant,
> WILLIAM CONGREVE.[15]

Whether the then princess appreciated the author's adulation is debatable as, by February 1697, the poor woman had given birth no less than fourteen times, with all but one being stillborn, miscarried or dying within two years of birth. Princess Anne was at the time just thirty-two years old, and would become pregnant a further three times, ending with one miscarriage and two stillbirths, the last born in January 1700. Anne became Queen in 1702 and, not surprisingly, died at the age of forty-nine, on 1 August 1714, following a stroke two days previously.

What a tragically sorrowful life Anne, the last Stuart monarch of Great Britain, had, enduring miserable ill health for most of it, including severe debilitating attacks of gout and multiple pregnancies with all but one ending in heartbreak. Even that sole survivor, Prince William, Duke of Gloucester, was a very sickly, weak child throughout his short life and succumbed to death, aged eleven, in 1700.

The year 1697 was a busy year for the Lincoln's Inn Fields Company, they putting on a total of six plays. On 8 April, following the success of

The Mourning Bride, Vanbrugh's excellent comedy *The Provoked Wife* was performed, this believed to be for the first time. This successful play ran for several days, with the generous Vanbrugh giving his third and sixth night profits to the players, as stated in the Epilogue. Mrs Bracegirdle, *then at the height of her charm,* took the part of Bellinda, niece to Lady Brute, with Mrs Barry as Lady Brute. Anne recited the Prologue and was joined by Elizabeth in the Epilogue, showing yet again their sheer popularity as leading ladies of the company:

EPILOGUE,

By another Hand.

Spoken by Lady Brute and Bellinda.
Lady B.
NO Epilogue!
Bell.
I Swear I know of none.
Lady.
Lord! How shall we excuse it to the Town?
Bell.
Why, we must e'en say something of our own.
Lady
Our own! Ay, that must needs be precious stuff.
Bell.
I'll lay my life they'll like it well enough.
Come Faith begin—
Lady
Excuse me, after you.
Bell.
Nay, pardon me for that, I know my Cue.
Lady
O for the World, I would not have Precedence.
Bell.
O Lord!
Lady
I Swear —
Bell.
O Fye!
Lady

I'm all Obedience.
First then, know all, before our Doom is fixt,
The Third day is for us —
Bell.
Nay, and the Sixt.
Lady
We speak not from the Poet now, nor is it
His Cause— (I want a Rhime)
Bell.
That we solicite.
Lady
Then sure you cannot have the hearts to be severe
And Damn us—
Bell.
Damn us! Let 'em if they Dare.
Lady
Why, if they should, what punishment Remains?
Bell.
Eternal Exile from behind our Scenes.
Lady
But if they're kind, that sentence we'll recal,
We can be grateful—
Bell.
And have wherewithall.
Lady
But at grand Treaties, hope not to be Trusted,
Before Preliminaries are adjusted.
Bell.
You know the Time, and we appoint this place;
Where, if you please, we'll meet and sign the Peace.[16]

At this time, Anne was twenty-six and in her prime, as an actress and a woman, charming all on and off the stage. Considering she was known for her virtue, she did however perform in some typically sexually-charged plays of the seventeenth century. How clever and perceptive she was to keep her acting persona completely separate from her everyday life.

Biographia Dramatica had this to say of *The Provoked Wife*:

THE PROVOK'D WIFE... by Sir John Vanbrugh. Acted at Lincoln's Inn Fields. 1697;... . This comedy has a great many fine scenes in it, and the character of Sir John Brute is very highly and naturally drawn. Yet it has in the language as well as conduct of it, too much loose wit and libertinism of sentiment to become the theatres of moral and virtuous nation; since no behaviour of a husband, however brutal, can vindicate a wife in revenging her cause upon herself, by throwing away the most valuable jewel she possesses, her innocence and peace of mind. Lady Brute's conduct, moreover, seems rather to proceed from the warmth of her own inclinations, than a spirit of resentment against her husband; nay, she seems so far to have lost even the very sense of honour, that a little matter appears capable of inducing her to turn panda to her niece Belinda. Had Lady Brute, indeed, appeared to the audience strictly virtuous through the whole transaction, yet had carried on such a deception to her husband, as to have alarmed all those suspicious of which a consciousness of his own behaviour towards her would authorize him in entertaining the belief, and then reformed him by a perfect clearing up of those suspicions, and, by showing him how near he might have been to the brink of a precipice, taught him to avoid for the future the path that was leading him towards it, the moral would have been complete; whereas, as it now stands, all that can be deduced from it is, that a brutish husband deserves to be made a cuckold; and that there can be no breach of virtue in giving him that desert, provided he can afterwards, either by the persuasions of his wife, or the bluster of her gallant, be soothed or frightened out of an intention of resenting it on her: a maxim of the most happy tendency to persons inclinable to gallantry and intrigue; since the same practices may equally answer against the good and indulgent, as against the surly and brutal husband. This play was one of those which were severely censured by Mr. Collier, on account of its immorality. When it was revived in 1725, the author thought proper to substitute a new scene, in the fourth act, in place of one in which, in the wantonness of his wit, he had made a rake talk like a rake in the habit of a clergyman; to avoid which offence he put the same debauchee into the undress of a woman of quality; and with this alteration it has ever since been performed.[17]

William Congreve, John Vanbrugh, John Dryden, Thomas D'Urfey and other playwrights all came under anti-theatrical attack regarding their dramatic works by Jeremy Collier's *A Short View of the Immorality and Profaneness of the English Stage…1699*. I was particularly curious as to what Collier had to say regarding characters in *The Provoked Wife* and *Love for Love*, with both Mrs Barry and Mrs Bracegirdle having acted in each play. Although omitting to name Congreve and Vanbrugh in the publication, Collier does on occasion mention Shakespeare, Jonson, Beaumont, Fletcher and D'Urfey, with Dryden's name appearing throughout. Collier was particularly venomous with regard to Vanbrugh's *The Provoked Wife*. In Chapter II, *The Profaneness of the Stage*, Collier remarks:

> …For when the Fit comes on them, they make no difficulty of Swearing at length. Instances of all these kinds may be met with in the *Old Batchelour, Double Dealer*, and *Love for Love*. And to mention no more, *Don Quixot*, the *Provok'd Wife*, and the *Relapse*, are particularly Rampant and Scandalous. The *English-Stage* exceed their Predecessors in this, as well as other Branches of Immorality. *Shakespear* is comparatively sober, *Ben Johnson* is still more regular; And as for *Beaumont* and *Fletcher,* in their Plays, they are commonly Profligate Persons that Swear, and even those are reprov'd for't. Besides, the Oaths are not so full of Hell and Defiance, as in the Moderns.[18]
>
> And if Religion signifies nothing (as I am afraid it does with some People) there is Law as well as Gospel, against *Swearing*. 3 *Jac*. I. *cap*. 2I. is expressly against the *Play-House*. It runs thus.
>
> FOR the preventing and avoiding of the great abuse of the holy Name of God in Stage-Plays, Enterludes, &c. Be it enacted by our Sovereign Lord, &c. That if at any time, or times, after the End of this present Session of Parliament, any Person or Persons do, or shall, in any Stage-Play, Enterlude, Shew, &c. Jestingly or Profanely, speak or use the Holy Name of God, or of Christ Jesus, or of the Holy Ghost, or of the Trinity, which are not to be spoken, but with Fear and Reverence; shall forfeit for every such Offence, by him or them committed Ten pound: The one Moiety thereof to the King's Majesty, his Heirs, and Successors; the other Moiety thereof to Him, or them, that will sue for the same in any Court of Record at Westminster, wherein no Essoin, Protection, or Wager of Law shall be allow'd.
>
> By this *Act* not only direct Swearing, but all vain Invocation of the Name of God is forbidden. This *Statute* well executed

would mend the *Poets*, or sweep the *Box:* And the *Stage* must either reform, or not thrive upon Profaneness.

Swearing in the *Play-House* is an ungentlemanly, as well as an unchristian Practice. The *Ladies* make a considerable par of the *Audience*. Now Swearing before Women is reckon'd a Breach of good Behaviour; and therefore a civil Atheist will forbear it. The Custom seems to go upon this Presumption; that the Impressions of Religion are strongest in Women, and more generally spread. And that it must be very disagreeable to them, to hear the Majesty of God treated with so little respect. Besides, Oaths are a boistrous and tempestuous sort of Conversation; generally the effects of Passion, and spoken with Noise, and Heat. Swearing looks like the beginning of a Quarrel, to which Women have an aversion; as being neither armed by Nature, nor disciplin'd by Custom for such rough Disputes. A Woman will start at a Soldier's Oath, almost as much as at the Report of his Pistol: And therefore a well-Bred Man will no more Swear than Fight in the Company of Ladies.[19]

Well, theologian Collier certainly doesn't hold his tongue when it comes to criticism! Goodness knows what the contemporary playwrights thought of that lambaste. But fortunately, we can see what William Congreve thought of Collier in a reply to his *Immorality of the English Stage*. Congreve published in 1698, *Amendments of M. Collier's false and imperfect citations, &c. from the Old Batchelour, Double Dealer, Love for love, Mourning Bride, by the author of those plays.* The publication itself is extremely lengthy, but brilliantly written by the talented Congreve, and hits on many of Collier's damning criticisms. On the title page there are various pieces in Latin, the most amusing one, loosely translated from Latin, reads thus:

> Graviter, & iniquo animo, maledicta tua paterer, si te scirem Iudicio magis, quam morbo animi, petulantia ista uti. Sed, quoniam in te neque modum, neque modestiam ullam animadverto, respondebo tibi: uti, si quam maledicendo voluptatem cepisti, eam male-audiendo amittas.

> I would suffer your curses severely, and with a wicked mind, if I had known you to use these things by judgment rather than from a disease of the mind, from wantonness. But, since in you

I do not notice any moderation, nor any modesty, I will reply to you: just as if you had taken pleasure in cursing, you would lose it by ill-hearing.

To give a flavour of its contents, here are the first few paragraphs of the *Amendments,* as to show it in its entirety would be a book in itself:

I Have been told by some, That they should think me very idle, if I threw away any time in taking notice ev'n of so much of Mr. Collier's late Treatise of the Immorality, &c. of the English Stage, as related to my self, in respect of some Plays written by me: For that his malicious and strain'd Interpretations of my Words were so gross and palpable, that any indifferent and unprejudic'd Reader would immediately condemn him upon his own Evidence, and acquit me before I could make my Defence.

On the other hand, I have been tax'd of Laziness, and too much Security in neglecting thus long to do my self a necessary Right, which might be effected with so very little Pains; since very little more is requisite in my Vindication, than to represent truly and at length, those Passages which Mr. Collier has shewn imperfectly, and for the most part by halves. I would rather be thought Idle than Lazy; and so the last Advice prevail'd with me.

I have no Intention to examine all the Absurdities and Falshoods in Mr. Collier's Book; to use the Gentleman's own Metaphor in his Preface, An Inventory of such a Ware-house would be a large Work. My Detection of his Malice and Ignorance, of his Sophistry and vast Assurance, will lie within a narrow Compass, and only bear a Proportion to so much of his Book as concerns my self.

Least of all, would I undertake to defend the Corruptions of the Stage; indeed if I were so inclin'd, Mr. Collier has given me no occasion; for the greater part of those Examples which he has produc'd, are only Demonstrations of his own Impurity, they only savour of his Utterance, and were sweet enough till tainted by his Breath.

I will not justifie any of my own Errors; I am sensible of many; and if Mr. Collier has by any Accident stumbled on one or two, I will freely give them up to him, Nullum unquam ingenium placuit sine venia. But I hope I have done nothing that can deprive me of the Benefit of my Clergy; and tho' Mr. Collier himself were the Ordinary, I may hope to be acquitted.

My Intention therefore, is to do little else, but to restore those Passages to their primitive Station, which have suffer'd so much in being transplanted by him: I will remove 'em from his Dunghil, and replant 'em in the Field of Nature; and when I have wash'd 'em of that Filth which they have contracted in passing thro' his very dirty hands, let their own Innocence protect them.

Mr. Collier, in the high Vigour of his Obscenity, first commits a Rape upon my Words, and then arraigns 'em of Immodesty; he has Barbarity enough to accuse the very Virgins that he has deflowr'd, and to make sure of their Condemnation, he has himself made 'em guilty: But he forgets that while he publishes their shame he divulges his own.

His Artifice to make Words guilty of Profaness, is of the same nature; for where the Expression is unblameable in its own clear and genuine Signification, he enters into it himself like the evil Spirit; he possesses the innocent Phrase, and makes it bellow forth his own Blasphemies; so that one would think the Muse was Legion.

To reprimand him a little in his own Words, if these Passages produc'd by Mr. Collier are obscene and profane, Why were they rak'd in and disturb'd unless it were to conjure up Vice, and revive Impurities? Indeed Mr. Collier has a very untoward way with him; his Pen has such a Libertine Stroke, that 'tis a question whether the Practice or the Reproof be the more licentious.

He teaches those Vices he would correct, and writes more like a Pimp than a P—. Since the business must be undertaken, why was not the Thought blanch'd, the Expression made remote, and the ill Features cast into Shadows? So far from this, which is his own Instruction in his own words, is Mr. Collier's way of Proceeding, that he has blackned the Thoughts with his own Smut; the Expression that was remote, he has brought nearer; and lest by being brought near its native Innocence might be more visible, he has frequently varied it, he has new-molded it, and stamp'd his own Image on it; so that it at length is become Current Deformity, and fit to be paid into the Devil's Exchequer.

I will therefore take the Liberty to exorcise this evil Spirit, and whip him out of my Plays, where-ever I can meet with him. Mr. Collier has revers'd the Story which he relates from Tertullian; and after his Visitation of the Play-house returns, having left the Devil behind him.

If I do not return his Civilities in calling him Names, it is because I am not very well vers'd in his Nomen clatures; therefore for his Foot pads, which he calls us in his Preface, and for his Buffoons and Slaves in the Saturnalia, which he frequently bestows on us in the rest of his Book, I will onely call him Mr. Collier, and that I will call him as often as I think he shall deserve it.[20]

It is very obvious from the above that William Congreve was certainly somewhat incensed by *Mr. Collier*!

But to a degree, one cannot help thinking that Collier at times had a point if the character of Major Rakish in Cibber's comedy *Woman's Wit; or, The Lady of Fashion* is anything go by. In the play, Lord Lovemore asks this question of Rakish: *Prithee, Major, how do you Manage your Pleasures, that you say they cost you nothing?* Rakish's reply: *I'll tell you, my Lord, I'll tell you how I spent the day before Yesterday: I got up, and Din'd with Sir Bartholomew Bumper, Drank my two Bottles and half with him by five a Clock. Then call'd in at the Play (Impudence my Ticket) pick'd up a Parson's Wife, gave her the Remains of an old Clap, and so pawn'd her at Philips's for three pints of Spirit of Clary... .*

I find Collier's sentiment of women *being neither armed by Nature, nor disciplin'd by Custom for such rough Disputes,* especially amusing. To the contrary, it seems that Restoration women, and notably the actresses, could hold their own, banter, joke and if needs be cause embarrassment to an irritating male spectator in the notorious pit. An example of this, albeit much later in the theatre than that of our subjects, concerned Mrs Oldfield when she was in a performance of *The Provok'd Husband; or, A Journey to London,* a comedy by Sir John Vanbrugh and Colley Cibber, in January 1728:

...In all the tumults and disturbances of the theatre on the first night of a new play, which was formerly a time of more dangerous service, to the actors, than it has been of late,

Mrs. Oldfield was entirely mistress of herself; she thought it her duty, amidst the most violent opposition and uproar, to exert the utmost of her abilities to serve the author. In the comedy of the Provoked Husband, Cibber's enemies tried all their power to get the play condemned. The reconciliation-scene wrought so effectually upon the sensible and generous part of the audience, that the conclusion was greatly and generously approved. Amidst a thousand applauses, Mrs. Oldfield came forward to speak the epilogue; but when she had pronounced the first line, —

Methinks I hear some powder'd critic say____

a man, of no distinguished appearance, from the seat next to the orchestra, saluted her with a hiss. She fixed her eye upon him immediately, made a very short pause, and spoke the words *poor creature*! loud enough to be heard by the audience, with such a look of mingled scorn, pity, and contempt, that the most uncommon applause justified her conduct in this particular, and the poor reptile sunk down with fear and trembling.[21]

What Collier doesn't seem to grasp is that women, and for that matter men too, were simply acting. They portrayed a character in a play that was often far removed from their own persona. The dramatists and playwrights wrote to entertain the audience, they knowing all too well of their spectators' near-the-knuckle appetites. An actress's licentious character when treading the boards was in many cases far removed from her life outside the theatre, with Mrs Bracegirdle proving this beyond doubt. Of course Mrs Barry, and others, *did* gain a certain reputation away from the theatre, but I believe she was no more promiscuous than the average Restoration woman, looking for adventurous sexual relations for financial gain, close companionship, or even a good marriage. I feel it was very unfair to look upon actresses as common street-strumpets when they were simply working hard to earn a lawful living. These actresses were professional women in their own right, celebrated for their talent in portraying many differing dramatic characters in both comedy and tragedy. In Collier's chapter *The Immodesty of the Stage*, he, as usual, goes overboard in his blinkered opinions:

Obscenity in any Company is a rustick uncredible Talent; but among women 'Tis particularly rude. Such Talk would be very affrontive in Conversation, and not endur'd by any Lady of Reputation. Whence then comes it to Pass that those Liberties which disoblige so much in Conversation, should entertain upon the *Stage*. Do the Women leave all the regards to Decency and Conscience behind them when they come to the *Play-House?* Or does the Place transform their Inclinations, and turn their former Aversions into Pleasure? Or were Their pretences to Sobriety elsewhere nothing but Hypocrisy and Grimace? Such Suppositions as these are all Satyr and Invective: they are rude Imputations upon the whole Sex. To treat the Ladys with such stuff, is no better than taking their Money to abuse them. It supposes their Imagination vitious, and their Memories ill furnishe'd: That they are practised in the Language of the Stews, and pleas'd with the Scenes of Brutishness. When at the same time the Customs of education, and the Laws of Decency, are so very cautious, and reserv'd in regard to Women:…

In this respect the *Stage* is faulty to a Scandalous degree of Nauseousness and Aggravation. For

1ˢᵗ. The *Poets* make *Women* speak Smuttily. Of this the Places before mention'd are sufficient Evidence: And if there was occasion they might be Multiplyed to a much greater Number: Indeed the *Comedies* are seldom clear of these Blemishes: And sometimes you have them in *Tragedy*. For Instance. The, *Orphans Monimia* makes a very improper Description; And the Royal *Leonora* in the *Spanish Friar,* runs a strange Length in the History of Love. And do Princesses use to make their Reports with such fulsom Freedoms? Certainly this *Leonora* was the first Queen of her Family… Are these the *Tender Things* Mr. *Dryden* says the Ladys call on him for? I suppose he means the *Ladys* that are too Modest to show their Faces in the *Pit*. This Entertainment can be fairly design'd for none but such. Indeed it hits their Palate exactly. It regales their Lewdness, graces their Character, and keeps up their Spirits for their Vocation: Now to bring Women under such Misbehaviour is Violence to their Native Modesty, and a Misrepresentation of their Sex. For Modesty as Mr. *Rapin* observes, is the *Character* of Women. To represent them without this Quality, is to make Monsters of them, and throw them out of their Kind…[22]

According to Colley Cibber, the immoralities of the stage plays had been creeping in somewhat *ever since King Charles his Time*. This was not an altogether surprising phenomenon, considering the blatant licentiousness often shown at the Royal Court. It no doubt became fashionable for dramatists and playwrights at that time to emulate by explicit prose the goings-on at the Palace of Whitehall. Even Cibber remarks that modest women were reluctant to attend a new comedy bare-faced, that is to say without wearing a mask, in case the play give *Risque of an Insult, to their Modesty*. He does remark however, that by the wearing of a mask such *Custom, however, had so many ill Consequences attending it, that it has been abolish'd these many Years.*

The Jacobean play *The Pilgrim*, originally by John Fletcher, had been revived and adapted during the Restoration by John Vanbrugh, with the play's Prologue and Epilogue penned by John Dryden. Cibber explains categorically the debased state of some prose, popular in Restoration plays, by naming Dryden as one whose *plays were more fam'd for their Wit, than their Chasity*. He then proceeds to print lines from Dryden's Epilogue in *The Pilgrim*, the updated version of which premiered at the Theatre Royal, Drury Lane on 29 April 1700. The production was also a benefit for Dryden, *but he dying on the third Night of its Representation, his Son attended the Run of it, and the Advantages accrued to his Family.*[23]

Dryden's Epilogue, probably one of the last things he ever wrote, is transcribed fully below. *The Parson* is obviously a reference to the Restoration dramatist's fiercest critic, Jeremy Collier:

EPILOGUE.

By Mr. DRYDEN.

Perhaps the Parson stretch'd a point too far,
When with our Theatres *he wag'd a War.*
He tells you, That this very Moral Age
Receiv'd the first Infection from the Stage.
But sure, a banish'd Court, with Lewdness fraught,
The Seeds of open Vice, returning, brought.
Thus Lodg'd, (as Vice by great Example thrives)
It first debauch'd the Daughters and the Wives.
London, *a fruitful Soil yet never bore*
So plentiful a Crop of Horns before.

The Poets, *who must live by Courts, or starve,*
Were proud, so good a Government to serve;
And mixing with Buffoons and Pimps profane,
Tainted the Stage, for some small Snip of Gain.
For they, like Harlots, *under* Bawds *profest,*
Took all th' ungodly Pains, and got the least.
Thus did the thriving Malady prevail,
The Court, it's Head, the Poets *but the Tail.*
The Sin was of our Native growth, 'tis true;
The Scandal of the Sin was wholly new.
Misses *there were, but modestly conceal'd;*
White-hall *the naked* Venus *first reveal'd.*
Who standing, as at Cyprus, *in her Shrine,*
The Strumpet was ador'd with Rites Divine.
'E're this, if Saints had any Secret Motion,
'Twas Chamber-Practice all, and Close Devotion.
I pass the Peccadillo's of their time;
Nothing but open Lewdness was a Crime.
A Monarch's *Blood was venial to the Nation,*
Compar'd with one foul Act of Fornication.
Now, they they wou'd Silence us, and shut the Door,
That let in all the bare-fac'd Vice before.
As for reforming us, which some pretend,
That work in England *is without an End:*
Well we may change, but we shall never mend.
Yet, if you can but bear the present Stage,
We hope much better of the coming Age.
What wou'd you say, if we shou'd first begin
To Stop the Trade of Love, behind the Scene:
Where Actresses *make bold with marry'd Men?*
For while abroad so prodigal the Dolt *is,*
Poor Spouse at home as ragged as a Colt is.
In short, we'll grow as Moral as we can,
Save here and there a Woman or a Man:
But neither you, nor we, with all our Pains,
Can make clean Work; there will be some Remains,
While you have still your Oats, *and we our* Hains.[24]

Following *The Provoked Wife,* on 1 May 1697, was performed *Intrigues at Versailles; or, A Jilt in all Humours,* a comedy by Thomas D'Urfey.

The roles of Dutchess de Sanserre, poetical, high-spirited and wanton, and Madam de Vandosme, a right jilt in all humours, were acted by Mrs Bracegirdle and Mrs Barry respectively.

The Poetical Register; or, The Lives and Characters of the English Dramatick Poets, by Giles Jacob, 1719, sized up the play thus:

> *The Intrigues at Versailles; or, A Jilt in all Humours*; a Comedy, acted at the Theatre in *Lincolns-Inn-Fields*, 1697. This Play likewise had not the Success the author desir'd; for in his Epistle to the two Sir *Charles Sidleys,* he condemns the Taste of the Town for not liking it, when they had approv'd others of his Plays of less Merit. The Thefts in this Play are numerous: *Tornezres* Disguise, and Count *Brisack's* falling in Love with his Wife's Gallant in Woman's Cloaths, are borrow'd from a Novel, entitled *The Double Cuckold*; *Vandesins* Character seems to be a Copy of *Olivia* in the *Plain-Dealer*, and *Mirtilla*, in Mrs *Behn's* Play, call'd, *The Amorous Jilt.*

A great many seventeenth-century comedy plays are set around love, intrigues and deception, and probably for many in the audience, these were everyday occurrences, and not at all shocking to them. But does our perception of seventeenth-century promiscuity stem a great deal from these outrageous plays? From the outset of stage performances, they were solely for entertaining the masses and no doubt the more excessively dramatic a tragedy or comedy was, the more the audience was enthralled. Perhaps life outside the glamour of theatre was, for the hoi polloi, a reality of everyday domestic drudgery just to keep body and soul together, and so the playhouse was, and has always been, a welcome, colourful respite from drab day-to-day routines.

A typical play that would have been popular with the audience was the comedy *Innocent Mistress* by novelist and playwright, Mrs Mary Pix (1666-1709). In this play at Lincoln's Inn on 18 June 1697, Anne took the part of Mrs Beauclair, a niece to Sir Charles Beauclair. *The Poetical Register* had this to say of the play, *This Play met with very good Success, tho' acted in the Summer Season. She has borrow'd some Incidents from other Plays, particularly Sir Fopling Flutter. And in A Comparison Between the Two Stages* (1702), it was said of Pix's play, *Tho' the Title calls this Innocent, yet it deserves to be Damn'd for its Obscenity.*

As winter approached, another work by Pix was performed, in late November; a comedy *The Deceiver Deceived*. In the play, the character of Ariana, the daughter of Melito Bondi, a Senator of Venice, was played by Anne, who once again duetted with Bowman in one of the songs which was written by D'Urfey, again with music by Eccles:

A DIALOGUE *between a* French *Beau, and a*
Coquett de Angletere.

Beau.　　WHEN vile *Stella* kind and *tendre*,
Recompense *five le Amour*;
You mine Heart have made me *rendre*,
If yours come not in *Retour*:
Black despair I can't *defendre*,
No, no, no I can't *defendre*,
Grief must kill me *tout les Jours*.

Coq.　　How can *Damon* Love another,
Who believes himself so fine;
He may talk and keep a pother,
But to change can ne'er incline:
So much Charm must slight all other,
Ay, ay, ay must slight all other,
He believes himself so fine.

Beau.　　Then adieu false *Esperanza,*
Tout les Plaisirs de Beau *Jours*;
Stella's Heart keeps at distance,
And disdains *le Cher* effort:
She *mon Ame* will ne'er advance,
No, no, no will ne'er advance,
Cruel Death then *prend mon Ceur*.

Coq.　　You a *Beau* and talk of dying,
'Tis a Cheat I'll ne'er believe,
You've such life in Self enjoying,
Death's a word you can't forgive:
Go, improve Deceit and Lying,
Ay, ay, ay but name no dying,
That's a Cheat I'll ne'er believe.

142

CHORUS.

He.	When, when will you prove me, to know
	The truth of a Passionate *Beau*;
She.	How, how shall I prove ye, to know
	The truth of a flashy Town *Beau*;
He.	By the Sighs. and the Tears, of the wretch,
She.	By his Paint, and his Powder and Patch;
He.	By his Mouth, and his very good Teeth,
She.	By his Nose, and his very bad Breath;
He.	By his Eyes, and the Air of his Face,
She.	When he Oagles, and looks like an Ass;
He.	*Par Dieu ma Avere*, each part my truth will shew.
She.	*Morbleau mon fou*, I never can think so.[25]

At this point, it might be worth considering hidden dangers that the players were unaware of, in the form of theatrical cosmetics.

Stage make-up was an essential part of the performance, as were lighting, scenery and backstage sound effects such as thunder, horses galloping etc. Even today, stage make-up is somewhat exaggerated, the purpose of which is so that the audience, particularly those at the back of the auditorium, can more clearly see the players' faces and expressions. If cosmetics were not applied, the faces of the thespians would look blank and almost totally expressionless. Of course, the pantomime dame is often seen with considerably exaggerated make-up, purposely to emphasise their comedic role. But thank goodness, the actor of today is, hopefully, in no danger whatsoever from any poisonous substances in the wearing of cosmetics.

But it was a very different story in the seventeenth century. Lead, mixed with vinegar, was used to achieve a base white face on which to apply rouge for cheeks and lips. The continual use of lead on the skin would, over time, give rise to lead poisoning. The rouge was vermilion-based and made from the mineral cinnabar, in other words, mercury sulphide and no less toxic than the lead product. These poisons, albeit slow-acting, took their toll on the body through years of use, with inevitable ill side effects of abdominal, joint and muscle pain, and the onset of fatigue, to mention a few. Eye make-up was also used in the playhouse to emphasise the eyes when viewed from a distance and they would be outlined in black, possibly using lamp black, soot or the ancient kohl, with blue eyeshadow sometimes being used. Coloured hair powder was also applied and goodness knows what that contained.

Close up, these cosmetics must have looked horrendous, more akin to a horror film than an amusing comedy. Taking into account that the practise of dental hygiene was as rare as hens' teeth, the whole ensemble must have looked, to be honest, quite frightful. Add to this the subject of personal cleanliness, which often amounted to no more than a daily washing of face and hands. Stage costumes were worn for many months on end and rarely ever had the benefit of washing-soap. Not forgetting the delightful mixture of vinegar and lead, what nasty odours must have been present in those crowded theatre tiring rooms? The compact audience gathering in a hot, stuffy, smoky atmosphere must have added further to the overall 'fragrant' ambience like to an underground sewer. No wonder the use of perfumes in the form of pomanders, perfumed gloves and fragranced handkerchiefs were popular as a stench barrier.

Anne Bracegirdle continued her celebrated career at Lincoln's Inn for the next eight years, with her last performance there being the premiere of Susanna Centlivre's *The Gamester*, on 22 February 1705.

Soon after, Mrs Bracegirdle, along with Betterton's Company, moved to the Queen's Theatre, Haymarket.

Chapter Fourteen

A Discomforting Rival

Having begun her career at the Theatre Royal, Drury Lane at the age of sixteen, in 1699, Mrs Anne Oldfield rose to become one of the highest-paid actresses of her time. She had been discovered by Irish dramatist George Farquhar (1677-1707), he hearing her reciting a play in a tavern; The Mitre, in St. James's. The tavern was run by Anne's aunt, a Mrs Voss, with whom Anne and her mother were living at the time, after Anne's father's untimely death at a young age. He had tragically left no estate for wife or daughter, after mortgaging several properties which he owned to buy a position in the Horse Guards.

Through Farquhar's discovery, Anne, at that young age, had been readily hired by Christopher Rich and she joined the cast of the Theatre Royal. Her debut there, almost a year later, was as Candiope in Dryden's tragicomedy, *Secret Love; or, The Maiden Queen.*

By 1706 Mrs Oldfield, like others before her, came into conflict with Drury Lane's management and promptly left to join the company of the Queen's Theatre, Haymarket. However, she did return to Drury Lane a couple of years later.

In another of Congreve's letters to his friend Keally, dated 10 September 1706, he describes the upheaval caused once again by the disagreeable Christopher Rich:

> ...The play-houses have undergone another revolution; and Swinny, with Wilks, Mrs Olfield, Pinkethman, Bullock, and Dicky, are come over to the Hay-Market. Vanbrugh resigns his authority to Swinny, which occasioned the revolt. Mr Rich complains and rails like Volpone when counterplotted by Mosea. My Lord Chamberlain approves and ratifies the desertion; and the design is, to have plays only at the Hay-Market, and operas only at Covent Garden. I think the design right to restore acting; but the houses are misapplied, which time may change. I have written an ode which I presented to the Queen, who received it very graciously...[1]

It was reported that the two Annes, Bracegirdle and Oldfield, became stage rivals, with Mrs Bracegirdle thirteen years older than Mrs Oldfield who was only twenty-two. The younger actress was very popular with the audience, the outcome of which was that the older thespian, the darling of the stage, was declining in stardom. In one particular play, *The Amorous Widow; or, The Wanton Wife*, by Thomas Betterton, it is believed that Bracegirdle and Oldfield each played the part of Mrs Brittle, on separate occasions. These episodes were looked upon by the admirers of each actress as a competition as to who would outshine the other in playing the character. Whoever instigated these ridiculous events should have a lot to answer for, as the outcome was that the audience favoured the younger of the actresses and therefore cut short the career of the brilliant Bracegirdle, causing a great loss to her beloved devotees:

> The long expected Night being come, the Senior Championess appear'd, attended with such a Croud of Beaux as might be expected from a long unrivall'd Superiority, and perform'd her Part, as usual to such Admiration, as inspir'd a Confidence into all her Friends, and made Mrs. Oldfield's well Wishers dread the Issue would not be in her favour. However, the next Night, when our Heroine graced the Stage, and had spoke but ten Lines, such was the gracefulness and beauty of her Person, so inchanting the harmony of her Voice and justness of her Delivery, and so inimitable her Action, that she charm'd the whole Audience to that Degree, they almost forget they had ever seen Mrs. Bracegirdle, and universally adjudged her the Preheminence; which very much disgusted her celebrated Antagonist; and Mrs. Oldfield's Benefit being allowed by Mr. Swinny to be in the Season before Mrs. Bracegirdle's, added so much to the Affront, that she quitted the Stage immediately. Ever since that time Mrs. Oldfield has maintained an undisputed Sovereignty over all her Contemporaries on every Theatre where-ever she perform'd.[2]

This preference was a serious disillusionment for the celebrated Bracegirdle and, as a consequence, in February 1707, after playing Lavinia in *The History And Fall Of Caius Marius*, a tragedy by Thomas Otway, Bracy, at the age of thirty-six, retired from the stage, to live out her days pleasantly in Howard Street, Strand.

It's a miracle that Anne Bracegirdle and the property in Howard Street managed to survive The Great Storm on 26 November 1703. This devastating extratropical cyclone struck central and southern England with such force, causing untold damage and destruction both on land and sea, including the destruction of the first Eddystone lighthouse. Some two thousand chimney stacks collapsed in London, Westminster Abbey's lead roofing was blown off, and on the Thames, some seven hundred ships were damaged by the force of the wind. Four thousand oaks in the New Forest were lost and ships were blown hundreds of miles off-course, with a report that one thousand seamen alone had died on the treacherous Goodwin Sands off the coast in Kent. The West-Country suffered extensive flooding with hundreds of people drowning on the Somerset Levels, along with sheep and cattle.

There is proof that Mrs Bracegirdle was living in Howard Street during the storm, by mention of her in a letter by William Congreve, written from London on 30 November 1703, to his friend Joseph Keally in Dublin. This letter is one of forty-three that Congreve wrote to him throughout his lifetime and in it, he gives a harrowing account of the storm's devastation in London and further afield. In the letter our neighbour is a reference to Anne Bracegirdle:

London Nov. 30.1703.

Dear Kelly,
I THINK it a tedious while since I heard from you; and though, to the best of my remembrance, I answered your last, yet I write again to put you in mind of your old friends, every one of whom has very narrowly escaped the hurricane on Friday night last. The public papers will be full of particulars. 'Tis certain, in the memory of man, never was any thing like it. Most of the tall trees in the Park are blown down; and the four trees that stood distinct before St James's, between the Mall and the Canal. The garden-wall of the priory, and the Queen's garden there, are both laid flat. Some great sash-windows of the banqueting-house have been torn from the frames, and blown so as they have never been found nor heard of. The leads of churches have some of them been rolled up as they were before they were laid on: others have been skimmed clever off, and transported cross the street, where they have been laid on other houses, breaking the roofs. The news out of the country is equally terrible; the roads being obstructed by the trees which lie cross. Anwick, Coventry, and most of the towns that my acquaintance have heard of, are in great

measure destroyed, as Bristol, where they say a church was blown down. It is endless to tell you all. Our neighbour in Howard's-street 'scaped well, though frighted, only the ridge of the house being stripped; and a stack of chimneys in the next house fell luckily into the street. I lost nothing but a casement in my man's chamber, though the chimneys of the Blue Ball continued tumbling by piece-meal most part of the night at Mr Porter's. The wind came down the little court behind the back parlour, and burst open that door, bolts and all, whirled round the room, and scattered all the prints; of which, together with the table and chairs, it mustered into one heap, and made a battery of 'em to break down the other door into the entry, whither it swept 'em; yet broke not one pane of the window which join'd to the back-court door. It took off the sky-light of the stairs, and did no more damage there. Many people have been killed. But the loss at sea is inconceivable, though the particulars are not many yet confirmed; and I am afraid poor Beaumont is lost. Shovel, they say, and Fairholm, are heard of. I hope you have been less sufferers. One should be glad to hear so from your own hands. Pray give my service to all friends. The King's-Bench walk buildings are just as before their roofs were covered. Tell that to Robin. I am, dear Keally, yours,

W. CONGREVE.[3]

The Mr Porter mentioned in the letter was Anne Bracegirdle's brother-in-law, Edward Porter, who was married to Anne's sister Frances. The Porters were great friends and neighbours of Congreve and were living in Surrey Street in close proximity to Mrs Bracegirdle and her mother in Howard Street and to Congreve in Arundel Street.

Howard Street was crossed by Norfolk Street, with Surrey Street to its west and Arundel Street to its east. The properties were built after 1678, when Arundel House with its surrounding gardens, owned by the Howards, Dukes of Norfolk, was demolished. A further demolition, of Howard Street and Norfolk Street, took place in the 1970s. Howard Street is clearly shown on The Map of London published in 1746 by the brilliant French-born surveyor John (Jean) Rocque (c.1704-1762). It lies close to the Strand and the Thames, with its neighbouring old Somerset House and gardens to its west and with St Clement Danes Church nearby.

By 1706, Congreve had moved permanently into the Porters' house in Surrey Street, as intimated in a letter to Keally written on 26 June 1706; *I am removed to Mr. Porter's in Surry-street, where I shall be glad to hear from you till I may hope to see you; which, believe me, is one of the things I wish the most heartily for in the world.* It is believed Congreve lodged there for over twenty years until his death, and during his time there housed his fine collection of books.

In a further letter of Congreve's to Keally, again from London, on 12 May 1708, there is an interesting sentence; *The legacy you have heard of is in part true, being one thousand pounds.* After further investigation, it transpires that this legacy was bequeathed to Anne Bracegirdle in the will of politician and courtier Robert Leke, 3rd Earl of Scarsdale (1654-1707). The will was dated 9 January 1702. It appears that he too was an admirer and friend of Anne, and might have replaced Congreve in her affections. But, as with Congreve, there is no proof that Leke's friendship with Anne was anything other than platonic. Nonetheless, one thing for certain is that Leke had been a friend to Mrs Bracegirdle for at least five years before she retired from the stage. Leke's will is in two parts; the main will and then a *Schedule of Legacies* attached, with Anne's legacy of one thousand pounds being the second-highest amount of eight legacies, and accompanied by a special note declaring, *I desire that this Legacy may be the first Money paid.* Those few words would seem to show the high regard the earl had for Anne, and could possibly indicate that their relationship was something very close. Having said that, even if there had been some sort of love intrigue between them, there would have been no shame in it, as Leke's wife, Mary Lewis, had died in 1684, with their only daughter Frances having died in 1681.

Apart from Anne's legacy, there was one to each of Leke's *Executors*, one to his *Neece Frances Leeke*, one to his *Neece Lucy Leeke*, one to *Collonell Ambrose Norton* and the last to a *Mr. Robert Bogg*. As can be seen, there were only two other women named in his will, they being of his family, so it would seem that Anne was a very special ladyfriend indeed. Leke's three executors were Sir Robert Davers, 2nd Baronet (c.1653-1722) of Rougham in Suffolk, John Digby Esq (1668-1728) of Mansfield Wood House in Nottinghamshire, M.P. for Newark and East Retford, and Ambrose Norton Esq (1646-1723) of St Margaret's Westminster in the County of Middlesex, presumably as also named *Collonell*. It does appear from Anne's friendship with the earl that even before her retirement she moved in high society circles.

At the University of Nottingham, in their manuscripts and special collections is held an anonymous and undated poem entitled *On Mrs Brasgirle*:

On M[rs] Brasgirle

May shee to Nations Scarsdall prove
an easy doteing Maid
May shee afected Mildmay Love
and bee by him betray'd
May shee to Walsh, that Awkward Beau
be lavish of her store
May shee Nere handsom Granbroke know
and yett be thought his whore
Yett sh'll in spite I wish her worst
and may shee fall this Lowe
May Berkly her last favours boast
and hee receive them too[4]

Those names in this unflattering satirical poem are intriguing but, apart from *Scarsdall*, it is very difficult to determine who they actually were. However, as a shot in the dark, two of them might, and that's a very tentative might, possibly relate to critic and poet William Walsh (1663-1708) and James Berkeley, 3rd Earl of Berkeley (c.1679-1736). Although the work is undated, the reference to Robert Leke, 3rd Earl of Scarsdale, must date it before his death in 1707.

The Earl of Scarsdale's legacy to Anne could not have been better timed, in view of her recent retirement, but as intimated earlier Anne did, along with her dear friend Elizabeth Barry, make one further special stage appearance, in 1709, in *Love for Love*, for dear old Betterton's benefit.

Mrs Bracegirdle wasn't the only actress to come out of retirement for one last performance. There was one who did just that in her eighty-fifth year whose name was Margaret (Peg) Fryer and later Mrs Vandenvelden.

Margaret's maiden name was Hall, she being baptised at St Giles, Cripplegate in the City of London on 2 December 1632. Her father was an Isaac Hall. At the age of twenty-seven, she married a Leonard Frier at St Giles on 10 November 1659. She became an actress, under the name of Peg Fryer during Charles II's reign, and seemingly quit the stage sometime during that period.

After the death of her first husband, Peg married John Baptist Vandenvelden at St James Duke's Place, London on 24 February 1690/1, and was afterwards purported to have kept a tavern in Tottenham Court Road.

In the year 1720, octogenarian Margaret was assigned a part at Drury Lane Theatre in *The Half-Pay Officers*, a farce by journalist, political activist and minor playwright Charles Molloy (d.1767). Her character, listed in the playbill, was that of Widow Rich, being played by Mrs Vandervelt. Astonishingly, at the end of the play, old Peg danced a jig! The play was a great success, running for some seven days. The dancing of her jig was, it would seem, the highlight of the whole performance and purposely designed to attract a substantial audience as will be seen from an except from the play's preface:

> THIS Thing was brought upon the Stage with no other Design, but that of shewing Mrs. FRYAR the House being willing to encourage any thing, by which it might propose to entertain the Town; therefore the Author, or rather the Transcriber, did not think himself any way concern'd in its Success, as to the Reputation of a Writer; I say Transcriber, the greatest Part of it being old: The Part of Mrs. Fryer is in an Old Play, call'd Love and Honour, which she acted when she was Young, and which was so imprinted in her Memory, she could repeat it every Word; and it was to an accidental Conversation with her, this Farce ow'd its Being; she acted with so much Spirit and Life, before two or three Persons who had some Interest with the House, that we judg'd it wou'd do upon the Stage; she was prevail'd upon to undertake it; upon which this Farce was immediately projected, and finish'd in Fourteen Days; it was got up with so much Hurry, that some of the Comedians, who are allow'd to be Excellent in their Way, had not time to make themselves Masters of their Parts; therefore not being perfect in the Dialogue, they could not act with that Freedom and Spirit, they are observ'd to do, upon other Occasions.[5]

There are two further accounts of this extraordinary event and their contents were well worth transcribing:

Theatrical anecdote.

In 1720, Charles Molloy, Esq., wrote a farce, called The Half-Pay Officers. It was brought out at Drury Lane Theatre, and to Mrs. Fryer, who had quitted the stage in the reign of King Charles the Second, was assigned the part of an old grandmother. In the play-bills was mentioned, the character of Lady Richlove to be performed by Peg Fryer, who has not appeared upon any stage these fifty years, which, as might be expected, drew a very crowded house. This character in the farce was supposed to be a very old woman, and Peg exerted her utmost abilities; and the farce being ended, she came again upon the stage to dance a jig at the age of eighty-five; she came tottering in, and at first seemed much fatigued, but all of a sudden the music striking up "The Irish Trot," she danced and footed it almost as nimbly as any wench of five-and-twenty, which performance was received with an universal roar of applause. Mrs. Fryer afterwards kept a public- house in Tottenham Court, and lived in full health till November, 1747, when she died at the age of 112 years.[6]

PEG FRYER

Was a favourite actress in the reign of Charles the Second, and after a long absence returned to the stage, merely by way of a visit, in the reign of George the First. Charles Molloy, Esq. took a farce, called the "Half-pay Officer," From a tragi-comedy of Sir William Davenant's, entitled "Love and Honour," and prevailed on Mrs. Fryer to take once more her original character of Lady Richlove which being that of an old woman, suited her years. Accordingly she was thus announced in the bills of Lincoln's-in-fields Theatre:— "Lady Richlove by the famous Peg Fryer, who has not appeared upon the stage for these fifty years, and who will dance a jig at the end of the farce." A few remembered her, and went to the theatre to see an old favourite; but most went out of curiosity to see Mrs. Fryer then (1720) eighty-five years of age. This extraordinary woman sustained her part with great spirit, and, was received with the most gratifying applause. But when she was to dance, she came on the stage, apparently quite exhausted by her exertions, and scarcely able to support herself, made her obedience to the audience, and was about to retire, when the orchestra struck up the Irish trot, and the animated old woman danced her promise jig with the nimbleness and the vivacity of five-and-twenty, laughing at the surprise of the audience, and receiving unbounded applause. Mrs. Fryer, after this, kept a tavern and ordinary at Tottenham-court; and her house was continually thronged with company, who went out of curiosity to converse with this extraordinary old woman.[7]

As for Anne Oldfield, she continued to act for the rest of her life, becoming *the* celebrated actress of her day, seemingly having to work a little harder than her forerunners, particularly where some Epilogues were concerned. On Monday 17 March 1712, Anne was acting the part of Andromache in *The Distrest Mother*, a tragedy by poet and politician Ambrose Philips (1674-1749). Apparently, the origin of the term 'namby-pamby', meaning affected, weak, and maudlin speech or verse, was a nickname first bestowed on Philips by poet, dramatist and songwriter Henry Carey (c.1687-1743), in his poem *Namby Pamby*, 1725. The term stemmed from Philips' tendency to feud with other poets. At the end of the performance, Anne recited the Epilogue, and astonishingly was requested by the audience to repeat it.

In correspondence printed in *The Spectator* on Tuesday 1 April 1712, the following comment appeared:

> ...The Audience would not permit Mrs. *Oldfield* to go off the Stage the first Night, till she had repeated it twice; the second Night the Noise of *Ancoras* was as loud as before, and she was again obliged to speak it twice: the third Night it was still called for a second time; and, in short, contrary to all other Epilogues, which are dropt after the third Representation of the Play, this has already been repeated nine times... .

Poor Anne must have been quite exhausted at the end of the play; just imagine having to recite the whole Epilogue twice on several more consecutive occasions:

EPILOGUE,

Written by Mr. *Budgell* of the *Inner-Temple*.

Spoken by Mrs. OLDFIELD.

I Hope you'll own, that with becoming art,
I've play'd my game, and topp'd the widow's part.

My spouse, poor man, could not live out the play,
But dy'd commodiously on wedding-day:
While I, his relict, made at one bold fling
Myself a princess, and young Sty a king.
YOU, Ladies, who protract a lover's pain,
And hear your servants sigh whole years in vain;
Which of you all would not on marriage venture,
Might she so soon upon her jointure enter?
'Twas a strange scape! Had Pyrrhus *liv'd till now,*
I had been finely hamper'd in my vow.
To dye by one's own hand, and fly the charms
Of love and life in a young monarch's arms!
'Twere an hard fate ____ ere I had undergone it
I might have took one night____ to think upon it.
But why, you'll say, was all this grief exprest
For a first husband laid long since at rest?
Why so much coldness to my kind protector?
____Ah, ladies! had you known the good man Hector!
Homer *will tell you (or I'm mis-inform'd)*
That, when enraged, the Grecian *camp be storm'd,*
To break the ten fold barriers of the gate,
He threw a stone of such prodigious weight,
As no two men could lift, not even of those
Who in that age of thund'ring mortals rose:
____It wou'd have sprain'd a dozen modern beaux.
At length howe'er I laid my weeds aside,
And sunk the widow in the well-dress'd bride.
In you it still remains to grace the play,
And bless with joy my coronation-day;
Take then, ye circles of the brave and fair,
The fatherless and widow to your care.

FINIS.[8]

Mrs Oldfield became seriously romantically involved with two men during her career. The first was Arthur Maynwaring (1668-1712), an English official and Whig politician by whom she bore a son, Arthur. A number of years after Maynwaring's death, Anne met Lieutenant General Charles Churchill (1679-1745), a British Army General and Member of Parliament whose father, Charles Churchill (1656-1714), also a British army officer, was the younger brother of statesman and famous soldier John Churchill, 1st Duke of Marlborough. Charles and the actress lived together for many years, with Anne giving birth to their son, Charles, born circa 1720 who died at least aged ninety in 1812.

Mrs Oldfield, at the age of thirty-seven, suffered bouts of chronic ill health after the birth of her second son from which she never fully recovered, this resulting in periodic absences from the theatre. Her final performance was on 28 April 1730, she performing one of her famous roles, that of Lady Brute in Vanbrugh's *The Provoked Wife*. At that time, the brave actress was suffering agonising pain in her abdomen and died a few months later, on 23 October.

Anne Oldfield had always been a finely dressed woman, and was ceremonially buried on 27 October, *in a very fine Brussels lace head, a holland shift and double ruffles of the same lace, a pair of new kid gloves, and her body wrapped in a winding-sheet*, in the south aisle of the nave of Westminster Abbey. It is said that her funeral was a magnificent affair and that the entire Drury Lane company was present.

Even after death, Mrs Oldfield didn't evade the satirist's pen. The ever-critical Alexander Pope penned these derogatory lines on the burial of Anne Oldfield in his *Epistles to several persons* (*Moral Essays*). Although Pope had the half-decency not to name her, it was patently clear at the time to whom it referred, his aspersions suggesting perhaps that their association had not been genial:

> "Odious ! in woollen ! 'Twould a saint provoke,"
> (Were the last words that poor Narcissa spoke)
> "No, let a charming chintz and Brussels lace
> Wrap my cold limbs, and shade my lifeless face:
> One would not, sure, be frightful when one's dead —
> And—Betty—give this cheek a little red."

The words *Odious! in woollen! 'Twould a saint provoke* allude to an Act of Parliament, passed in 1666, for *burying in woollen only* in an effort to support the English wool trade. If a person was buried in anything other than wool, a fine of five pounds was imposed on their estate, with half of this fine allocated to the poor of the parish and the remainder to the informant. There was a clever loophole however; a family member could put themselves forward as an informant, so effectively only half the fine would be paid!

Chapter Fifteen

A Long and Happy Retirement with the Inevitable Consequence

Unlike Mrs Oldfield, Anne Bracegirdle was blessed with good health throughout her long life and was able to enjoy many years of retirement in Howard Street, where she relished the company of many old and new friends including notables of her generation.

By the winter of 1747, Anne had reached her seventy-sixth year, and the frailty of old age had inevitably caught up with her. On 28 November that year she made her last will and testament, which would benefit those of her remaining family, who were few:

> **This is the last Will** and Testament of me Anne Bracegirdle of the Parish of Saint Clements in the County of Middlesex Spinster I Will that all my debts and Funeral Expenses be first paid I give to the poor of Saint Clements parish aforesaid Ten pounds to be distributed by my Executrix herein after mentioned in such shares and proportions as she shall think proper I give to my Nephew Justinian Bracegirdle Four Hundred pounds Item I give unto Mrs Ann Lodge of the Parish of Saint Clement Danes aforesaid Spinster the Sum of One Hundred pounds All which Legacies I Will shall be paid within Six months after my decease I desire to be buried in a Leaden Coffin in Westminster Abby but if I die in the Country in the Parish Church where I shall die I give and bequeath unto my Neice Martha Bracegirdle all the rest and residue of all and singular my personal Estate whatsoever I Nominate and Appoint my said Neice Martha Bracegirdle Executrix of this my last Will and Testament In Witness whereof I have hereunto set my Hand and Seal this Twenty eighth day of November One Thousand Seven Hundred and Forty Seven A: Bracegirdle Signed Sealed and Delivered Published and Declared by the said Anne Bracegirdle as and for her last Will and Testament in the presence of Rob[t]. Judman.[1]

After Anne's death, on 12 September 1748, it appears from the following document that the validity of the testator's signature had been questioned:

> Appeared personally Elizabeth Parker of the parish of St. Clement Danes in the County of Middlesex Spinster and made oath that she knew and was well acquainted with Anne Bracegirdle late of the parish of St. Clement Danes aforesaid Spinster deceased in her the said deceased's life time having lived with her as a servant for the space of eight years before her death and has often seen her write and subscribe her Name and thereby became well acquainted with her manner and Character of Hand Writing and Subscription And that having now seen and perused the last Will and Testament of the said deceased hereto annexed beginning - This is the last Will and Testament of me Anne Bracegirdle - and ending - In Witness whereof I have hereunto set my Hand and Seal this twenty eighth day of November One Thousand Seven Hundred and Forty Seven - and Subscribed A Bracegirdle - She verily beleives the said Name A. Bracegirdle or Subscription thereto to be of the proper Hand Writing of the said deceased. E: Parker Same Day the said Elizabeth Parker was sworn to the Truth of the Premisses before me. Robt. Chapman Surrogate Pres^t. John Caesar. NS.

> **This Will** was proved a London before the Worshipfull Robert Chapman Doctor of Laws Surrogate of the right Worshipfull John Betterworth Doctor of Laws Master Keeper or Commissary of ther Prerogative Court of Canterbury lawfully constituted on the twelfth day of September in the year of Our Lord One Thousand Seven Hundred and Forty eight by the Oath of Martha Bracegirdle Spinster the Neice of the said deceased and Sole Executrix named in the said Will to whom Administration was graned of all and singular the Goods Chattels and Credits of the said deceased she being first Sworn duly to Administer.[2]

The said Elizabeth Parker had left the employ of Anne Bracegirdle in 1742, six years prior to her employer's death:

> Middx
> Eliz: Parker aged upw^{ds}. of 60 Y^{rs}. upon her Oath saith she was never married & that she lived a Yearly by hired Servt. with

M^{rs}. Bracegirdle in Heward Street in the Parish of St Clement Danes in the County of Middx at the Yearly Wages of £5 for 8 Years or thereabouts & hath left her s^d. Service ab^t. 2 Years since which time she hath not Rented ten pounds a Year paid Parish Taxes lived with any person as a Yearly hired Servt. For one Year or otherwise gained a Settlem^t. in any other Place to her knowledge or beleif
Sworn Febry 19th 1744}
before}   E. Parker

Tho Lane.[3]

Mrs Bracegirdle's niece, Martha, who was the daughter of Hamlett Bracegirdle, the youngest brother of Anne, had been resident for many years with her in Howard Street. Following her aunt's demise, Martha, then aged thirty-seven and of no small means, would certainly have been a very attractive proposition for marriage to an attentive bachelor:

> 1748 Nov. 30 John Grimaldeston, of Hammersmith, co. Midd., B., & Martha Bracegirdle, of St Clement Danes, Co, Midd., S. Licence.[4]

It appears that although Martha married late in life, she did produce two children, a daughter Ann Bracegirdle Grimbaldeston, who was baptised at St Clement Danes on 30 October 1749, and John baptised on 7 March 1752, also at St Clement Danes.

By 1793, Martha was an eighty-two-year-old frail widow and had made her will in October that year. In the will, it is interesting to see that forty-five years after her aunt's demise Martha was still benefiting from the actress's will. She was still in possession of the leased house in Howard Street and at this time resided at another property, in the parish of St Luke Old Street. It is also surprising that Martha's son, John, was bequeathed the paltry legacy of ten pounds, whereas her daughter, Ann Bracegirdle Grimbaldeston received the whole of her mother's estate. At this time she was aged forty-four and also a widow, by the name of Anderson. Her husband John had died in 1786 and was buried at St Clement Danes.

Both Ann Bracegirdle Grimbaldeston and her brother married in the same year, each by licence. John married Ann Griffiths at St Clement Danes, on 25 February 1775, with the bride's father and John's sister as witnesses. Later, Ann married John Anderson at St Marylebone,

Westminster on 4 July, with one of the witnesses being a Jane Griffiths, a relative of John's wife.

One can only surmise that son John had either made his own fortune or did not turn out the son Martha would have been proud of.

Here is the will of Martha Grimbaldeston:

> **In the Name of God Amen** I Martha Grimbaldeston of Paridise Street in the Parish of Saint Luke Old Street in the County of Middlesex Widow being of sound and perfect mind and memory blessed be Almighty God for the same but considering the uncertainty of this mortal life I resign my soul into the hands of my Alwise Creator and Redeemer to make and publish this my last Will and Testament in manner and form following that is to say after payment of all my just Debts and Funeral Expenses and the proving of this my Will I Give and Bequeath unto my son John Grimbaldeston the sum of ten pounds which said Legacy or sum of ten pounds I direct to be paid within three months after my Decease and I hereby Give and Bequeath to my Dear Daughter Ann Bracegirdle Grimbaldeston otherwise Anderson all my Interest in the Lease of a House in Howard Street in the Strand in the County of Middlesex and also my Leasehold House and Premises in Paridise Street aforesaid where I now Dwell and all my Money invested in the Funds on Government Security with all my Plate Silver China Books Pictures Household Goods Money and Securities for Money's And all the Rest Residue and Remainder of my Personal Estate Goods and Chattels of what kind or nature soever I Give and Bequeath the same to my said Daughter Ann Bracegirdle Grimbaldeston otherwise Anderson whom I appoint whole and Sole Executrix of this my Will only requesting my old Friend Walter Tothill of Bedford Street Bedford Row in the Parish of Saint Andrew Holborn in the County of Middlesex Gentleman to Assist her +[in the margin '+*in the execution thereof and if she thinks fit to admit him to join with her*] as Executor and to Administer with her to this my last Will and Testament and I hereby revoke and make void all other and former Wills by me heretofore made and declare this and this only to be and contain my last Will and Testament and given under my hand and seal this twentieth Day of October in the year of our Lord one thousand seven hundred and ninety

three Martha Grimbaldeston Signed sealed published and Declared by the above named Martha Grimbaldeston to be her last Will and Testament in the Presence of us who have hereunto subscribed our names as Witnesses in the presence of the Testatrix Jane Thompson. Paul Street Moorfields Stephen Wilkins.: Paul Street Moorfields

This Will was proved at London the Fifteenth Day of November in the year of our Lord one thousand seven hundred and ninety three before the Worshipful James Henry Arnold Doctor of Laws and Surrogate of the Right Honourable Sir William Wynne Knight also Doctor of Laws Master Keeper or Commissary of the Prerogative Court of Canterbury lawfully constituted by the Oaths of Ann Bracegirdle Grimbaldeston otherwise Anderson Widow the Daughter of the Deceased and Walter Tothill the Executors named in the said Will to whom Administration of all and singular the Goods Chattels and Credits of the said Deceased was granted having been first sworn duly to Administer.[5]

The four hundred pounds bequeathed to Anne's nephew, Justinian, then aged fifty-one and only surviving son of her second eldest brother, John, was a substantial sum to have inherited. This should have ensured the legatee a more than comfortable lifestyle to the end of his days but research reveals this was not the case. Whether through poor investment, debt, the loss of a loved one or simply the temptations of city life, the standing of this one-time favoured nephew sank to the depths. Fortunately, his admiring aunt never knew of his misfortunes, but the old actress would have been appalled to have read the following:

London, to wit.

Be it remembred That on the 19th. Day of June 1752 in the 26th. Year of his present Majesty's Reign Justinian Bracegirdle a person under a Degree of a Gentleman was convicted before me one of His Majesty's Justices of the Peace for the City of London, of Swearing ten prophane Oaths in the parish of Saint Sepulchre London

Given under my Hand and Seal the Day and Year first above written.

T: Cokayne.[6]

A gentleman in the parish of St Sepulchre he might have been, but in what circumstances was he living? For poor Justinian, eleven years later, met a sad demise; *10th February 1763 Justinian Bracegirdle in Chick Workhouse aged 62.*[7] However, according to his christening, sixty-six years should have been the recorded age.

The honourable reputation of Anne Bracegirdle has so far proven unblemished. Her admirable stage career and spinster friendships in later life with the worthies of her generation speak volumes to her personable character:

> …Horace Walpole was among the number of her associates, as we learn from a letter of his to Horace Mann in 1742, wherein he says:
>
> "Now I talk of players, tell Mr Chute that his friend Bracegirdle breakfasted with me this morning. As she went out, and wanted her clogs, she turned to me and said - 'I remember at the playhouse they used to call - Mrs. Oldfield's chair! Mrs. Barry's clogs! And Mrs. Bracegirdle's pattens.'"
>
> A few years after this, according to Bellchambers, she "retired" to the house of the Mr. Chute mentioned in the foregoing letter. And on the 18th of September 1748 she died, aged eighty-five years, and was buried in the east cloister of Westminster abbey.[8]

The reference to her age as eighty-five years was clearly incorrect and no doubt taken from the inscription on her tomb in Westminster Abbey. This inscription has in the past led to confusion regarding her date of birth and in fact, it should have read seventy-seven years (1671-1748). At least her request to be buried at the Abbey was honoured.

Even in her old age, Anne still had energy and wit enough to banter with her good friend Colley Cibber:

> …On one occasion, a group of her visitors were discussing the merits of Garrick, whom she had not seen, and Cibber spoke disparagingly of his Bayes, preferring in that part his own pert and vivacious son, Theophilus. The old actress tapped Colley with her fan; "Come, come, Cibber," she remarked; "tell me if there is not something like envy in your character of this young gentleman. The actor who pleases everybody must be a man of merit." Colley smiled, tapped his box, took a pinch, and,

catching the generosity of the lady, replied: "Faith, Bracey, I believe you are right; the young fellow *is* clever!"[9]

I feel it appropriate to give the great Colley Cibber the honour of having the final say on the celebrated Bracy:

> I come now to the last, and only living Person, of all those whose Theatrical Characters I have promis'd you, Mrs. *Bracegirdle*; who, I know, would rather pass her remaining Days forgotten, as an Actress, than to have her Youth recollected in the most favourable Light I am able to place it; yet, as she is essentially necessary to my Theatrical History, and, as I only bring her back to the Company of those, with whom she pass'd the Spring and Summer of her Life, I hope it will excuse the Liberty I take, in commemorating the Delight which the Publick receiv'd from her Appearance, while she was an Ornament to the Theatre.
>
> Mrs. *Bracegirdle* was now, but just blooming to her Majority; her Reputation, as an Actress, gradually rising with that of her Person; never any Woman was in such general Favour of her Spectators, which, to the last Scene of her Dramatick Life, she maintain'd, by not being unguarded in her private Character. This Discretion contributed, not a little, to make her the *Cara*, the Darling of the Theatre: For it will be no extravagant thing to say, Scarce an Audience saw her, that were less than half of them Lovers, without a suspected Favourite among them: And tho' she might be said to have been the Universal Passion, and under the highest Temptations; her Constancy in resisting them, serv'd but to increase the number of her Admirers: And this perhaps you will more easily believe, when I extend not my Encomiums on her Person, beyond a Sincerity that can be suspected; for she had no greater Claim to Beauty, than what the most desirable *Brunette* might pretend to. But her Youth, and lively Aspect, threw out such a Glow of Health and Chearfulness, that, on the Stage, few Spectators that were not past it, could behold her without Desire. It was even a Fashion among the Gay, and Young, to have a Taste or *Tendre* for Mrs. *Bracegirdle*. She inspired the best Authors to write for her, and two of them, when they gave her a Lover, in a Play seem'd palpably to plead their own Passions, and make their private Court to her, in fictitious Characters. In all the chief Parts

she acted, the Desirable was so predominant, that no Judge could be cold enough to consider, from what other particular Excellence she became delightful. To speak critically of an Actress, that was extremely good, were as hazardous, as to be positive in one's Opinion of the best Opera Singer. People often judged by Comparison, where there is no Similitude, in the Performance. So that, in this case, we have only Taste to appeal to, and of Taste there can be no disputing. I shall therefore only say of Mrs. *Bracegirdle*, That the most eminent Authors always chose her for their favourite Character, and shall leave that uncontestable Proof of her Merit to its own Value. Yet let me say, there were two very different Characters, in which she acquitted herself with uncommon Applause: If any thing could excuse that desperate Extravagance of Love, that almost frantick Passion of *Lee's Alexander the Great*, it must have been, when Mrs. *Bracegirdle* was his *Statira*: As when she acted *Millamant*, all the Faults, Follies, and Affectation of that agreeable Tyrant, were venially melted down into so many Charms, and Attractions of a conscious Beauty. In other Characters, where Singing was a necessary Part of them, her Voice and Action gave a Pleasure, which good Sense, in those Days, was not asham'd to give Praise to.

She retir'd from the Stage in the Height of her Favour from the Publick, when most of her Contemporaries, whom she had been bred up with, were declining, in the Year 1710, nor could she be perswaded to return to it, under new Masters, upon the most advantageous Terms, that were offer'd her; excepting one Day, about a Year after, to assist her good Friend Mr. *Betterton*, when she play'd *Angelica*, in *Love for Love*, for his Benefit. She has still the Happiness to retain her usual Chearfulness, and to be, without the transitory Charm of Youth, agreeable.[10]

Epilogue

When Hart and Mohun, Mrs. Marshall and Nell Gwyn, Betterton and Smith, Mrs. Barry and Mrs. Bracegirdle acted what Dryden, Wycherley, Otway, and Congreve wrote the theatre with all its drawbacks had reached a zenith of brilliance which was certainly not sustained in the Hanoverian era and which will probably never again be so fully compassed and achieved.

The Restoration Theatre, by Montague Summers. 1934.

The Restoration era was an exciting time for all those who embraced it and for some, as with our two actresses, a time of welcome independence.

In the public theatre, for the first time, women had the freedom to be on an equal footing with their male stage counterparts, if not in monetary terms then in their acting prowess. This was proved time and time again, with the popularity that many of the actresses gained during their long hard-working careers.

Choosing to become an actress or if, as in the case of Barry and Bracegirdle, the stage chose *them*, this was not the easiest job in the world, as has been seen. Nonetheless, though their world was often looked upon as something being of a dubious nature, it must be said that it was a far better choice than other, particularly immoral occupations.

As young girls, who one could loosely call orphaned, Elizabeth and Anne had the protection of their respective theatre guardians, Lady Davenant and Thomas and Mary Betterton, together with that of a large family of theatre employees.

The shock of moving from a secure family home to a house with the largest curtains in the street must have been something very frightening, but also a little magical, and after all, it was a *play* house. Young eyes would espy in every room, in every corner, nook and cranny, stage props of all shapes and sizes, costumes of luxurious materials, hats, boots, shoes, and weapons of death; a whole kaleidoscope world. Life in the streets and alleyways of London must have seemed very dull indeed, compared to the inner sanctum of their enchanting 'home'.

Mrs Barry was thirteen years Mrs Bracegirdle's senior and, with both girls coming from similarly troubled family backgrounds, they must have become very close friends early on, with Elizabeth taking the lead in protecting her theatre step-sister.

Evidence of the ancestral roots of Mrs Barry is sparse to say the least, as has been intimated. To date, it has never been conclusive as to who her family really were. She might have belonged to a family of Irish Barrys, or in fact a family of Oxfordshire Barrys. And although exhaustive research has been undertaken to 'unearth' her ancestors, alas no conclusive evidence has yet come to light. But in the case of Mrs Bracegirdle, documentation of her ancestral roots turned out to be in abundance, and has proven once and for all that Anne was born and bred in Northamptonshire, and not Wolverhampton as is sometimes suggested.

It is most irritating that while contemporaries of Elizabeth wrote about her looks, her stature, the colour of her eyes and the slight defect in her mouth, they made no mention of her accent. If only someone had just intimated that Mrs Barry talked with such and such an accent, it might have given some tantalising clue as to her roots. Sadly, the only written evidence of her family is from the unreliable source of Edmund Curll. And then, there is the despicable Robert Gould, who penned these scurrilous lines on Elizabeth; ...*What I shall speak must be beneath the Rose. Her mother was a common Strumpet known, Her Father half the Rabble of the Town. Begot by Casual and Promiscuous Lust,...* There may be some truth in both Curll's and Gould's accounts of her background but, with their wildly differing versions, it's impossible to consider either as representing her true ancestry. Naturally, one would like to think of Curll's account as the truer but sadly, to date, there is no conclusive evidence that Mrs Barry came from *an ancient family and good estate.* However, it must be borne in mind that it *was* Curll who seemed to be the first to mention Mrs Barry's acting tutelage by Lord Rochester, which *is* generally believed to be true.

As Elizabeth and Anne matured into adulthood, they both exhibited a natural talent for thespianism and became two of the most revered actresses of their generation. Yet their lives outside of the playhouse were very dissimilar, with Elizabeth's reputation being that of a supposed *mercenary whore* and with Anne's being that of a supposed *pious angel.* How true their characters really were can only be gleaned from historic hearsay, and one is very reluctant to wholly believe all that one reads. Nonetheless, the old adage *no smoke without fire* might give some indication as to the truths or otherwise of their lives. I will leave that conundrum for the reader to ponder upon.

Although their lives seemed very different beyond the workplace, they must have enjoyed living as independent women and not, as with many of their contemporary females, in married life or as a servant in domestic drudgery. Even though Mrs Barry bore at least one child, that of Rochester, she was, as far as we know, never officially wed to any man. As regards Mrs Bracegirdle, although there were rumours that she and Congreve might have married, documentary evidence of this has so far never come to light and my guess, believing those rumours to be completely unfounded, is that it never will.

It's remarkable to think that Elizabeth and Anne were working actresses for thirty-seven and twenty-seven years respectively; that amounts to a lot of rehearsals, a lot of performances, and hundreds of changes of costume, not to mention applying make-up umpteen times. Their dedication to their art is something to be admired, with the tenacity to perform day after day, treading the boards in front of either an appreciative or sometimes a hostile audience, all requiring a great deal of stamina and bravery.

Then there were the critics; the good, the bad and the ugly of them. And we have seen how blatantly hostile some of those critics could be. For female actresses in particular, it must have been very hard indeed to overcome such harsh broadsides, especially when those critical satires were aimed at their sexual conduct in a most derogatory and vile manner. On the other side of the coin, it must have been most rewarding for the players to read a praiseworthy piece on their day's performance.

With their careers spanning many years, it gave them an amount of monetary security throughout their working lives and beyond, enabling them to live without the fear of poverty.

The wills of Mrs Barry and Mrs Bracegirdle go to show that at the end of their lives they were women of some wealth and in Barry's case with an estate in Newbury too. Anne's wealth continued for many years after her death by way of benefiting her beloved niece.

All this points to the fact that Elizabeth and Anne were not merely common actresses, as some regarded them, but were shrewd women who knew the value of independent wealth, giving them self-esteem and self-assured confidence in a then dictatorial, male world.

To overcome those dreadful events; one having a child abducted by a former lover, and the other almost being abducted herself by a love-crazed captain culminating in the murder of a dear friend, reveals that Elizabeth's and Anne's lives were not entirely socially secure. They must have been well aware that celebrity status could give rise to unwanted incidents, which to this day is still sadly evident.

There is very little documented about Elizabeth and Anne following their retirement, apart from references to Elizabeth retiring to Acton and telling of her tragic death, and to Anne breakfasting in the company of Walpole.

The type of company that Elizabeth enjoyed in her days of retirement living in Acton can only be surmised from the people mentioned in her will. Apart from the two gentlemen named therein, the rest were women. Does this reveal that in her later life she preferred the female friendships without the complications of male adoration and their love intrigues towards her? She had no doubt learned, from past experiences with the male sex, that their initial infatuations with *the famous Mrs. Barry* were not long-lasting or sincere. But it appears that Gabriel Ballam was an exception, they knowing each other for possibly fifteen years, and he benefiting from her *Estate at Newbury consisting of mills*. It is a great pity that there is no correspondence between Elizabeth and Gabriel, which would certainly have thrown some light on their relationship. There could well have been personal letters between them but, as is often the case with a deceased's estate, goods and chattels etc. they are disposed of in various directions, while personal papers can be seen as having no value whatsoever and are unceremoniously destroyed. This is evidenced by the only known extant letter written by Mrs Barry, in reply to a letter from The Right Honourable the Lady Lisburne. How wonderful it would be to have read Lisburne's letter, and to know the reason for Mrs Barry's reply; *I obeyed your Ladyships commands to Mr Batterton and Mrs Bracegirdle who returned their humble service and thanks for soe great a favour*. What was that great favour? As a researcher, one does live in hope of unearthing more and who knows, the descendants of Mary Sayer might one day hold the key. By the same token, descendants of *Ann Bracegirdle Grimbaldeston otherwise Anderson*, might have tucked away, in some dusty corner of an attic, remnants of personal correspondence etc. of *the darling of the stage*. Such a find could well put to rest, once and for all, speculation on Mrs Bracegirdle's supposed relationship with William Congreve.

Had Elizabeth Barry been blessed with longevity, like her friend Anne Bracegirdle, one likes to contemplate what reminiscences those two stalwarts of the London Stage would have enjoyed, sat by a warming winter's fire, sparking memories by the dozen.

'I remember at the playhouse they used to call Mrs. Oldfield's chair! Mrs. Barry's clogs! And Mrs. Bracegirdle's pattens!'

Repertoire of Plays performed by Mrs Barry and/or Mrs Bracegirdle

Abramule; or, Love and Empire – *Joseph Trapp* (1679-1747)
Adventures In Madrid – *Mary Pix* (1666-1709)
Alcibiades – *Thomas Otway* (1652-1685)
Almyna; or, The Arabian Vow – *Delarivier Manley* (c.1663-1724)
Alphonso King of Naples – *George Powell* (c.1668-1714)
Ambitious Slave; or, A Generous Revenge – *Elkanah Settle* (1648-1724)
Amphitryon – *Jean-Baptiste Poquelin (Molière)* (1622-1673)
As You Find It – *Charles Boyle, 4th Earl of Orrery* (1674-1731)
Aureng Zebe; or, The Great Mogul – *John Dryden* (1631-1700)
Beauty in Distress – *Peter Anthony Motteux* (1663-1718)
Boadigea Queen of Britain – *Charles Hopkins* (c.1664-c.1700)
Bussy D'Ambois; or, The Husbands Revenge – *Thomas D'Urfey* (1653-1723)
Cleomenes, the Spartan Hero – *John Dryden*
Comical History of Don Quixote, Part I – *Thomas D'Urfey*
Cyrus the Great; or, The Tragedy of Love – *John Banks* (c.1650-1706)
Distress'd Innocence; or, The Princess of Persia – *Elkanah Settle*
Don Sebastian, King Of Portugal – *John Dryden*
Edward IV With the Fall of Mortimer, Earl of March – author not certain, but possibly written by *John Bancroft* (d.1696) and *William Mountfort* (c.1664-1692)
False Friend; or, The Fate of Disobedience – *Mary Pix*
Fatal Friendship – *Catharine Trotter* (c.1679-1749)
Friendship Improved; or, The Female Warrior – *Charles Hopkins* (c.1664-c.1700)
Hamlet, Prince Of Denmark – *William Shakespeare* (1564-1616)
Henry II. With the Death of Rosamond – Authorship uncertain
Heroic Love – *George Granville, Lord Lansdowne* (1666-1735)
Innocent Mistress – *Mary Pix*
Intrigues at Versailles; or, A Jilt in all Humours – *Thomas D'Urfey*

Iphigenia – *John Dennis* (1658-1734)

Irene; or, The Fair Greek – *Charles Goring (date not known)*

Julius Caesar – *William Shakespeare*

King Arthur; or, The British Worthy – *John Dryden*

King Edward III – attributed in part to *William Shakespeare* and *Thomas Kyd* (1558-1594)

King Lear, and his Three Daughters – Altered from William Shakespeare – *NahumTate* (1652-1715)

Liberty Asserted – *John Dennis*

Love Betrayed; or, The Agreeable Disappointment – *William Burnaby* (1673-1706)

Love for Love – *William Congreve* (1670-1729)

Love for Money; or, The Boarding School – *Thomas D'Urfey*

Love Triumphant; or, Nature will Prevail – *John Dryden*

Love's a Jest – *Peter Anthony Motteux*

Love's Victim; or, The Queen of Wales – *Charles Gildon* (c.1665-1724)

Lover's Luck – *Thomas Dilke* (b.c.1699)

Lucius Junius Brutus Father of His Country – *Nathaniel Lee* (c.1653-1692)

Macbeth – *William Shakespeare*

Marriage a La Mode – *Colley Cibber* (1671-1757)

Measure for Measure; or, Beauty the Best Advocate – Altered from William Shakespeare by *Charles Gildon*

Othello, Moor Of Venice – *William Shakespeare*

Queen Catharine; or, The Ruines of Love – *Mary Pix*

Rule a Wife and have a Wife – *John Fletcher* (1579-1625)

She Ventures and he Wins – Authorship uncertain

She Wou'd If She Cou'd – *Sir George Etherege* (c.1636-c.1692)

Sir Anthony Love; or, The Rambling Lady – *Thomas Southerne* (1660-1746)

Sophonisba – *James Thomson* (c.1700-1748)

Squire Trelooby – *Congreve, Vanbrugh* (1664-1726) and *William Walsh* (1662-1708)

Successful Strangers – *William Mountfort*

Tamerlane – *Nicholas Rowe* (1674-1718)

The Adventures Of Five Hours – *Sir Samuel Tuke, 1st Baronet* (c.1615-1674)

The Ambitious Stepmother – *Nicholas Rowe*

The Amorous Bigotte – *Thomas Shadwell* (c.1642-1692)

The Amorous Widow; or, The Wanton Wife – *Thomas Betterton* (1635-1710)

The Atheist; or, The Second Part of the Souldiers Fortune – *Thomas Otway* (1652-1685)

The Beau Defeated; or, The Lucky Younger Brother – *Mary Pix*

The Biter – *Nicholas Rowe*

The British Enchanters; or, No Magick Like Love – *George Granville, Lord Lansdowne*

The Careless Husband – *Colley Cibber*

The City Heiress; or, Sir Timothy Treatall – *Aphra Behn* (1640-1689)

The Committee; or, The Faithful Irishman – *Sir Robert Howard* (1626-1698)

The Confederacy – *Sir John Vanbrugh*

The Constant Nymph; or, The Rambling Shepheard. Author not known.

The Country Wake – *Thomas Doggett* (c.1640-1721)

The Deceiver Deceived – *Mary Pix*

The Destruction of Troy – *John Banks*

The Double Dealer – *William Congreve*

The Double Distress – *Mary Pix*

The Duke of Guise – *John Dryden and Nathaniel Lee*

The Fair Penitent – *Nicholas Rowe*

The Fatal Marriage; or, The Innocent Adultery – *Thomas Southerne*

The Feigned Courtizans; or, A Night's Intrigue – *Aphra Behn*

The Female Vertuosos – *Thomas Wright* (fl.1693)

The Fickle Shepherdess – *Thomas Randolph* (1605-1635)

The French Conjuror – *Thomas Porter* (1636-1680)

The Gamester – *Susanna Centlivre* (c.1669-1723)

The History and Fall of Caius Marius – *Thomas Otway*

The Indian Emperor; or, The Conquest of Granada by the Spaniards – *John Dryden*

The Injured Lovers; or, The Ambitious Father – *William Mountfort*

The Jew Of Venice – *George Granville, Lord Lansdowne*

The Ladies Visiting Day – *William Burnaby* (1673-1706)

The Lady's Last Stake; or, The Wife's Resentment – *Colley Cibber*

The London Cuckolds – *Edward Ravenscroft* (c.1654-1707)

The Loves of Mars and Venus – *Peter Anthony Motteux*

The Loving Enemies – *Lewis Maidwell* (1650-1716)

The Maid's last Prayer; or, Any rather than Fail – *Thomas Southerne*

The Maid's Tragedy – *Francis Beaumont* (1584-1616) and *John Fletcher*

The Man of Mode; or, Sir Fopling Flutter – *Sir George Etherege*

The Marriage-Hater Match'd – *Thomas D'Urfey*

The Married Beau; or, The Curious Impertinent – *John Crowne* (1641-1712)

The Mistakes – *Joseph Harris* (c.1650-1715)

The Mourning Bride – *William Congreve*

The Old Bachelor – *William Congreve*

The Orphan; or, The Unhappy Marriage – *Thomas Otway*

The Platonick Lady – *Susanna Centlivre*
The Princess of Cleve – *Nathaniel Lee*
The Princess of Parma – *Henry Smith* (date not known)
The Provoked Wife – *Sir John Vanbrugh*
The Rape; or, The Innocent Impostors – *Nicholas Brady* (1659-1726)
The Revenge; or, A Match in Newgate – *Aphra Behn*
The Revolution of Sweden – *Catharine Trotter*
The Richmond Heiress; or, A Woman Once in the Right – *Thomas D'Urfey*
The Rival Queens; or, The Death of Alexander the Great – *Nathaniel Lee*
The Rover; or, The Banish'd Cavaliers – *Aphra Behn*
The Royal Convert – *Nicholas Rowe*
The Royal Mischief – *Delarivier Manley*
The Scornful Lady – *Francis Beaumont* and *John Fletcher*
The Scowrers – *Thomas Shadwell*
The She-Gallants – *George Granville, Lord Lansdowne*
The Soldier's Fortune – *Thomas Otway*
The Spanish Friar; or, The Double Discovery – *John Dryden*
The Squire of Alsatia – *Thomas Shadwell*
The Temple of Love – *Peter Anthony Motteux*
The Traytor – *James Shirley* (1596-1666) with alterations, amendments and
    additions written by
Anthony Rivers (date not known)
The Unhappy Favourite; or, The Earl of Essex – *John Banks*
The Volunteers; or, The Stock-jobbers – *Thomas Shadwell*
The Way of the World – *William Congreve*
The Widow Ranter; or, The History of Bacon in Virginia – *Aphra Behn*
The Wives' Excuse; or, Cuckolds Make Themselves – *Thomas Southerne*
The Wrangling Lovers; or, The Invisible Mistress. *Edward Ravenscroft*
Titus and Berenice – *Thomas Otway*
Tom Essence; or, The Modish Wife – Ascribed to *Thomas Rawlins*
    (c.1620-1670)
Treacherous Brothers – *George Powell*
Ulysses – *Nicholas Rowe*
Valentinian – Adapted from *Fletcher* by *John Wilmot, Earl of Rochester*
    (1647-1680)
Venice Preserved; or, A Plot Discover'd – *Thomas Otway*
Vertue Betrayed; or, Anna Bullen – *John Banks*
Zelmane; or, The Corinthian Queen – Authorship uncertain, possibly
    Mountfort or *Pix*

Bibliography

All Saints Church, Spelsbury, *Extract from a pamphlet*, Copyright Incumbent and Parochial Church Council of the Parish Church of Spelsbury. 2005.

Berkeley, George-Monck, Esq., *Literary Relics: Containing Original Letters from King Charles II. King James II. The Queen of Bohemia, Swift, Berkeley, Addison, Steel, Congreve, The Duke of Ormond and Bishop Rundle. To which is prefixed, An Inquiry into The Life of Dean Swift*. London. MDCCLXXXIX.

Besant, Sir Walter, *London in the Eighteenth Century*. 1901.

Betterton, Thomas, *The history of the English stage, from the Restauration to the Present Time…* London. 1741.

Brown, Mr., *Amusements Serious and Comical Calculated for the Meridian of London*. London. 1700.

Brown, Thomas and Gould, Robert, *Love Given Over; or, A Satyr against the pride, lust and inconstancy &c. of woman.*, London: Printed for R. Bentley and J. Tonson. 1686.

Brown, Thomas, *The Third Volume of the Works of Mr. Tho. Brown. Being Amusements…* London. 1719.

Burnet, Gilbert, D.D., *Some Passages of the Life and Death of the Right Honourable John Earl of Rochester, Who died the 26th of July, 1680.* Written by his own Direction on his Death-Bed. London. 1660.

Butler, Samuel, *The Posthumous Works of Mr. Samuel Butler, (Author of Hudibras). Written in the time of the Grand Rebellion, and in the reign of King Charles II. Being a collection of satire, speeches, and reflections upon those times.* 3rd edition. London. MDCCXXX.

Cibber, Colley, *An Apology for the Life of Mr. Colley Cibber, Comedian, and late patentee of the Theatre-Royal: with an historical view of the stage during his own time.* 1740.

Collier, Jeremy, M.A., *A Short View of the Immorality and Profaneness of the English Stage…* London. MDCXCIX.

Cooper, Susan Margaret, *Roger Bridgwater* (1694-1754): "An Old Actor & An Honest Man" – Richard Cross – Theatre Prompter – 1754. 2020.

D'Urfey, Thomas, *Collin's walk through London and Westminster, A poem in burlesque.* 1690.

D'Urfey, Thomas, *Wit and Mirth: or Pills to Purge Melancholy...* Vol. II London. 1719.

Davies, Thomas, *Dramatic Miscellanies...* Vol III Dublin. 1784.

Dennis, John, *Letters upon several occasions written by and between Mr. Dryden, Mr. Wycherly, Mr.----, Mr. Congreve, and Mr. Dennis, published by Mr. Dennis with a new translation of select letters of Monsieur Voiture.* London: Printed for Sam. Briscoe. 1696.

Editor of Wit & Wisdom, *The Funniest Jest Book in the World, being a superior collection of all the Well-Seasoned Jests, Curious Relations, Strange Stories, Sprightly Sayings, Droll Doings, Funny Tales, Witticisms, Epigrams and Recitations.* Liverpool. 1847.

Egerton, William Esq., *Faithful Memoirs of the Life, Amours and Performances, of That justly celebrated, and most eminent actress of her Time, Mrs. Anne Oldfield. Interspersed with several other Dramitcal Memoirs.* London. MDCCXXXI.

Fyvie, John, *Tragedy Queens of the Georgian Era.* 1908.

Genest, Rev. John, *Some Account of the English Stage, from the Restoration in 1660 to 1830.* Vol.II. Bath. 1832.

Gent. A. G., *The Rake Reform'd: A Poem in a Letter to the Rakes of the Town.* London. MDCCXVIII.

Gildon, Charles, *The Life of Mr. Thomas Betterton, The late Eminent Tragedian...* London. 1710.

Gosse, Edmund W, *Seventeenth-Century Studies. A contribution to The History of English Poetry.* London. 1883.

Granville, George, *The Dramatic Works of the Right Honourable George Granville, Lord Lansdowne.* Glasgow. MDCCLII.

Harding, S. and E., Published by, *The Biographical Mirrour.* London. Pall Mall. 1795.

Highfill, Philip H Jr. Burnim, Kalman A. and Langhans, Edward A., *A Biographical Dictionary of Actors, Actresses, Musicians, Dancers, Managers & Other Stage Personnel in London, 1660-1800.* 1973.

Hooker, Edward Niles, edited by, *The Critical Works of John Dennis.* Volume II. 1711-1729. Baltimore, The John Hopkins Press. 1943

Jacob, Giles, *The Poetical Register; or, the Lives and Characters of the English Dramatick Poets.* London. 1719.

Jones, Stephen, *Biographia Dramatica; or, A Companion to the Playhouse:...* Vol III. London. 1812.

Knapp, Andrew and Baldwin, William, *The Newgate Calendar:* Vol. II. 1825.

Latham, R and Matthews, W, Edited by, *The Diary Of Samuel Pepys*. A New And Complete Transcription. 1983.

Macaulay, Lord, *The History of England from the Accession of James the Second*. Volume. V. 1914.

Magalotti, Lorenzo, *Travels of Cosmo The Third, Grand Duke of Tuscany, through England. During the reign of King Charles the Second (1669)*. London. 1821.

Overcome, Sam. Vincent, Samuel. Dekker, Thomas, *The young gallant's academy; or, Directions how he should behave himself in all places and company as in an ordinary, in a play-house, in a tavern, as he passes along the street all hours of the night, and how to avoid constables interrogatories: to which is added, the character of a town-huff: together with the character of a right generous and well-bred gentleman, ca. 1572-1632*. London: Printed by J.C. for R. Mills… 1674.

Oxberry, W, of the Theatre Royal Drury-lane. *The Actor's Budget; consisting of Monologues, Prologues, Epilogues and Tales, Serious and Comic:…* London. 1820.

Serjeantson, The Rev. R.M. M.A., *A History of the Church of All Saints Northampton*. 1901.

Several Persons, *Prologue at Oxford. A Collection of Poems Written upon several Occasions…* London, Printed for Tho. Collins. 1673.

Seymour, Robert Esq., *Survey of the Cities of London and Westminster Borough of Southwark and parts adjacent*. Vol II. London. MDCCXXXV.

Steele, Sir Richard, *The Theatre…* London. MDCCXCI.

Summers, Montague, *The Restoration Theatre*. 1934.

The Works of the Earls of Rochester, Roscomon, and Dorset:… London. 1735.

Thornton, Thomas Esq., *The Works of Thomas Otway in three volumes…* Vol. III. 1813.

Unknown, *Authentick Memoirs of the Life of that celebrated Actress Mrs. Ann Oldfield. Containing a genuine Account of her Transactions from her Infancy to the time of her Decease…* The Fifth Edition. London. 1730.

Wilmot, John, *The Works of John Earl of Rochester…* Fourth Edition. London. 1732.

Wilson, Charles, *Memoirs of the Life, Writings, and Amours of William Congreve Esq*. London. 1730.

Wilson, John, *Court Satires of the Restoration*. Ohio State University Press. 1976.

Wivell, Abraham, *An inquiry into the History, Authenticity, & Characteristics of the Shakespeare Portraits...* London. 1827.

Wright, James, believed to be, *The Old English Drama. Vol. I.* London. MDCCCXXX.

Written and collected by several hands, *A Pacquet from Will's: Or a New Collection of Original Letters on several subjects;...* London. Printed for Sam. Briscoe, and sold by John Nutt near Stationers-Hall. 1701.

Appendix I

A pindarique ode, humbly offer'd to the Queen, on the victorious progress of Her Majesty's arms, under the conduct of the Duke of Marlborough. To which is prefix'd, a discourse on the pindarique ode. By Mr. Congreve: London: printed for Jacob Tonson, 1706.

http://name.umdl.umich.edu/004807842.0001.000

ODE.

I.
Daughter of Memory, Immortal Muse,
Calliope; what Poet wilt thou chuse
Of ANNA's Name to Sing?
To whom wilt thou thy Fire impart,
Thy Lyre, thy Voice, and tuneful Art;
Whom raise Sublime on thy Aetherial Wing,
And Consecrate with Dews of thy Castalian Spring?

II.
Without thy Aid, the most aspiring Mind
Must flag beneath, to narrow Flights confin'd,
Striving to rise in vain:
Nor e'er can hope with equal Lays
To celebrate bright Virtue's Praise.
Thy Aid obtain'd, even I, the humblest Swain,
May climb Pierian Heights, and quit the lowly Plain.

III.
High in the Starry Orb is hung,
And next Alcides Guardian Arm,
That Harp to which thy Orpheus Sung,

Who Woods, and Rocks, and Winds cou'd Charm.
That Harp which on Cyllenes shady Hill,
When first the Vocal Shell was found,
With more than Mortal Skill
Inventer Hermes taught to sound.
Hermes on bright Latona's Son,
By sweet Persuasion won,
The wond'rous Work bestow'd;
Latona's Son, to thine
Indulgent, gave the Gift Divine:
A God the Gift, a God th' Invention show'd.

I.
To that high-sounding Lyre I tune my Strains;
A lower Note his Lofty Song disdains
Who Sings of ANNA's Name.
The Lyre is struck! the Sounds I hear!
O Muse, propitious to my Pray'r!
O well known Sounds! O Melody, the same
That kindled Mantuan Fire, and rais'd Maeonian Flame!

II.
Nor are these Sounds to British Bards unknown,
Or sparingly reveal'd to one alone:
Witness sweet Spencer's Lays
And witness that Immortal Song,
As Spencer sweet, as Milton strong,
Which humble Boyn o'er Tiber's Flood cou'd raise,
And mighty William Sing, with well-proportion'd Praise.

III.
Rise, Fair Augusta, lift thy Head,
With Golden Tow'rs thy Front adorn;
Come forth, as comes from Tithon's Bed
With chearful Ray the ruddy Morn.
Thy lovely Form, and fresh reviving State,
In Crystal Flood of Thames survey;
Then bless thy better Fate,
Bless ANNA's most Auspicious Sway.

While distant Realms and neighb'ring Lands,
Arm'd Troops and hostile Bands
On ev'ry Side molest,
Thy happier Clime is Free,
Fair CAPITAL of Liberty!
And Plenty knows, and Days of Halcyon Rest.

I.

As Britain's Isle, when old vex'd Ocean roars,
Unshaken sees against her Silver Shoars
His foaming Billows beat;
So Britain's QUEEN, amidst the Jars
And Tumults of a World in Wars,
Fix'd on the Base of Her well-founded State,
Serene and safe looks down, nor feels the Shocks of Fate.

II.

But Greatest Souls, tho' blest with sweet Repose,
Are soonest touch'd with Sense of others Woes.
Thus ANNA's mighty Mind,
To Mercy and soft Pity prone,
And mov'd with Sorrows not her own,
Has all her Peace and downy Rest resign'd,
To wake for Common Good, and succour Human-kind.

III.

Fly, Tyranny, no more be known
Within Europa's blissful Bound;
Far as th' unhabitable Zone
Fly ev'ry hospitable Ground.
To horrid Zembla's Frozen Realms repair;
There with the baleful Beldam, NIGHT,
Unpeopl'd Empire share,
And rob those Lands of Legal Right.
For now is come the promis'd Hour,
When Justice shall have Pow'r;
Justice to Earth restor'd!
Again Astrea Reigns!
ANNA Her equal Scale maintains,
And MARLBRÔ wields Her sure deciding Sword.

I.

Now could'st thou soar, my Muse, to Sing the MAN
In Heights sublime, as when the Mantuan Swan
Her tow'ring Pinions spred;
Thou should'st of MARLBRÔ Sing, whose Hand
Unerring from his QUEEN's Command,
Far as the Seven-mouth'd Ister's secret Head,
To save th' Imperial State, Her hardy Britons led.

II.

Nor there thy Song should end; tho' all the Nine
Might well their Harps and Heav'nly Voices join
To Sing that Glorious Day,
When Bold Bavaria fled the Field,
And Veteran Gauls unus'd to yield,
On Blenheim's Plain imploring Mercy lay;
And Spoils and Trophies won, perplex'd the Victors way.

III.

But cou'd thy Voice of Blenheim Sing,
And with Success that Song pursue;
What Art cou'd Aid thy weary Wing
To keep the Victor still in view?
For as the Sun ne'er stops his radiant Flight,
Nor Sets, but with impartial Ray
To all who want his Light
Alternately transfers the Day:
So in the Glorious Round of Fame,
Great MARLBRÔ, still the same,
Incessant runs his Course;
To Climes remote, and near,
His Conq'ring Arms by turns appear,
And Universal is his Aid and Force.

I.

Attempt not to proceed, unwary Muse,
For O! what Notes, what Numbers could'st thou chuse,
Tho' in all Numbers skill'd;
To Sing the Hero's matchless Deed,
Which Belgia Sav'd, and Brabant Free'd;

To Sing Ramillia's Day! to which must yield
Cannae's Illustrious Fight, and Fam'd Pharsalia's Field.

II.
In the short Course of a Diurnal Sun,
Behold the Work of many Ages done!
What Verse such Worth can Raise?
Lustre and Life, the Poet's Art
To middle Vertue may impart;
But Deeds sublime, exalted high like These,
Transcend his utmost Flight; and mock his distant Praise.

III.
Still wou'd the willing Muse aspire,
With Transport still her Strains prolong;
But Fear unstrings the trembling Lyre,
And Admiration stops her Song.
Go on, Great Chief, in ANNA's Cause proceed;
Nor sheath the Terrors of thy Sword,
'Till Europe thou hast freed,
And Universal Peace restor'd.
This mighty Work when thou shalt End,
Equal Rewards attend,
Of Value far above
Thy Trophies and thy Spoils;
Rewards even Worthy of thy Toils,
Thy QUEEN's just Favour, and thy COUNTRY's Love

FINIS.

Appendix II

The Will of William Congreve

In the Name of God Amen This is the last Will of mee William Congreve of the parish of St Clement Danes Westminster in the County of Middlesex Esqr made the Twenty Sixth day of February Anno Dni 1725 and first I desire and direct that my Funerall shall be privately performed without the least Ostentation and the place where I referr to my Executor to appoint. I Give to the Severall persons herein after named the respective Legacyes following (That is to say) To

My intention is that the following Legacys be given to the respective persons herein named as if they were insert in the blank Spare left in this Will for that purpose Imprimis I give & bequeath to Ann Jellet twenty pounds a year during her life. Item to William Congreve Son to Coll: Willm Congreve of Highgate & my Godson three hundred pounds to Mrs Ann Congreve Daughter to my late Kinsman Coll: Ralph Congreve of Clarges Street two hundred pounds To Mrs Ann Bracegirdle of Howard Street two hundred pounds. to Mrs Frances Porter Fifty pounds Item to Mrs Deborah Rooke one hundred pounds with all my linnen and apparel for other less legacys I leave them as Specified in a Codicill enclosed in the duplicate of this Will & left in the Custody of the Dutchess of Marlborough.

All the rest and residue of my Estate the same consisting in personall things only (not having any Lands or other Reall Estate) I give and bequeath to the Dutchess of Marlborough the now Wife of Francis Earl of Godolphin of Godolphin in the County of Cornwall But not so as to vest in him the said Earl of Godolphin the Equitable right and Interest of such rest and residue But that the same & every part thereof and the Interest produce and benefitt thereof shall and may at all times from and after my Decease bee had and received by her the said Dutchess Namely Henrietta D^{ts} of Marlborough to her Sole and Separate use & wherewith her said Husband or any after taken Husband of her the said Dutchess of Marlborough shall not intermeddle or have any controuling power over nor shall the said rest and residue on the Interest and produce thereof bee lyable to the Debts and Incumbrances of the said Earl of Godolphin of any after taken Husband of her the said Dutchess of Marlborough in any Wise But shall be had and received Issued and payd as Shee the said Dutchess of Marlborough Shall by Writeing under her hand from time to time Direct and appoint and her owne acquittance shall bee a Sufficient discharge for all or any part of the Estate soe given to her as aforesaid and in confidence of the honesty and Justice of him the said Francis Earl of Godolphin I do hereby Constitute and Appoint him the Sole Executor of this my Will in Trust for his said Wife as aforesaid In Witness whereof I have hereunto Subscribed my name and Sett my Seale the day and yeare aforesaid Wm Congreve Signed Sealed and Declared by the said William Congreve the Testator to bee his last Will in the presence of us Timo: Hiplin Thos. Swan.

In the Name of God Amen This is the last Will of mee William Congreve of the parish of Saint Clement Danes Westminster in the County of Middlesex Esqr made the Twenty Sixth day of February Anno Dni 1725 and first I desire and direct that my Funerall shall be privately performed without the least ostentation and the place where I referr to my Executor to appoint. I give to the Severall persons hereinafter named the respective Legacyes following (that is to say) To

Legacys intended to be inserted in Blank Space of this Will and which I desire may be payd tho any thing should prevent my inserting them with my own hand in manner as I have filled up the other Blanks in the same Imprimis to Ann Jellet twenty pounds a year for her life Item to my Godson William Congreve son of Coll Wm Congreve of Highgate three hundred pounds Item to Ann Congreve daughter of the Late Coll Ralph Congreve of Clarges Street two hundred pounds Item to Mrs Ann Congreve her Mother & to Coll Willm Congreve of Highgate each twenty pounds Item to Mrs Ann Bracegirdle of Howard Street two hundred pounds Item to Mrs Deborah Rook one hundred pounds and all my wearing apparrel and Linnen of all sorts Item to Mrs Frances Porter fifty pounds Item to Peter Walter Esqr of St Margets Westminster twenty pounds Item to Richard Ld Viscount Cobham and Richard Ld Viscount Shannon twenty pounds each Item to Charles Mein Esqr and Mr Edward Porter and Mr Joshua White twelve pounds each Item to her Grace Henrietta Dutchess of Newcastle I give & bequeath the Dutchess of Marlbroughs picture by Kneller Item to the Lady Mary Godolphin youngest Daughter to the Dutchess of Marlborough I give & bequeath her Mothers picture Enamelld in Miniature together with my white brillant Diamond Ring Item to Coll Charles Churchill twenty pounds together with my gold headed Cane Item to all and each of my Domestic Servants a years Wages & proper Mourning Item to the poor of the parish ten pounds

All the rest and residue of my Estate the same consisting in personall things only (not having any Lands or other reall Estate) I Give and Bequeath to Henrietta Dutchess of Marlborough the now Wife of Francis Earl of Godolphin of Godolphin in the County of Cornwall But not Soe as to Vest in him the said Earl of Godolphin the Equitable right & Interest of such rest and residue But that the same and every part thereof and the Interest produce and benefit thereof shall and may att all times from and after my decease be had and received by her the said Dutchess of Marlborough to her Sole and Separate use and wherewith her said Husband or any after taken Husband of her the said Dutchess of Marlborough shall not intermeddle or have any controuleing power over nor shall the said rest and residue or the Interest and produce thereof bee lyable to the Debts and incumbrances of the said Earl of Godolphin or of any after taken Husband of her the said Dutchess of Marlborough in any wise But shall be had and received issued and payd as shee the said Dutchess of Marlborough shall by Writeing under her hand from time to time direct and appoint and her owne Acquittance shall be a Sufficient discharge for all or any part of the Estate soe given to her as aforesaid and in Confidence of the Honesty and Justice of him the said Francis Earl of Godolphin I doe hereby constitute and appoint him the Sole Executor of this my Will In Trust for his said Wife as aforesaid In Witness whereof I have hereunto subscribed my name and Sett my Seale the day and yeare aforesaid William Congreve Signed Sealed and Declared by the said William Congreve the Testator to bee his last Will in the presence of us William Humpstone George Thorpe Jonathan White

Whereas I William Congreve did by my last Will and Testament bearing date the Sixth day of February 1725 affix a Schedule of Legacys written in my own hand over a blank spare left for that purpose in the said Will I do hereby revoke and anull those Legacys excepting such as are bequeathed to persons related to me & bearing my own name as also what is therein Bequeathed to Mrs Ann Jellet and Mrs Ann Bracegirdle which said Legacys I do hereby Confirm & I do hereby revoke and anull all other Legacys therein mentioned or in the Counterpart of the said Will more at large set down which Counterpart is by me left in the Custody of her Grace Henrietta Dutchess of Marlborough my Sole Executrix as is Specified in the said Will and Counterpart thereof. be it understood that my intention is by this Writing to revoke those Legacys not herein Confirmed as above mentioned in such manner only as to leave them absolutely in the power and determination of the above named Henrietta Dutchess of Marlborough my Sole Executrix either to pay or refuse to pay them to take from them or add to them as she shall Judge the persons therein named especially my Domestic Servants therein mention'd or not mention'd may have Merited of me William Congreve Signed & Sealed in presence of Joseph Lee William Humpstone.

29 January 1728.

Which day appeared personally Thomas Snow of Saint Clements Danes in the County of Middlesex Goldsmith and John Paltock of the same parish Goldsmith and by virtue of their Oaths Deposed that they Severally knew and were well acquainted with William Congreve late of the parish of St Clements Danes in the County of Middlesex Esqr deceased and with his handwriting Character and manner of Writing having severall times seen him Write, and having seen and perused a Codicil annexed to the last Will and Testament of the said deceased beginning thus (my intention is that the following Legacys be given to the respective persons herein named) and ending thus (and left in the Custody of the Dutchess of Marlborough) and having also seen and perused another Codicil enclosd in the Duplicate of the said Will beginning thus (Legacys intended to be inserted in Blank Space of this Will) and ending thus (Item to the poor of the parish Ten pounds) these Deponents do beleive that the said Codicills and oath of them were totally wrote by and are the proper handwriting of the said William Congreve deceased... [*followed by four witnesses Tho Snow, John Paltock, G Saul and Tho: Tyllott, accompanied by Latin phrases.*]

Endnotes

Prologue

1. 'September 1642: Order for Stage-plays to cease.', in *Acts and Ordinances of the Interregnum*, 1642-1660, ed. C H Firth and R S Rait (London, 1911), pp. 26-27. *British History Online* www.british-history.ac.uk/no-series/acts-ordinances-interregnum/pp26-27 [accessed 22 December 2021].
2. *Some Seventeenth Century Allusions to Shakespeare and his Works Not Hitherto Collected*. London. 1920. p. 8.
3. *The Old English Drama. Vol. I*. London. MDCCCXXX. pp. xviii-xxi.

Part I: Mrs Elizabeth Barry (1658-1713)

Chapter One: Restoration Theatre and Its Environs

1. *The Rake Reform'd A Poem in a Letter to the Rakes of the Town*. By A.G. Gent. London. MDCCXVIII. pp. 11-13.
2. *The Third volume of the Works of Mr. Tho. Brown….London*. 1719. pp. 277-278.
3. *The Restoration Theatre* by Montague Summers, 1934, p.78.
4. *The Young King; or, The Mistake. As acted at the Duke's Theatre*. Written by Mrs. A. Behn. London. MDCXCVIII.
5. The Works of the Earls of Rochester, Roscomon, and Dorset:… London. 1735. pp. 47-48.
6. *Love given over; or, A Satyr against the pride, lust and inconstancy &c. of woman* Brown, Thomas, 1663-1704., Gould, Robert, d. 1709? London: Printed for R. Bentley and J. Tonson 1686. http://name.umdl.umich.edu/A41693.0001.001
7. *The young gallant's academy; or, Directions how he should behave himself in all places and company as in an ordinary, in a play-house, in a tavern, as he passes along the street all hours of the night, and how to avoid constables interrogatories: to which is added, the character of a*

185

town-huff: together with the character of a right generous and well-bred gentleman, by Sam. Overcome.Vincent, Samuel. Dekker, Thomas, ca. 1572-1632. London: Printed by J.C. for R. Mills...,1674. https://quod. lib.umich.edu/e/eebo2/A64976.0001.001/1:5.4?rgn=div2;view=toc

8. *Amusements Serious and Comical Calculated for the Meridian of London.* By Mr. Brown. London. 1700. pp. 48-50.

9. *Prologue at Oxford. A. Collection of Poems Written upon several Occasions By several Persons. London,* Printed for Tho. Collins. 1673. https://quod. lib.umich.edu/e/eebo/A33849.0001.001/1:82?rgn=div1;view=fulltext

10. *Travels of Cosmo The Third, Grand Duke of Tuscany, through England. During the reign of King Charles the Second* (1669), London. 1821. pp.190-191.

11. *Roger Bridgwater* (1694-1754). Susan Margaret Cooper. 2020. pp. 108-109.

12. *The Stage: A Poem. Inscrib'd to Joseph Addison, Esq;* by Mr. Webster, of Christ-Church, Oxon. London. 1713. pp. 22-24.

13. Project Gutenberg's *The Tatler, Volume 1, 1899*, by George A. Aitken.

14. *Thyestes a tragedy, translated out of Seneca to which is added mock-thyestes, in burlesque,* by F. W. Gent. Seneca, Lucius Annaeus, ca. 4 B.C.-65 A.D., J. W. fl. 1674. London : Printed by T. R. and N. T. for Allen Banks... :, 1674. https://quod.lib.umich.edu/e/eebo2/ A59185.0001.001?view=toc

15. *Dramatic Miscellanies:...* Thomas Davies, Dublin. Vol. III. M,DCC,LXXXIV. pp. 48-49.

16. *Dramatic Miscellanies:...* Thomas Davies, Dublin. Vol. III. M,DCC,LXXXIV. p. 182.

17. *London in the Eighteenth Century.* Sir Walter Besant. 1901. p. 343.

18. *Biographia Dramatica; or, A Companion to the Playhouse...* Vol. III. London, 1812. pp. 249-250.

Chapter Two: Mrs Barry's Roots

1. *A Biographical Dictionary of Actors, Actresses, Musicians, Dancers, Managers & Other Stage Personnel in London, 1660-1800.* Philip H. Highfill, Jr., Kalman A. Burnim, and Edward A. Langhans. Volume 4. Corye to Dynion. p. 166.

2. *The Restoration Theatre* by Montague Summers, 1934, p.319.

3. *The Restoration Theatre* by Montague Summers, 1934, p.317.

4. *The Works of Thomas Otway in three volumes...* Vol. III. Thomas Thornton, Esq. 1813. p.320.

Chapter Three: Would She Make an Actress?

1. *An Apology for the Life of Mr. Colley Cibber, Comedian, and late patentee of the Theatre-Royal: with an historical view of the stage during his own time.* Colley Cibber. 1740. p. 94.
2. *The history of the English stage, from the Restauration to the Present Time…* Thomas Betterton. London,. 1741. pp. 14-15.
3. *The Works of John Earl of Rochester…* Fourth Edition. London. 1732. pp. 164-165.

Chapter Four: The Famous Mrs Barry

1. Shadwell, Thomas, *The Squire of Alsatia…* The Third edition, (London: For James Knapton, 1692) http://access.bl.uk/item/viewer/ark:/81055/vdc_100043379954.0x000001
2. *The Life of Mr. Thomas Betterton, The late Eminent Tragedian….* London. 1710. pp.7-9.
3. *The Critical Works of John Dennis* edited by Edward Niles Hooker. Volume II. 1711-1729. Baltimore, The John Hopkins Press. 1943. p.248.
4. *A Biographical Dictionary of Actors, Actresses, Musicians, Dancers, Managers & Other Stage Personnel in London*, 1660-1800. Philip H. Highfill, Jr., Kalman A. Burnim, and Edward A. Langhans. Volume 1. Abaco to Belfille. p.315.
5. *The History of the English Stage, from the Restauration to the Present Time…* Thomas Betterton. London,. 1741. pp. 53-54.
6. *Some Passages of the Life and Death of the Right Honourable John Earl of Rochester, Who died the 26th of July, 1680.* Written by his own Direction on his Death-Bed, by Gilbert Burnet, D.D. London. 1660. p. 158.
7. *Extract from a pamphlet,* All Saints Church, Spelsbury. Copyright Incumbent and Parochial Church Council of the Parish Church of Spelsbury, 2005

Chapter Five: Not a Very United Company

1. *An Apology for the Life of Mr. Colley Cibber, Comedian, and Late Patentee of the Theatre-Royal.* Written By Himself. London. 1740. pp. 72-73.

2. *Dramatic Miscellanies...* by Thomas Davies Vol III Dublin. 1784. p. 201.
3. Crown, *Darius King of Persia. A tragedy, etc,* (London: R. Bentley, 1688) <http://access.bl.uk/item/viewer/ark:/81055/vdc_00000002A6AE>
4. *A Biographical Dictionary of Actors, Actresses, Musicians, Dancers, Managers & Other Stage Personnel in London,* 1660-1800. Philip H. Highfill, Jr., Kalman A. Burnim, and Edward A. Langhans. Volume 1. Abaco to Belfille. p.319.

Chapter Six: Nice and Settled at Lincoln's Inn Fields

1. *The Poetical Register; or, the Lives and Characters of the English Dramatick Poets....*London. 1719. p.43.
2. Etherege, George, *The Man of Mode: or, Sr. Fopling Flutter.* A comedy. By Sir George Etherege, (London, Great Britain: printed in the year, 1711) <http://access.bl.uk/item/viewer/ark:/81055/vdc_100045967832.0x000001>
3. *The Dramatic Works of the Right Honourable George Granville, Lord Lansdowne.* Glasgow. MDCCLII.
4. *The Dramatic Works of the Right Honourable George Granville, Lord Lansdowne.* Glasgow. MDCCLII.
5. *The Library Chronicle of the Friends of the University of Pennsylvania Library.* Volume XVI. Fall 1949 – Summer 1950.

Chapter Seven: Fame Brings Its Price

1. *The Posthumous Works of Mr. Samuel Butler, (Author of Hudibras). Written in the time of the Grand Rebellion, and in the reign of King Charles II. Being a collection of satire, speeches, and reflections upon those times.* 3rd edition, London. MDCCXXX. pp. 121-122.
2. *Court Satires of the Restoration.* John Harold Wilson. Ohio State University Press. 1976. p.78.
3. *Court Satires of the Restoration.* John Harold Wilson. Ohio State University Press. 1976. pp.220-221.
4. *Letters and related papers re: will of Anne Lee, deceased, who has left her estate to her husband Thomas Wharton.* 1685-1686. Oxfordshire History Centre. E36/18/6/W/1.
5. *Indenture.* Copy of Deed to lead uses of a fine dated 4th May 1685. A/CSC/1512. London Metropolitan Archives.

6. *Seventeenth-Century Studies. A contribution to The History of English Poetry.* By Edmund W. Gosse. London. 1883. p. 278.

7. https://crrs.ca/new/wp-content/uploads/2012/11/OV17-Staging-Islam.pdf pp. 46-46

8. *Measure for measure; or, Beauty the best advocate as it is acted at the theatre in Lincolns-Inn-Fields: written originally by Mr. Shakespear, and now very much alter'd, with additions of several entertainments of musick.* https://quod.lib.umich.edu/e/eebo/A59508.0001.001/1:5?rgn=div1;view=fulltext

9. *Some Account of the English Stage, from the Restoration in 1660 to 1830.* Vol. II. Bath. 1832. pp. 463-464.

10. *An Apology for the Life of Mr. Colley Cibber, Comedian, and Late Patentee of the Theatre-Royal.* Written By Himself. London. 1740. pp. 93-95.

11. *The history of the English stage, from the Restauration to the Present Time...* Thomas Betterton. London,. 1741. pp. 21-22.

12. *The history of the English stage, from the Restauration to the Present Time...* Thomas Betterton. London,. 1741. pp. 22-23.

13. *A Biographical Dictionary of Actors, Actresses, Musicians, Dancers, Managers & Other Stage Personnel in London, 1660-1800.* Philip H. Highfill, Jr., Kalman A. Burnim, and Edward A. Langhans. Volume 2. Belfort to Byzand. p. 261.

14. *Court Satires of the Restoration.* John Harold Wilson. Ohio State University Press. 1976. p. 206.

Chapter Eight: Mrs Barry's Latter Stage Years

1. 'The Haymarket Opera House', in *Survey of London: Volumes 29 and 30, St James Westminster, Part 1*, ed. F H W Sheppard (London, 1960), pp. 223-250. British History Online www.british-history.ac.uk/survey-london/vols29-30/pt1/pp223-250 [accessed 22 December 2021].

2. Vanbrugh, John, *The Confederacy, etc,* (London: J. & R. Tonson, 1751)<http://access.bl.uk/item/viewer/ark:/81055/vdc_100025260313.0x000001>

3. *Literary Relics: Containing Original Letters...By* George-Monck Berkeley, Esq. London. MDCCLXXXIX. p. 342.

4. *A Pacquet from Will's: Or a New Collection of Original Letters on several subjects;...* Written and collected by several hands. London.

Printed for Sam. Briscoe, and sold by John Nutt near Stationers-Hall, 1701. pp.42-43.

5. *A Pacquet from Will's: Or a New Collection of Original Letters on several subjects;...* Written and collected by several hands. London. Printed for Sam. Briscoe, and sold by John Nutt near Stationers-Hall, 1701. pp. 43-45.

6. *A Pacquet from Will's: Or a New Collection of Original Letters on several subjects;...* Written and collected by several hands. London. Printed for Sam. Briscoe, and sold by John Nutt near Stationers-Hall, 1701. pp. 46-48.

7. *Letters upon several occasions written by and between Mr. Dryden, Mr. Wycherly, Mr.----, Mr. Congreve, and Mr. Dennis, published by Mr. Dennis with a new translation of select letters of Monsieur Voiture.* London: Printed for Sam. Briscoe, 1696. pp.24-27 https://quod.lib. umich.edu/e/eebo/A35671.0001.001?view=toc

8. *A Pacquet from Will's: Or a New Collection of Original Letters on several subjects;...* Written and collected by several hands. London. Printed for Sam. Briscoe, and sold by John Nutt near Stationers-Hall, 1701. pp. 49-50.

9. Project Gutenberg's *The Tatler,* Volume 1, 1899, by George A. Aitken

10. *Survey of the Cities of London and Westminster Borough of Southwark and parts adjacent* – Robert Seymour Esq., Vol II. London. M,DCC,XXXV. p. 583.

11. *An inquiry into the History, Authenticity, & Characteristics of the Shakespeare Portraits,...* London 1827. pp.47-48.

12. *Will of Mary Betterton, Widow of Saint Martin in the Fields, Middlesex.* 10 March 1711. PROB 11/526/281. The National Archives.

13. *An Apology for the Life of Mr. Colley Cibber, Comedian, and late patentee of the Theatre-Royal: with an historical view of the stage during his own time.* Colley Cibber. 1740. p. 96.

Chapter Nine: A Welcome Retirement But a Tragic Death

1. Diane K Bolton, Patricia E C Croot and M A Hicks, 'Acton: Growth', in *A History of the County of Middlesex: Volume 7, Acton, Chiswick, Ealing and Brentford, West Twyford,* Willesden, ed. T F T Baker and C R Elrington (London, 1982), pp. 7-14. *British History Online* www.british-history. ac.uk/vch/middx/vol7/pp7-14 [accessed 22 December 2021].

2. *Will of Elizabeth Barry, Spinster.* 07 November 1713. PROB 11/536/276. The National Archives.

3. *Will of Elizabeth Barry, Spinster.* 07 November 1713. PROB 11/536/276. The National Archives.

4. *Will of Richard Barrow, Gentleman of King Street Saint James, Middlesex.* 30 December 1723. Reference: PROB 11/594/414. The National Archives.

5. *The Biographical Mirrour.* London. Published by S. and E. Harding, Pall Mall. 1795. p. 30.

PART II: Mrs Anne Bracegirdle (1671-1748)

Chapter Ten: Unlocking Anne's Ancestry

1. *The state of Northampton from the beginning of the fire Sept. 20th 1675 to Nov. 5th represented in a letter to a friend in London and now recommended to all well disposed persons in order to Christian-charity and speedy relief for the said distressed town and people.* Pearse, Edward, 1631-1694. https://quod.lib.umich.edu/e/eebo2/A56816.0001.001/1:3?rgn=div1;view=fulltext

2. *A History of the Church of All Saints Northampton* – The Rev. R.M. Serjeantson, M.A. 1901 Northampton pp.323- 324.

3. Sourced from Northamptonshire Records Office.

4. Proceedings of the Society of Antiquities of London. November 17, 1870, to April 3, 1873. Second Series, Vol. V. p. 461.

5. *Reports from Commissioners Charities* Vol XII 1826. p. 280.

Chapter Eleven: The Play House, Anne's New Home

1. *The History of England from the Accession of James the Second.* By Lord Macaulay. Volume. V. 1914. pp.2268-2270.

2. *The History of England from the Accession of James the Second.* By Lord Macaulay. Volume. V. 1914. p. 2266.

Chapter Twelve: Fresh-faced Anne Bracegirdle, the Darling of the Stage

1. *Congreve, William, The Old Bachelor...* The seventh edition, (London: R. W, 1707) <http://access.bl.uk/item/viewer/ark:/81055/vdc_100086416886.0x000001>

2. *The Newgate Calendar:* by Andrew Knapp and William Baldwin. Vol. II. 1825. p. 15.

Chapter Thirteen: A Happy Company at Lincoln's Inn Fields

1. *Literary Relics: Containing Original Letters*...By George-Monck Berkeley, Esq. London. MDCCLXXXIX. pp. 325-327.
2. *Literary Relics: Containing Original Letters*...By George-Monck Berkeley, Esq. London. MDCCLXXXIX. p. 374.
3. *Literary Relics: Containing Original Letters*...By George-Monck Berkeley, Esq. London. MDCCLXXXIX. p. 378.
4. *Memoirs of the Life, Writings, and Amours of William Congreve Esq.* Charles Wilson. London. 1730. Preface p. 13.
5. *Memoirs of the Life, Writings, and Amours of William Congreve Esq.* Charles Wilson. London. 1730. Preface p. 11.
6. *Tragedy Queens of the Georgian Era* (1908). John Fyvie pp. 26.
7. *The Third Volume of the Works of Mr. Tho. Brown. Being Amusements...* London. 1719. p. 39.
8. *Love's a Jest. A Comedy, as it is Acted at the New Theatre In Little-Lincolns Inn-Fields*...London. MDCXCVI.
9. *Love's a Jest. A Comedy, as it is Acted at the New Theatre In Little-Lincolns Inn-Fields*...London. MDCXCVI.
10. *Love's a Jest. A Comedy, as it is Acted at the New Theatre In Little-Lincolns Inn-Fields*...London. MDCXCVI.
11. *A Biographical Dictionary of Actors, Actresses, Musicians, Dancers, Managers & Other Stage Personnel in London, 1660-1800.* Philip H. Highfill, Jr., Kalman A. Burnim, and Edward A. Langhans. Volume 2. Belfort to Byzand. p. 201.
12. Motteux, Peter Anthony, *The Loves of Mars and Venus, etc,* (1697) <http://access.bl.uk/item/viewer/ark:/81055/vdc_100026356857.0x000001>
13. Congreve, William, *The Mourning Bride, etc,* ([The Hague]: T. Johnson, 1711) <http://access.bl.uk/item/viewer/ark:/81055/vdc_100022850911.0x000001>
14. The Lives and Characters of the English Dramatick Poets....London. 1719. pp. 43-44
15. Congreve, William, *The Mourning Bride, etc,* ([The Hague]: T. Johnson, 1711) <http://access.bl.uk/item/viewer/ark:/81055/vdc_100022850911.0x000001>

16. *The Provok'd Wife a comedy, as it is acted at the new theatre in Little Lincolns-Inn-Fields* 1697, by Sir JohnVanbrugh. https://quod.lib. umich.edu/e/eebo/A65060.0001.001/1:5?rgn=div1;view=fulltext

17. *Biographia Dramatica; or, A Companion to the Playhouse:...* Vol III. London. 1812. pp. 184-185.

18. *A Short View of the Immorality and Profaneness of the English Stage...* Jeremy Collier, M.A. London. MDCXCIX. p. 57.

19. *A Short View of the Immorality and Profaneness of the English Stage...* Jeremy Collier, M.A. London. MDCXCIX. pp. 58-60.

20. *Amendments of M. Collier's false and imperfect citations, &c. from the Old batchelour, Double dealer, Love for love, Mourning bride, by the author of those plays.* Congreve, William, 1670-1729. London:Printed for J. Tonson,1698. http://name.umdl.umich.edu/A34297.0001.001

21. *Dramatic Miscellanies...* by Thomas Davies Vol III Dublin. 1784. pp. 260-261.

22. *A Short View of the Immorality and Profaneness of the English Stage...* Jeremy Collier, M.A. London. MDCXCIX. pp.7-9.

23. *Faithful Memoirs of the Life, Amours and Performances, of That justly celebrated, and most eminent actress of her Time, Mrs. Anne Oldfield....* William Egerton Esq. London. MDCCXXXI. p.2.

24. Fletcher, John, *The pilgrim, a comedy: as it is acted at the Theatre-Royal in Drury-Lane. Written originally by Mr. Fletcher: and now very much alter'd, with several additions. Likewise a prologue, epilogue, dialogue and masque:* written by... Mr. Dryden, (Dublin: printed by A. Rhames for W. Smith,1724) <http://access.bl.uk/item/viewer/ark:/81055/vdc_100038615624.0x000001>

25. *Wit and Mirth: or Pills to Purge Melancholy...* Vol. II London. 1719. pp. 126-127.

Chapter Fourteen: A Discomforting Rival

1. *Literary Relics: Containing Original Letters...*By George-Monck Berkeley, Esq. London. MDCCLXXXIX. pp. 348-349.

2. *Authentick Memoirs of the Life of that celebrated Actress Mrs. Ann Oldfield...* The Fifth Edition... London. 1730. pp. 21-22.

3. *Literary Relics: Containing Original Letters...*By George-Monck Berkeley, Esq. London. MDCCLXXXIX. pp.332-334.

4. *On Mrs Brasgirle.* Anonymous undated poem. University of Nottingham. Manuscripts and Special Collections. Pw V 1255.

5. Molloy, Charles, *The half-pay officers : a comedy: as it is acted by His Majesty's servants*, (London: 1720) <http://access.bl.uk/item/viewer/ark:/81055/vdc_100022695770.0x000001>

6. *The Funniest Jest Book in the World, being a superior collection of all the Well-Seasoned Jests, Curious Relations, Strange Stories, Sprightly Sayings, Droll Doings, Funny Tales, Witticisms, Epigrams and Recitations.* Liverpool. 1847. p.5.

7. *The Actor's Budget; consisting of Monologues, Prologues, Epilogues and Tales, Serious and Comic:...* by W. Oxberry, of the Theatre Royal Drury-lane. London. 1820. p. 177.

8. *Philips, Ambrose, The Distrest Mother* : A tragedy. By Mr. Amb. Philips, (London, Great Britain: printed for T. Caslon, T. Lowndes, W. Nicoll, and S. Bladon, 1767) <http://access.bl.uk/item/viewer/ark:/81055/vdc_100036710441.0x000001>

Chapter Fifteen: A Long and Happy Retirement with the Inevitable Consequence

1. *Will of Anne Bracegirdle, Spinster of Saint Clement Danes, Middlesex.* 12 September 1748. PROB 11/764/361. The National Archives.

2. *Will of Anne Bracegirdle, Spinster of Saint Clement Danes, Middlesex.* 12 September 1748. PROB 11/764/361. The National Archives.

3. *St Clement Danes, Pauper Settlement, Vagrancy and Bastardy Examinations.* London Lives, 1690-1800, LL ref: WCCDEP358180293 3rd November 1742 – 15th October 1745 (www.londonlives.org,), Westminster Archives Centre, Image 293 of 391.19th February 1745

4. *Register Book of marriages. Parish of St George, Hanover Square, County of Middlesex.* John H Chapman. Vol I. 1725-1787. London. p. 40.

5. *Will of Martha Grimbaldeston, Widow of Saint Luke Old Street, Middlesex.* 15 November 1793. PROB 11/1238/209. The National Archives.

6. *City of London Sessions: Sessions Papers – Justices' Working Documents. 26th September 1751 – 8th December 1752* LL ref: LMSLPS150630118. (www.londonlives.org,) London Metropolitan Archives. Image 118 of 213. 19th June 1752

7. *Parish of St Sepulchre, Middlesex, London.* London Metropolitan Archives.

8. *Tragedy Queens of the Georgian Era.* John Fyvie. London. 1908. pp. 32-33.

9. *"Their Majesties Servants" or Annals of The English Stage....*by Dr. Doran, F.S.A., London. 1865. p. 60.

10. *An Apology for the Life of Mr. Colley Cibber, Comedian, and late patentee of the Theatre-Royal: with an historical view of the stage during his own time.* Colley Cibber. 1740. pp.100-102.

Index

People

Addison, Joseph, 2, 7, 20, 24, 186

Anne, Countess of Rochester, 57, 58, 63

Anne, Princess, Royal Highness, 126, 128

Anne, Queen, 83-85, 128

Arbuthnot, Dr John, 116, 126

Aston, Anthony, 34, 99, 118

Ballam, Gabriel, Gent, 73-79, 87, 167

Ballam, Jonadab, 73

Ballam, Patience, 73

Banks, John, 35

Barrow, Richard, 87-89, 191

Barry, Edward, 29-31

Barry, Mrs Elizabeth, xv, 2, 24, 29-32, 34-37, 41-43, 45, 46, 48, 49, 51-54, 57-73, 79-91, 102, 103, 109, 110, 112, 113, 123, 124, 129, 132, 137, 141, 150, 161, 164-167, 190, 191

Barry, Robert Esq., 29-31

Beaumont, Francis, 72, 132, 148

Behn, Aphra, 7, 35, 43, 44, 83, 103, 141, 185

Berkeley, James, 3rd Earl of Berkeley, 150

Betterton, Mary [formerly Saunderson], 37, 82-85, 102, 103, 164, 190

Betterton, Thomas, 23, 25, 29, 31, 32, 37, 39-41, 43, 53, 54, 56, 58, 64, 65, 70, 71, 79-83, 85, 102, 103, 124, 144, 146, 150, 163, 164, 187, 189

Blackmore, Sir Richard, 125, 126

Bowtell, Elizabeth [Boutell], 67-69, 103

Bowman, John [Bowen], 53, 119, 121-123, 142

Bracegirdle Grimbaldeston, Ann [later Anderson], 158-160, 167

Bracegirdle, Mrs Anne, xv, 2, 53, 58, 79-81, 84, 87, 90, 91, 94, 99, 100, 102-104, 106, 107, 110, 111, 113-119, 123, 124, 129, 132, 137, 141, 144, 146-150, 156-158, 161-167, 181-183, 194

Bracegirdle, Elizabeth [Anne's sister], 99

Bracegirdle, Frances [Anne's sister], 99, 148

Bracegirdle, Hamlett [Anne's brother], 94, 99, 158

Bracegirdle, Honnor [Anne's sister], 99

Bracegirdle, John [Anne's brother], 99

Bracegirdle, Justinian [Anne's brother], 99

Bracegirdle, Justinian [Anne's nephew], 156, 160, 161

Bracegirdle, Justinian [Brastgerdle] [Anne's father], 98, 99, 102, 117, 118

Bracegirdle, Justinian [Rector], 99, 100

Bracegirdle, Martha [Anne's sister], 99

Bracegirdle, Martha [nee Furnis] [Anne's mother], 98, 117

Bridgwater, Roger, 17, 186

Brown, Thomas, 5, 7, 10, 12, 83, 118

Burgess, Captain Elizeus, 5

Carey, Henry, 153

Cary, John Esq, 63

Catherine, Queen, xi

Centlivre, Susanna [Susanna Carroll], 59, 144

Charles I, King, x, xi, 29, 37

Charles II, King [also Prince Charles], viii, x, xi, xv, 7, 23, 24, 35, 37, 46, 84, 94, 123, 150, 152, 188

Churchill, Charles [Charles's father], 154

Churchill, Colonel Charles, 182

Churchill, John, 1st Duke of Marlborough, 7, 155, 176

Churchill, Lieutenant General Charles, 154

Churchill, Sarah, Duchess of Marlborough, 71

Chute, Mr, 161

Cibber, Colley, 24-26, 46, 66, 67, 72, 82, 85, 86, 136, 137, 139, 161, 162, 187, 189, 190, 195

Cibber, Theophilus, 161

Clerke, Elizabeth, 36

Cochrane, John, 4th Earl of Dundonald, 89

Cochrane, Lady Anne, 89

Collier, Jeremy, 74, 75, 131-137, 139, 193

Congreve, Mary [nee Browning], 113

Congreve, Colonel William, 113

Congreve, William, 24, 53, 65, 70, 72, 75, 90, 103, 109, 113-118, 124-126, 128, 131-133, 136, 145, 147-149, 164, 166, 167, 182, 190-193

Cosimo III, Prince, of Tuscany, 15

Cromwell, Oliver, Protector, viii, x, 94

Cromwell, Richard, viii

Crowne, John, 51, 112

Curll, Edmund, 29, 30, 116, 165

Custis, John, 87, 88, 90

D'Urfey, Thomas, 14, 82, 131, 132, 140, 142

Davenant, John, x

Davenant, Lady Mary [Lady D'Avenant], 30, 31, 58, 164

Davenant, Sir William [William D'Avenant], x-xiv, 30, 37, 54, 83

Davers, Sir Robert, 2nd Baronet, 149

Dekker, Thomas, 11, 186

Dennis, John, 41, 58, 64, 75-78, 187, 190

Dering, Charles, 57

Digby, John Esq, 149

Doggett, Thomas, 53, 84

Douglas, James, 4th Duke of Hamilton and 1st Duke of Brandon KG KT, 106

Dryden, John, 3, 46, 54, 56, 66, 67, 73, 78, 81, 85, 131, 138, 139, 164, 190, 193
Du Tremblay, Henrietta Maria, 30

Eccles, John, 114, 121, 142
Edward IV, King, 111
Elizabeth, Countess of Sandwich, 88
Estcourt, Sir William, 57
Etherege, Sir 'gentle' George, 41, 57, 188

Fane, Charles Fane, 1st Viscount Fane, 5
Fane, Henry Bourchier, 5
Farquhar, George, 145
Fenton, Elijah, 17
Fielding, Beau, 27
Finger, Gottfried [Godfrey], 114, 123
Flecknoe, Richard, ix, 2
Fletcher, John, xi, 48, 72, 132, 139, 193
Frier, Leonard, 150
Fryer, Margaret [Peg] [nee Hall] [later Mrs Vandenvelden], 150-153
Fulwood, Mr, 27

Gay, John, 126
George I, King, 71, 118
George, Prince of Denmark and Norway, Duke of Cumberland, 57
Gildon, Charles, 64, 65
Godolphin, Francis, 2nd Earl of Godolphin, 181-183
Godolphin, Henrietta, 2nd Duchess of Marlborough, 113, 115, 181-184
Godolphin, Lady Mary, 113, 182

Goring, Henry, 57
Gosse, Sir Edmund William CB, 63, 64, 189
Gould, Robert, 9, 10, 31, 165, 185
Granville, George, 1st Baron Lansdowne, 52, 54, 55, 188
Grimbaldeston, John, 158, 159
Grimbaldeston, Martha [nee Bracegirdle], 156-160
Gwyn, Nell [Eleanor] [Pretty, witty, Nellie], xv, 64, 103, 164

Halifax, Lord, 117
Hall, Isaac, 150
Hamilton, James, 5th Duke of Hamilton, 89
Harley, Robert, 1st Earl of Oxford and Earl Mortimer, 126
Hart, Charles, 39-41, 164
Hawker, Thomas, 87
Hawker, Mrs, 87
Henry I, King, 111
Henry, Matthew, 126
Hill, Captain Richard, 104, 105
Hogarth, William, 111, 112
Howe, Ruperta [Hughes], xv
Hughes, Margaret [Peg], xv

Jacob, Giles, 141
James I, King, xi
James II, King [also James Duke of York], xiii, 35, 121
Jeffreys, Judge George, 1st Baron Jeffreys, 57

Keally, Joseph, 72, 114, 115, 145, 147-149
Keck, Robert, 83
Killigrew, Sir Robert, xi

Killigrew, Thomas Esq, x, xi, xiii, xiv, 13, 41
King, Mr, 26
Kneller, Sir Godfrey, 1st Baronet, 89, 182
Kynaston, Edward, xi, 37, 39-41, 46-48
Kynaston, Reverend, 48

Lambe, Henry, 89
Lambe, Anne, 89
Lee, Anne, 63, 188
Lee, Edward Henry, 1st Earl of Lichfield, 63
Lee, John, 46
Lee, Nathaniel, 46, 67
Leke, Robert, 3rd Earl of Scarsdale, 117, 149, 150
Leveson, Sir William, 52
Lewis, Mary, 149
Locke, John, 126

Magalotti, Count Lorenzo, 15
Malet, Elizabeth, 35
Manley, Delarivier, 64
Mann, Horace, 161
Mary, of Modena, Duchess of York, 35
Maynwaring, Arthur, 154
Meggs, Mary [Orange Moll], 13
Milton, John, x
Mohun, Charles, 4th Baron Mohun, 104-107, 109
Molloy, Charles Esq, 151, 152, 194
Molyneux, William, 126
Monck, General George, 1st Duke of Albemarle, 37
Montagu, Edward Richard, Viscount Hinchingbrooke, 88, 89

Montagu, Edward, 3rd Earl of Sandwich, 88
Motteux, Peter Anthony [Pierre Antoine], 119, 121, 123, 192
Mountfort, Edward [Susanna's son], 109
Mountfort, Elizabeth [Susanna's daughter], 109
Mountfort, Mary [Susanna's daughter], 109
Mountfort, Susanna [Susanna's daughter], 109
Mountfort, Susanna [nee Percival] [later Verbruggen], 109, 112
Mountfort, William, 103-105, 107
Murray, Anne, 89

Nichol, Mr, 84
Norton, Ambrose Esq, 149
Nosworthy, Edward, 57

Oldfield, Anne, 27, 103, 136, 137, 145, 146, 153-156, 161, 167, 193
Orrery, Earl of, 35
Otway, Capt. Thomas, 7, 32, 33, 42, 65, 66, 102, 146, 164, 186
Overton, Abigail [nee Stackhouse], 87, 88
Overton, Philip, 88

Page, Baron, 88
Page, Mr, 105
Parker, Elizabeth, 157, 158
Parnell, Thomas, 126
Payne, Henry Nevil, 3
Pearse, Edward, 94, 191
Pepys, Samuel, xi, 16, 20, 22, 23, 25, 46, 47
Percival, Mr, 108

Philips, Ambrose, 153, 194
Pix, Mary, 141, 142
Pope, Alexander, 126, 155
Porter, Edward, 148, 149, 182
Porter, Frances, 181, 182
Purcell, Daniel, 114
Purcell, Henry, 108, 109, 114

Radd, Mrs, 104
Rhodes, John, 37
Rich, Christopher, 51, 53, 70, 112, 113, 145
Rich, Mrs John, 17
Rocque, John [Jean], 148
Rosco, James, 17
Rowe, Nicholas, 72, 117, 118
Rupert, Prince of the Rhine, Count Palatine, Duke of Cumberland, xv

Sackville, Charles, 6th Earl of Dorset, 10, 38, 53
Salisbury, Bishop of, 42
Sayer, James, 88
Sayer, Mary [formerly Overton], 88, 167
Sedley, Sir Charles, 5th Baronet, 47, 48
Settle, Elkanah, 107
Shadwell, Thomas, 38, 103, 187
Shakespeare, William, ix, x, 64, 80, 83, 85, 132, 185, 189, 190
Slingsby, Lady Mary, 46
Slingsby, Sir Charles, 46
Smith, Anthony M.A., 73, 74
Southerne, Thomas, 42, 109
St. John, Henry, 4th Baronet, 1st Viscount, 54, 56, 57, 61
St. John, Henry, 1st Viscount Bolingbroke, 126

Steele, Sir Richard, 2, 17 18, 20, 24, 78
Stewart, Frances [nee Howard], Duchess of Lennox and Richmond, Countess of Hertford, x
Stonehouse, Francis, 57
Swift, Jonathan, 7, 126

Underhill, Cave, 53, 121
Unwin, William, 73

Vanbrugh, Giles, 71
Vanbrugh, Sir John, 70, 71, 103, 113, 129-132, 136, 139, 145, 155, 189
Vandenvelden, John Baptist, 150
Verbruggen, John Baptista, 64, 109
Vincent, Samuel [Sam. Overcome], 11, 186
Voss, Mrs, 145

Walpole, Horace, 118, 161, 167
Walsh, William, 150
Watts, Isaac, 126
Webb, Edmund, 57
Weldon, John, 114
Wharton, Thomas, 1st Marquess of Wharton, 62, 63, 188
William III, King [William of Orange], 5, 54, 71
William, Prince, Duke of Gloucester, 128
Wilmot, John, 2nd Earl of Rochester [Lord Rochester], xi, 8, 34-36, 41-46, 48, 57, 58, 61, 63, 68, 88, 90, 165, 166, 185, 187
Wilmot, Mallet, Lady Lisburne, 58, 59, 167

Wilson, Charles Esq, 115, 116
Wolseley, Robert, 48
Wycherley, William, 65, 77,
    164, 190

Theatres
Cockpit, Drury Lane, 37
Dorset Garden Theatre, 32, 35, 37,
    39-43, 45, 70, 102, 114, 120
Duke's Theatre, xi, 7, 23, 37,
    38, 40, 41, 46, 57, 102, 103,
    122, 185
King's Theatre, xi, 15, 20, 37,
    39-41, 46, 47, 103
Lincoln's Inn Fields Theatre, 27,
    37, 39, 40, 53, 54, 56, 58, 59,
    70, 76, 113, 119, 124, 125, 128,
    130, 141, 144, 189, 192, 193
Queen's Theatre, Haymarket, 70,
    72, 79, 85, 144, 145
Theatre Royal, Drury Lane, 13,
    17, 20, 25, 27, 39, 46, 57, 70,
    72, 79, 103, 111, 112, 123,
    139, 145, 151, 187, 189, 190,
    193-195

Churches
All Saints, Northampton, 94, 98,
    101, 191
All Saints, Spelsbury, 45, 187
St Andrew's, Great Billing, 99
St Clement Danes, Westminster,
    46, 105, 108, 109, 148, 156-158,
    181, 182, 184, 194
St George the Martyr,
    Southwark, 112
St Giles, Cripplegate, London, 150
St Giles, Northampton, 94, 99
St James Duke's Place,
    London, 150

St James Garlickhythe, x
St James, Gretton,
    Northamptonshire, 99
St Martin-in-the-Fields,
    London, 109
St Mary's, Acton, 89
St Marylebone, Westminster,
    158, 159
St Olave's, Southwark, 73
St Saviour, Southwark, 73
St Sepulchre, 101

Places
Acton, 86, 89, 91, 167, 190
Acton Wells, 86
Bartholomew Fair, 111
Bedlam Hospital, Moorfields, 46
Church Brampton, 100
Covent Garden, 2, 27, 48, 73, 74,
    76, 112
Drury Lane, 2, 21, 27, 105
Howard Street, Strand 104, 113,
    146-148, 156, 158, 159,
    181, 182
Newbury, 72, 73, 87, 166, 167
Northampton, 94-99, 101, 117,
    118, 191
Priory of the Hospital of
    St. Bartholomew, 111
Saracen's Head, Northampton 118
Southwark, 73, 190
Southwark Fair, 111
St James's Park, 48
St Margaret's Westminster, 149
Town Mills, Newbury, 72, 88, 167

Plays
Alcibiades, 32
Amorous Widow; or, The Wanton
    Wife, The, 146

Aureng-zebe, 3, 22
Biter, The, 72
Careless Husband, The, 72
Cleomenes, 66, 67
Confederacy, The, 71, 189
Cyrus the Great, 21
Darius King of Persia, 51, 188
Deceiver Deceived, The, 142
Distrest Mother, The, 153, 194
Don Quixot [Comical History of Don Quixote], 132
Double Dealer, The, 132, 133, 193
Duke of Guise, The, 46, 51
Fatal Marriage; or, The Innocent Adultery, The, 42
Gamester, The, 59, 144
Half-Pay Officers, The, 151, 152, 194
Heroic Love, 54-56
History and Fall of Caius Marius, The, 146
Injured Lovers; or, The Ambitious Father, The, 103
Innocent Mistress, 141
Intrigues at Versailles; or, A Jilt in All Humours, The, 140, 141
Judgement of Paris, The, 114
King Arthur, 125
Libertine, The, 27
Love and Honour, 151, 152
Love for Love, 53, 79, 81, 113, 132, 133, 150, 163, 193
Love's a Jest, 119, 121, 123, 192
Loves of Mars and Venus, The, 123, 192
Loyal Subject, The, xi
Maid's Last Prayer; or, Any Rather Than Fail, The, 109
Maid's Tragedy, The, 47, 72, 82

Man of Mode; or, Sir Fopling Flutter, The, 41, 42, 54, 141, 188
Mariamne, 17
Married Beau; or, The Curious Impertinent, The, 51, 112
Measure For Measure; or, Beauty the Best Advocate, 64, 189
Morning Ramble; or, The Town Humour, The, 3
Mourning Bride, The, 31, 53, 124-126, 129, 133, 192, 193
Mustapha, 35
Old Bachelor, The, 109, 110, 132, 133, 191 193
Orphan; or, The Unhappy Marriage, The, 42, 43, 102
Pilgrim, The, 139, 193
Provok'd Wife, The, 70, 130, 132, 193
Provok'd Husband; or, A Journey to London, The, 136
Revenge; or, A Match at Newgate, The, 43
Rinaldo and Armida, 18, 58, 76
Rival Queens; or, The Death of Alexander the Great, The, 67, 104, 163
Rover; or, The Banish'd Cavaliers, The, 35
Royal Mischief, The, 64
Scornful Lady, The, 27
Secret Love; or, The Maiden Queen, 145
She Would if She Could, 16
Siege of Rhodes, The, x
Spanish Friar; or, The Double Discovery, The, 85, 138
Spanish Tragedy, The, 25
Squire of Alsatia, The, 38, 187

Stage Mutiny, The, 112

Thyestes, 24, 186

Unhappy Favourite; or, The Earl of
Essex, The, 35

Valentinian, 48, 49

Venice Preserved; or, A Plot
Discover'd, 42

World in the Moon, The, 107

Young King; or, The Mistake, The,
7, 185